Understanding Learning and Teaching
in Secondary Schools

PEARSON

We work with leading authors to develop the strongest
educational materials in education bringing cutting-edge
thinking and best learning practice to a global market.

Under a range of well-known imprints, including Longman,
we craft high-quality print and electronic publications which
help readers to understand and apply their content,
whether studying or at work.

To find out more about the complete range of our
publishing, please visit us on the World Wide Web at:
www.pearsoned.co.uk.

Understanding Learning and Teaching in Secondary Schools

Edited by
Alison Hramiak and **Terry Hudson**

Longman
is an imprint of

Harlow, England • London • New York • Boston • San Francisco • Toronto
Sydney • Tokyo • Singapore • Hong Kong • Seoul • Taipei • New Delhi
Cape Town • Madrid • Mexico City • Amsterdam • Munich • Paris • Milan

Pearson Education Limited
Edinburgh Gate
Harlow
Essex CM20 2JE
England

and Associated Companies throughout the world

Visit us on the World Wide Web at:
www.pearsoned.co.uk

First edition published 2011

© Pearson Education Limited 2011

ISBN 978-1-4058-9944-4

British Library Cataloguing-in-Publication Data
A catalogue record for this book is available from the British Library

Library of Congress Cataloguing-in-Publication Data
A catalog record for this book is available from the Library of Congress

10 9 8 7 6 5 4 3 2 1
15 14 13 12 11

Typeset in 9.5/12.5 pt Giovanni by 75
Printed by Ashford Colour Press Ltd., Gosport

This book is dedicated to Amelie and Isaac Nottage
and Michael and Ben Hramiak

Brief contents

Detailed contents

9 Assessment and feedback

Helen Boulton

10 Behaviour management in the classroom

Phil Spencer

Part 3 HOW SCHOOLS ARE ORGANISED   187

11 The mentoring process   189

Helen Cook

12 School structures, leadership and management   206

Stephen Holden and Terry Hudson

13 Collaborative working   223

Alison Hramiak and Terry Hudson

Preface

Teaching is both an art and a science. As a profession, it is individualistic in nature, and humanistic in the way it is undertaken. Every day is different and has its own rewards, though some days the rewards are harder to find than others. In this respect, it has similarities with the other noble professions of medicine and law. Teaching is a roller coaster of a ride. The profession provides constant ups and downs, day in day out – with all the thrills and spills that come with it.

This book is intended to support you during your training, and encourage you to look beyond your own classroom to draw on ideas and inspiration from those who have researched and written about education, and those who successfully work with learners in the UK and beyond. We hope that you find it useful, and that, once qualified, you appreciate that you are still just starting the fascinating journey towards being a truly exceptional teacher. Good luck in getting there.

Guided tour

Learning outcomes enable you to focus on the key themes that will be introduced within each chapter.

Practical tasks in the chapter are realistic activities that will not only improve your practice but can help you work towards collecting the necessary evidence required to meet QTS standards.

Challenge your thinking features are intended to be both thought-provoking and at times contentious to encourage reflection and debate.

Case studies help to apply theory discussed in the book to real classroom situations and practice.

Case study

A trainee teacher was called in to university from placement to attend an Academic Conduct Panel. Unbeknown to the trainee, the work that he had lent to one of his housemates had been copied – it being very easy to email electronic copies of assignments to friends for them to look at.

The first third of his assignment had been copied word for word and used by his house-mate, who was behind on the assignment and worried that she would miss the deadline for the work. A very nervous and horrified trainee was stunned when he discovered what had been done with his work.

It was only when the marker had looked at the references and seen that the wrong Ofsted report had been used by the copier, that the alarm was raised and the two assignments were then carefully checked to see what had been copied from where.

As a result of this, the guilty party was forced to resubmit and the work capped. The innocent trainee teacher never again let others see his work in this way.

Stop and reflect

Think back over your most recent week of teaching. Analyse:
- How many hours did you spend planning lessons?
- How many hours did you spend teaching lessons?
- How many hours did you spend thinking about making the lessons better?

Evaluate how well you feel you undertake reflective practice.
- What makes reflective practice truly critical?

Stop and reflect boxes throughout each chapter are designed to encourage you to think deeply and critically about yourself and your own practice, as a trainee and as a teaching professional.

Critical synthesis boxes take your reading and learning to a deeper level, extending your knowledge on selected topics, in line with Master's-level study.

Critical synthesis

The work of Dewey is regarded by many as being influential in developing ideas about reflective practice. Indeed some regard Dewey as the father of 'modern reflective practice' and suggest that Schön, Kolb and others applied Dewey's ideas. Critically review some of the work of Dewey. Useful background can be found in Mark Smith's useful summary (http://www.infed.org/thinkers/et-dewey.htm). For an analysis of some of the original ideas you can read Dewey (1933).
- Analyse the work of Dewey, Schön, Kolb and Boud. Identify where Schön, Kolb and Boud might have been influenced by Dewey's thinking.
- Do you agree with those who claim that Dewey should be regarded as the father of 'modern reflective practice'?

Further reading

Davitt, J. (2005) *New Tools for Learning: Accelerated learning meets ICT*, Stafford: Network Education Press.

Ofsted (2001) 'Managing Support for the Attainment of Pupils from Minority Ethnic Groups', available from *www.ofsted.gov.uk*

Pachler, N. (ed.) (2007) *Mobile Learning, Towards a Research Agenda*, London: Institute of Education.

Potts, P. Armstrong, F. and Masterton, M. (eds) (2000) *Equality and Diversity in Education: Learning, Teaching and Managing in Schools*, London: Routledge.

QCA 'A language in common – assessing English as an additional language', available from *www.qca.org.uk*.

Warlick D.F. (2004) *Redefining literacy for the 21st century*, Worthington, Ohio: Linworth Publishers.

Warlick, D. (2005) *Classroom blogging: A teacher's guide to the Blogosphere*, Raleigh: The Landmark Project.

Web resources

http://audacity.sourceforge.net/ – to download voice recording software
http://elgg.net/
http://www.becta.org.uk/

Further reading and **Web resources** are included at the end of each chapter, directing you to specific references and links, directly related to material in that chapter.

About the authors

Helen Boulton is Principal Lecturer and Learning and Teaching Coordinator (LTC) in the School of Education at Nottingham Trent University (NTU). She coordinated the PGCE (Secondary) Information Communications Technology course for nine years and also the PGCE 14–19 programme for two years. Prior to working at NTU, she was ICT coordinator for 10 years at a large 11–18 comprehensive school in North Nottinghamshire. She is actively involved in teacher training, both face-to-face and on-line, and runs regular training sessions for ICT teachers who are supporting her students as part of the PGCE. Helen's research interests include e/blended learning and teaching, the application of new technologies to learning, and work-based learning. Her current research focuses on using Web 2.0 technologies to develop reflective practice for teacher trainees and she is researching the transition into HE relating specifically to assessment and feedback. Helen is a member of the national committee for The Association for Information Technology in Teacher Education, a Fellow of the Higher Education Academy and chairs an ESCalate Special Interest Group on Assessment and Feedback.

Helen Cook is a Senior Lecturer at Sheffield Hallam University where she is the course leader for the Religious Education PGCE. She also contributes to the Citizenship PGCE programme, leads a generic education module for secondary trainees and supports students following the Graduate Teacher Programme (GTP) and Teach First routes into teaching.

Prior to this, Helen taught RE in schools in the East Midlands and had responsibility in schools for supporting ITT students and managing NQT Inductions.

Dr Alison Hramiak is a Senior Lecturer at Sheffield Hallam University, and is the Course Leader for the 14–19 ICT PGCE. She also teaches on a number of CPD programmes at Master's level and above, and also on the EdD programme at the university. She was the Faculty Teaching Fellow for Assessment and Feedback. She has taught in FE colleges, schools and universities, and also in the private sector, over the last 20 years. She is widely published nationally and internationally in conferences and academic journals and has also written a book, with other authors, on using virtual learning environments (VLEs) in secondary schools. Her research interests include e/blended learning and teaching, the application of new technologies to learning, and ICT and pedagogy with respect to teacher training. She is a member of the national committee for Information Technology in Teacher Education (ITTE) and co-edits their national newsletter. She is also a Fellow of the Higher Education Academy and a member of the Universities' Council for the Education of Teachers (UCET) committee for secondary teacher education.

Steve Holden was educated at John Port School in Derbyshire to 1974. He enjoyed a four-year BEd (Hons) course at Dudley College and University of Birmingham (1974–78) and is still celebrating being awarding the coveted 'Prize for Outstanding Teaching' following his three teaching practices. From September 1978 to 2007 Steve taught in Sheffield schools. During his 29-year career he has been a teacher of Business and Economics (and many other subjects); Head of Careers; Senior Sixth Form Tutor; Head of Sixth Form; Assistant Head Teacher; ITT mentor; and Senior Mentor Coordinator. Steve joined the staff of Sheffield Hallam University in September 2007 as Secondary Partnership Leader and is now the Head of Partnership in Education across all phases.

Terry Hudson is the Regional Executive Director of the Teach First Initiative in Yorkshire and Humber. He was, until recently, Head of Post Compulsory and Secondary Education and Training at Sheffield Hallam University.

Terry was a science teacher for 12 years, holding a range of middle and senior management posts in Newcastle and Derbyshire. He also worked for Derbyshire LEA on the Advisory staff and was a Fulbright exchange teacher teaching chemistry and physics at high school and college level in Colorado, USA. His HE experiences include: Science Lecturer; CPD Coordinator for the Centre for Science Education; Programme Leader for secondary ITT, Head of PCASO area and member of the Divisional Management Team. Terry has also acted as External Examiner and Chief External Examiner at other universities.

During his time at Sheffield Hallam University, Terry has managed and participated in a wide range of national and international projects – including Support for Supply Teacher and Returners (TTA), Pupil Researcher Initiative (Research Councils) and a TEMPUS project aimed at restructuring science education with the Slovak Republic (EU).

In addition, Terry has published over 100 books and articles including secondary school curriculum resources, research papers and books for teachers and trainee teachers. He has also acted as consultant to a wide range of publishers and companies, including Zenith Entertainment for the BBC.

Keith Shelton was, until recently, a Principal Lecturer and the LTA (Learning, Teaching and Assessment) and Teaching Skills Lead in the Department of Teacher Education at Sheffield Hallam University and is a Fellow of the Higher Education Academy. He joined the University in 1990, having previously been responsible for Teacher Education and Training Programmes in a large college of arts and technology, and was involved in the training of youth and community workers in Doncaster, Wakefield and Rotherham.

He was the Course Leader of the PgC in Learning and Teaching in Higher Education (LTHE), having previously been Programme Leader of the University Course for New Teaching Staff, the MA in Learning and Teaching in Higher Education and the Certificate in Education: Post-Compulsory Education and Training. He is involved in teaching on the PgC LTHE, the Professional Development Programme in Education; supervising MA dissertation and project students; and running programmes of workshops for associate lecturers and graduate teaching assistants. He recently worked with the University's Learning and Teaching Institute in the development and implementation of a Professional Development Framework for University Teaching Staff.

Keith was a member of the governing body of his local school for over 20 years, where as chair, he was involved in recruiting staff to a number of school appointments, ranging from Headteacher and Deputy Headteacher, Teachers, Caretaking and Learning Support Staff.

Phil Spencer is the course leader for the PGCE ICT 11–16 course at Sheffield Hallam University. Prior to this, for many years he was a teacher and Head of Department in a challenging north Sheffield school. Phil is currently researching the use of audio/video for self-reflection and is writing a book on surviving your teaching placement.

Acknowledgements

The Editors would like to thank the contributing authors for their hard work and dedication in putting this book together and our families and friends for their support and patience during the writing of this book, without whom it would not have been possible. We would also like to thank the editorial team at Pearson Education.

Publisher acknowledgements

We are grateful to the following for permission to reproduce copyright material:

Figure 15.1 from www.qcda.gov.uk

Tables 8.1, 8.2 from www.nationalstrategies.standards.dcsf.gov.uk; Table 9.2 from Assessment and the Secondary School Teacher, Routledge (MacIntosh and Hale 1976)

In some instances we have been unable to trace the owners of copyright material, and we would appreciate any information that would enable us to do so.

Chapter 1

Introduction

Theme 3 – How schools are organised

In this part of the book, Chapters 11 to 18, school structures and management are covered, giving you insight into how schools are organised with particular reference to you as a trainee or beginning teacher. Chapter 11 deals with you and your mentor and the processes behind the relationship between you and them. This is probably the most important relationship of your training year, and as such, it is vital that you know how to develop and nurture it to get the most out of it in the short time that you have it.

In Chapters 12 to 17 the book concentrates on describing in detail how schools are organised and how you can work within these structures as a teacher and as a member of the school. Chapter 12 covers the ways in which schools are structured as educational organisations. The various ways that the work of teachers and other professionals within schools is coordinated to have maximum benefit for learners are discussed, and you will be encouraged to examine and reflect on the management structures existing within the organisations within which you work.

Following on from this, Chapter 13 covers the many ways you might be able to work in collaboration with other trainees and teachers, and indeed with the many different roles associated with a school. This chapter gives ideas about how to collaborate on a face-to-face basis, and also details how you might collaborate with others using the latest technology to do so, and how you might extend this to using these ideas within your own teaching for your own students.

Chapters 14, 15 and 16 are closely linked, and cover areas of the curriculum that you might initially feel are beyond your own remit, and therefore not worth too much attention at this time. A teacher, however, is part of the school, and not just a subject specialist teacher. You will be expected to be part of the team that teaches more pastoral aspects, possibly doing so as part of your role as a form tutor, perhaps also including citizenship during this time. You would also be expected to understand the curriculum outside your own area and to be aware of the new developments in the work-related and vocational areas of the school curriculum. These chapters ensure that you are fully prepared for this.

In Chapter 17 a wider picture of teaching is described giving the reader an overview of what we can learn from education and schooling beyond our shores. The use of international league tables is discussed, and some of the parameters used to make international comparisons are considered. The main focus of the chapter is to encourage you to reflect on how we can learn from good practice in other countries, but without making shallow comparisons.

The final chapter of the book is dedicated solely to helping you to get your first teaching post. In this chapter you will find very practical and pragmatic guidance on applying for and being interviewed for your first role in teaching. Much of what is written here can also be used in subsequent job applications. As you might expect, this chapter has a slightly different structure as it is the only chapter that does not demand M-level thinking and further study – but it does encourage you to highlight your skills and knowledge in this area throughout the application process.

How to use this book effectively

As stated earlier, teachers and trainee teachers are busy people. We appreciate that you are busy in school getting ready to teach in classrooms, and you are also are busy as learners, researching and writing academic reports and essays for the qualification on which you have enrolled. Therefore, it is crucial that you use the time you have available for studying very wisely. The structure of the book has been outlined above so that you can use it primarily as a reference book. While we hope that you read much of the book, we would be naive to think that you would feel that you had the time initially to read all of it from cover to cover and, indeed, some chapters will be more valuable and relevant later in your course as you have more personal professional experiences to draw on. To this end, then, each chapter has been described in such a way as to guide you to where you might need to read and learn.

As well as the above, in each chapter you will find both practical and reflective tasks for you to do to aid your understanding of the topics you are reading about. The 'Stop and reflect' tasks have been designed to assist you in your development as reflective thinkers and practitioners – an innate requirement of the teaching profession at all stages – from trainee to very experienced leaders in schools. These boxes are intended to make you think deeply and critically about yourself and your own situation as a trainee and as a teaching professional. We would advise you to do as many of these as you can while reading the book in order to get the most out of each chapter.

The purpose of 'Practical tasks' included in each chapter is to provide you with realistic activities that are directly related to your training and practice. They provide you with activities that can assist in your collection of evidence for your QTS standards, and also for your own teaching. The intention is that, in doing the practical tasks, your own practice will improve as a result.

As mentioned earlier in this introduction, there are also 'Critical synthesis' boxes in each chapter which serve to push you that little bit further in the areas covered in that chapter and facilitate your learning at Master's level. As with the other extra tasks and activities throughout the book, take the time to look at these, and explore the avenues they send you down, to give yourself more and more practice at working at this level. There are also boxes in Chapters 2 to 17 that are called 'Challenge your thinking'. These, as you might imagine, are designed to encourage you to reflect on some possibly contentious issues or viewpoints. The intention is to create a virtual seminar discussion where things might get heated and the status quo questioned. We hope you enjoy them – or at least stop to question prior views before moving on.

In using this book as advised above, you should find that you will develop yourself as a reflective practitioner and as a professional teacher. You should also find that your own continuing professional development progresses, as does your relationship with the learners in your care, and the part you play in the school in which you teach. The chapters contain case studies to help you to apply your knowledge to realistic situations, and each chapter also provides the references used in the chapter. Throughout the book you are encouraged to undertake further reading about each topic covered. This is done by specific references to additional texts and by encouraging you to explore the internet for additional materials and information. You should investigate the topics you are most interested in, using these in order to become better informed both as a teacher and as a learner. Remember: good teachers never stop learning.

Part 1

YOU AS A LEARNER

Chapter 2

Becoming a reflective practitioner

Learning outcomes

By the end of this chapter you will have an understanding of:

→ What reflective practice is and what it is not

→ How to apply models and processes of reflective practice to your professional work

→ How to understand the value and importance of reflective practice

→ How to use feedback from others to enhance your professional practice

→ The need to synthesise information during reflective practice and use to target set and action plan effectively

Introduction

The aim of this chapter is to introduce you to key models and ideas related to reflective practice and to provide approaches to help you to reflect critically on your work. This will help you to become a more effective teacher, not only during your training course but beyond.

Why is reflective practice so important? Boud *et al.* (1985) stress that effective learning does not take place unless you do reflect. They point out what you probably already know about your own learning: by thinking of a moment in time or a particular situation over and over again, you gain new insights into the situation. You begin to see it from different points of view. Kolb (1984) also describes reflection as an essential element of learning. Kolb will be mentioned again later in the chapter. You may already be familiar with his experiential learning cycle.

There are many definitions of reflective practice and, indeed, many approaches to undertaking it. Key definitions, models and approaches will be discussed in this chapter, and the references at the end of the chapter will lead you to further reading.

What is reflective practice?

Good teachers are skilled reflective practitioners – they always aim to improve their practice. Never satisfied, they question themselves and reflect on their work in an effort to find better ways of working with learners. However, doing this by just thinking back can have limited value. By improving your reflective practice you can make much better use of your experiences and ensure that you are exploring as many ways as possible to review what you are doing, how you are doing it and how you might do it better.

Why review/reflect on your teaching?

Reflecting on your teaching is an essential activity to help you to:

- Understand what happens in your teaching sessions
- Understand the effect of what you do
- Identify your strengths and weaknesses
- Learn about yourself
- Learn about your learners
- Learn about teaching and learning
- Develop strategies for developing your teaching.

Practical task

Think back to an episode or experience that you have learned from. Write down the lessons you learned and how you reflected on the experience.

● Did you write anything down?

● Did you discuss your experiences with anyone?

● Was your learning informed by feedback from others?

● How long after the experience did you apply your learning?

Reflective practice can be defined as 'a set of abilities and skills, to indicate the taking of a critical stance, an orientation to problem solving or state of mind' (Moon, 1999, p. 63). This seems to indicate that the reflective practitioner must develop specific skills and abilities, and apply these in a problem-solving way to arrive at useful professional conclusions. These abilities and skills will be explored later, but it is important to emphasise the state of mind of the reflector. This isn't an activity to be undertaken as a task imposed by others – rather it is the desire to dig, to question, not to be satisfied with what is, that makes the true reflective practitioner.

With reference to educational reflection, probably close to your hearts, Cowan (1999) emphasises that reflection is akin to thinking about your own learning. Cowan goes on to state that learners reflect when they both analyse and then generalise from that thinking. This raises the important point that reflection involves linking your experiences to wider situations – possibly even relating it to wider theories and practice. This means that reading can help your reflective practice.

A danger of reflection that is carried out without any depth of thinking, or reference to other viewpoints, such as colleagues, students or research literature, is that we sometimes only see what we want to see. Biggs (1999, p. 6) explains this beautifully:

'. . . a reflection in a mirror is an exact replica of what is in front of it. Reflection in professional practice, however, gives back not what it is, but what it might be, an improvement on the original.'

So, no easy definition can be used to explain reflective practice. It clearly involves thinking about experiences critically with a view to improving practice. It also is informed by reading and the view of others, so the practitioner is simply not reflecting back the 'exact replica' of what is in front. True reflective practice should be challenging and related to problem solving. Perhaps Fade (2005) most concisely provides us with a definition that will serve a useful purpose in this chapter:

'Reflection involves describing, analysing and evaluating our thoughts, assumptions, beliefs, theories and actions.'

True reflective practice is not lesson evaluation. Thinking back over experiences is important, but limited. Any learning from this process will be enhanced through gathering evidence from a variety of sources in order to examine your work more critically. Sources of evidence to enhance your reflective practice will be discussed later in the chapter.

However, you already know that teaching is a time-consuming process and that schools and colleges are busy places. This means that time for reflection appears to be limited.

Take care. The busy nature of where you work makes it even more essential that you find time and space for reflection. Being busy is no excuse for making the same mistakes over and over again, or not innovating to enhance learning for your students. It might mean becoming very familiar with models of reflective practice that can be undertaken efficiently and effectively. This chapter will help.

Stop and reflect

Think back over your most recent week of teaching. Analyse:

● How many hours did you spend planning lessons?

● How many hours did you spend teaching lessons?

● How many hours did you spend thinking about making the lessons better?

Evaluate how well you feel you undertake reflective practice.

● What makes reflective practice truly critical?

Ideas about reflective practice

The term 'reflective practitioners', first used by Schön in his key publications during the 1980s, has been the focus for much research since. Schön used the term to describe professional working and professional practice. Indeed, Schön's work will feature a great deal in this chapter and he has certainly been highly influential in the development of professional practice and reflective practice in many fields.

Schön (1983, 1987) describes two types of reflection:

● Reflection in action (thinking on your feet)

● Reflection on action (retrospective thinking).

Throughout his work Schön points out that reflection is used by professionals when faced by unique situations. This means that existing theories and approaches cannot simply be applied.

Critical synthesis

The work of Dewey is regarded by many as being influential in developing ideas about reflective practice. Indeed some regard Dewey as the father of 'modern reflective practice' and suggest that Schön, Kolb and others applied Dewey's ideas. Critically review some of the work of Dewey. Useful background can be found in Mark Smith's useful summary (http://www.infed.org/thinkers/et-dewey.htm). For an analysis of some of the original ideas you can read Dewey (1933).

● *Analyse the work of Dewey, Schön, Kolb and Boud. Identify where Schön, Kolb and Boud might have been influenced by Dewey's thinking.*

● *Do you agree with those who claim that Dewey should be regarded as the father of 'modern reflective practice'?*

Reflecting in action

Somerville and Keeling (2004) describe reflection in action as 'the hallmark of the experienced professional'. As the reflection is taking place while the activity or experience is ongoing, this means examining your own behaviour and that of others while in a situation (Schön, 1987). Somerville and Keeling (2004) highlight the following skills needed for reflection in practice:

● Being a participant observer in situations that offer learning opportunities
● Attending to what you see and feel in your current situation, focusing on your responses and making connections with previous experiences
● Being 'in the experience' and, at the same time, adopting a 'witness' stance as if you were outside it.

Reflection on action

Reflection on action is possibly the form of reflection you are most familiar with. This is when you reflect on experiences and situations that occurred in the past. The purpose is to use your analytical skills to draw conclusions from a range of sources of information in order to devise and test more effective ways of acting in the future.

Both reflection in action and reflection on action have become crucial to professional development. This explains why both are encouraged throughout and beyond professional development and training courses. Indeed, it has been stated that a key role of effective mentoring is to encourage reflective practice (Atherton, 2009).

> 'Indeed, it can be argued that "real" reflective practice needs another person as mentor or professional supervisor, who can ask appropriate questions to ensure that the reflection goes somewhere, and does not get bogged down in self-justification, self-indulgence or self-pity!'

(Atherton, 2009)

Stop and reflect

● Select an experience you have recently had as a teacher.
● Write down a list of the thoughts you can remember while the experience was happening.
● Would you classify this as reflection in action?
● Write down a list of the thoughts you have had since the experience that you have used to improve your teaching.
● Would you classify this as reflection in action?

You will know from this activity, if not before, that reflective practice is a very active process. It is not an event and it draws on theoretical concepts and previous learning. A number of authors stress this and point out that it is a positive process that leads to an action plan (Kemmis, 1985; Reid, 1993). Reflection is a personal, internalised process resulting in change and new learning (Johns, 1995).

Kolb's Experiential Learning Cycle

Though most commonly referred to within the context of student learning, the experiential learning cycle is a useful way to consider reflective processes. Kolb (1976, 1985) proposed a cyclical model of four sequential stages:

● Concrete experience (learners immersed in new experiences)
● Reflective observation (learners reflect on experiences)
● Abstract conceptualisation (new ideas and theories result from reflections)
● Active experimentation (new ideas used to solve problems).

The cyclical nature of this problem-solving model is best seen in diagrammatic form (see Figure 2.1).

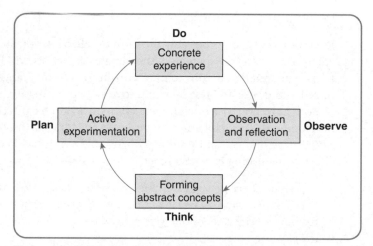

Figure 2.1 **Kolb's Experimental Learning Cycle**

Though Shön and Kolb provide us with useful models to help us to understand reflective practice, both have their critics. Finger and Asún (2000) have commented that such models of reflective practice require mistakes to have been made. These authors argue that it is possible to short circuit the cycle and arrive at new ideas, approaches and theories. They call this 'theories in action'. Such reflective practice not only looks at improving existing systems and approaches, but starts from the premise of questioning these directly. This can lead to more fundamental change, but is more challenging.

Zwozdiak-Meyers Dimensions of Reflective Practice

Another useful model for understanding reflective practice contains nine dimensions (Zwozdiak-Meyers, 2009). This incorporates ideas from Schon, Kolb and others on reflective practice but also includes the notion of 'teacher as researcher' – a concept developed by Stenhouse (1975). This involved teachers becoming engaged in action research into their own practice. Findings from such research can provide a rich source of evidence to inform reflective practice. In addition, the Zwozdiak-Meyers Dimensions

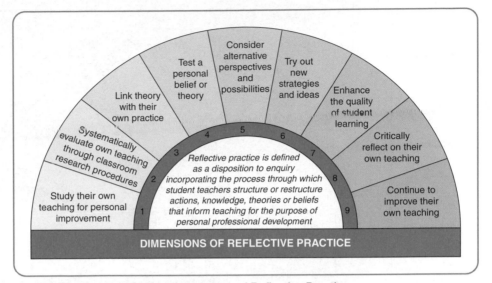

DIMENSIONS OF REFLECTIVE PRACTICE

Text inside figure:

Study their own teaching for personal improvement

Systematically evaluate own teaching through classroom research procedures

Link theory with their own practice

Test a personal belief or theory

Consider alternative perspectives and possibilities

Try out new strategies and ideas

Enhance the quality of student learning

Critically reflect on their own teaching

Continue to improve their own teaching

Reflective practice is defined as a disposition to enquiry incorporating the process through which student teachers structure or restructure actions, knowledge, theories or beliefs that inform teaching for the purpose of personal professional development

Figure 2.2 Zwozdiak–Meyers Dimensions of Reflective Practice

of Reflective Practice (see Figure 2.2) also incorporate the ideas of Hoyle and John (1995) who explored the ideas of 'extended professionals' and 'restricted professionals'.

Stop and reflect

- Study and analyse the nine dimensions shown in Figure 2.2.
- Which of the dimensions have you commonly used as part of your reflective practice?
- Which of the dimensions have you never used as part of your reflective practice?
- Select two you have not used and attempt to incorporate them into your processes for reflective practice.

Who can help with reflective practice?

As has already been stated, reflective practice is a personal, internalised process resulting in change and new learning (Johns, 1995). However, this does not mean it is a lonely activity. Indeed, it is enhanced through interaction with others.

Imagine you are looking at a particular issue as part of your reflective process. You look from your own viewpoint (experiences, prejudices, expectations and understanding) as if you are looking at the hub of a wheel along one of the spokes. The wheel would be much stronger with many spokes. In other words, can you try to reflect on the issue from other viewpoints? These can include student voice, mentor comments, observation reports and discussions with others. An effective reflective practice wheel might contain some or all of the spokes shown in Figure 2.3. You will be able to think of others.

Finally, when thinking of the various models of reflective practice, do not underestimate your ability to just sense what is right. This is what Schön calls 'intuition, insight

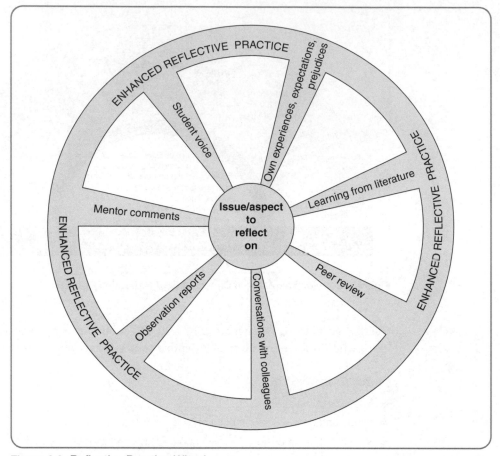

Figure 2.3 Reflective Practice Wheel

and artistry' (Schön, 1983). He also goes on to remind us that we can aspire to being 'thoughtful, wise and contemplative' in our reflective practice.

Some techniques to consider

In order to reflect effectively it is hoped you are taking yourself through a learning cycle. Your focus is likely to be on what happened during your teaching sessions and what you can learn from this to help you in your future teaching sessions. It is common practice in teaching to undertake reflective practice – the key issues are to ensure that this reflective practice is critical and that it has genuine impact on your future work. You are no doubt heavily engaged in this activity, so reflect on which of the following issues and strategies you use and consider. The content of your reflections is likely to include such things as:

● **You**: What you did, why you did what you did, the effect it had, what you are learning about yourself, what you might do next.

- **Students**: What they did, why they did as they did, the effect it had, what you are learning about individuals and what you are learning about them as a learning group, what are their future needs.
- **Learning**: What you are learning about how individuals (best) learn, what helps and hinders learning.
- **Teaching**: What effect does your teaching have, how does it influence learning, how can you develop and improve your teaching and manage the learning environment better so that learning is optimised?

You might want to focus on particular or key incidents/events which occurred during your teaching and use these as the basis of your reflection. Here are some techniques that you may be using. As you read the list think about which are known to you and which you might wish to evaluate as possibly beneficial.

Critical conversations

When discussing your work with others try to encourage them to ask critical questions. These include:

- What were you aiming to do when you did that?
- What theories or models informed your actions?
- Why did you choose that particular strategy?
- What would you change next time and why?

Good mentors will ask this sort of question. If you are not asked such questions very regularly then ask them of yourself.

Critical conversations take time to prepare but can be highly effective for both people involved

Source: Education Photos

Practical task

- Design five more critical questions that could be asked about your work.
- Share them with your mentor or an experienced colleague so they can comment on them.
- Ask yourself the questions regularly.

Feedback

You will have received feedback from a range of people and in different ways. Using feedback sensibly to inform reflective practice is not easy but it can be very effective. Somerville and Keeling (2004) provide some very useful advice. This is summarised below:

- Feedback can be both verbal and non-verbal.
- It may cover behaviour, skills, values, relationships to others.
- Feedback is central to the process of reflection.
- It is vital to check you have accurately understood the feedback.
- Don't hesitate to ask others how they perceive a particular incident.
- Don't hesitate to ask for feedback but select someone who can be trusted to give an honest answer and whose opinion you value.
- Good feedback will challenge your thoughts in a supportive and non-threatening manner.
- You do not have to accept the feedback but give it your consideration.
- Ask for feedback from more than one person who has participated in the same experience.

Feedback is of no use if you do not use it to inform your reflective practice, so think carefully about what others are saying to you and writing about you. In this way, all feedback is positive as it is helping you to learn.

Reflective logs or diaries

You may already be keeping a paper or on-line reflective log or journal. This is also sometimes called an 'e-portfolio'. If you have experience of this, you will no doubt have appreciated that writing down your thoughts and ideas is an excellent way to help you to formulate new ideas. In addition to acting as evidence that you are reflecting (important in many training situations and certainly linked to standards), it also has the more valuable purpose of changing the way you think about things. The act of committing your thoughts to paper (or laptop) does actually lead to different thought processes.

An interesting point to consider is the level of formality of the reflective writing. You may be keeping a blog or even writing down your reflections on Facebook or similar social networking sites. Be careful with these though. These can be very informal sites and your writing will likewise be informal. In contrast, an assessed portfolio or journals may lead you to more formal, almost academic, writing. You may wish to reflect on which medium you find allows the most honest output.

- Are you also influenced by the audience?
- Do you reflect differently through your writing if it is either informal (for yourself or selected friends) or formal (for assessment purposes)?

You may have already discovered that it can be extremely valuable, though not always comfortable, to allow other people to read your reflections and comment on them. They can act as a valuable agenda for discussions with colleagues and, especially, mentors. You will also be able to look back over your log or diary to follow your training and development journey. This can be very encouraging, as you may not recognise the great gains you are making in your professional development. Always celebrate success. It is too easy to focus on the problems, especially if you have written the reflections soon after the event. Read back over your reflections after a few days or even weeks – you are allowed to add to them.

Some useful techniques are to:

- write one adjective to describe your experiences for the lesson and then another one for what you are going to do next time to make it better
- try putting down the best thing that happened during a lesson and the worst
- don't cross anything out – look back on it later and add.

Rich pictures

Occasionally it is very useful to try to represent an area you are reflecting on as a picture. This isn't an attempt to be accurate or skilled as an artist. It is meant to unlock parts of your brain not normally used to reflect on issues. By allowing yourself to just set off and draw what comes into your head you may find interesting and unusual links arising. This technique can also be used with small groups – a large poster can be produced without discussion or consultation and then the outcome discussed.

Practical task

- Think back to the first experience you ever had teaching a class.
- Draw your reflections of that experience.
- Do not write any words at all.
- When you have finished step back and just look at the picture for a while.
- Now, try to interpret it.

Using metaphors

Metaphors are very powerful in trying to explain or describe situations, ideas or organisations. Using metaphors can be very revealing. For example, a teacher who describes her school as a broken-down car is telling us a lot about the school and her level of satisfaction. Even if she described the school as a well-oiled machine, we would be left pondering the nature of relationships there and the leadership style!

Making sense of our experiences through the use of metaphor can help with our reflective practice and encourage us to look at things differently. Try it!

Reading

Do not underestimate the value of reading the literature on the issues you are focusing on. If you are reflecting on behaviour issues, there is a great deal of underpinning theory that could change the way you look at the issue. One important value of getting to grips with some wider theories is that you will find yourself applying them in new situations. Your reading will also allow you to set your reflections in a wider context.

Synthesis

To really get the maximum benefit from your reflective practice you will need to synthesise all of the information you are gathering and make sense of it. You will need to link your thoughts with feedback from others and the literature. See if you can draw links between any of the comments or ideas. The secret is to identify connections between the many different aspects of your reflective practice. Try to write summaries and then think about what these mean to your practice. Do any surprise you? Will any mean changes in your practice? Why?

Finally, make sure that your reflective practice results in clear plans for action. These plans need to be constantly reviewed as you develop. Plans should be challenging – but with realistic targets, success criteria and opportunities to celebrate the success.

Target	Actions to be taken	Evidence for need	How will I know when I have met the target? (success criteria)	Timescale	Resources needed

Figure 2.4 Example of an action plan

Practical task

- Look at the example of an action plan in Figure 2.4.
- Make a copy and then complete it to show a specific area of your work that you have been reflecting on. How does this type of plan relate to your existing action planning processes?
- Think about the evidence you have been using to help you to reflect more critically.
- Are there any additional sources or approaches to reflective practice you could use from now?
- Write down three challenging but realistic targets and success criteria. Add a timescale.
- Monitor your plan and modify it as you continue to reflect.

Challenge your thinking

The following is the abstract of a paper entitled: 'Reflective practice: Realising its potential' by Lynn Clouder (Clouder, 2000).

'One criticism of reflective practice is its association with the production of individual knowledge. The assumption inherent in this critique is that the introspective nature of reflection denies benefit to the profession at a wider level. However, this view is problematic because it ignores the dialogical potential of reflective practice. The importance of intersubjectivity and the potential for "communities of practice" to enhance learning and professional awareness have been overlooked. From an educational perspective it is vital that professional socialisation of undergraduate students incorporates strategies that facilitate dialogical reflection rather than focusing solely on written reflection.'

- Read the abstract.
- Critically reflect on the content. Do you agree that an emphasis on individual critical reflection has made the process introspective?
- What are your experiences of a 'community of practice' informing and influencing your critical reflection?
- What mechanisms are in place to help you to share ideas to help you to form your critical reflections? Are there any additional ones that you would suggest?
- The article refers to physiotherapy students in training. What can we learn from other professions about reflective practice?

Case study

Alison has a topic to teach that should take a total of eight periods. The students are in Year 9 and she has been told that they are a potentially disruptive group but typical of the school. Alison has just started her second school experience having taught in her first school for eight weeks. Despite this lack of experience, Alison is very confident and hard working and was told during her first placement that her planning was excellent and her lessons good. This school was in the leafy suburbs of a town and noted for its high examination scores.

During her first lesson with the Y9 group Alison realises that the students are noisy and many are not paying attention. Several students leave their seats, shout and two run out of the classroom. Alison ends up shouting for most of the lesson. Her mentor, who has observed the lesson, offers feedback that is constructive, but she also makes it clear that the planning for the lesson was not detailed enough and the behaviour of the students was far from satisfactory. In the mentor's opinion very little effective learning took place. Alison reflects upon her lesson and becomes extremely critical of her own performance. As she prepares to teach the group again she becomes very worried and doesn't sleep well. She is often in tears and has a crisis of confidence. Alison claims that she will never be able to cope and she is seriously considering leaving the course. Her mentor needs to step in and try to offer appropriate support.

Consider the experiences that Alison has had since starting her training as a teacher.

- What are some of the issues raised by her different performance in the two schools she has worked in?
- What advice could you give to Alison to enhance her lesson planning and behaviour management skills?
- If you were Alison's mentor, how might you encourage her to undertake a more balanced and productive approach to reflective practice?
- Are there any strategies and sources of information and feedback she could use?

Summary

The purpose of this chapter was to give you a brief overview of what reflective practice is and what it is not. You should now be aware that reflective practice is a complex learning process aimed at analysing professional practice, approaches and beliefs with a view to enhancing that practice. You will have studied some of the key models and processes of reflective practice and understood its value and importance. The chapter also summarised some pragmatic approaches to reflective practice, including using feedback from others to enhance your professional practice and the value of reflective logs and diaries. Finally, the crucial need to synthesise the different sources of information used in your reflective practice to make connections and draw conclusions was emphasised. Reflective practice should always result in effective action planning.

References

Atherton, J. S. (2009) *Learning and Teaching; Reflection and Reflective Practice* [on-line] UK: Available: *http://www.learningandteaxching.info/learning/reflecti.htm*. Accessed 8 November 2009.

Biggs, J. (1999) *Teaching for quality learning at university*, Buckingham: Open University.

Boud, D., Keough R. and Walker D. (1985) *Reflection: Turning experience into learning*, London: Kogan Page.

Clouder, L. (2000) 'Reflective practice: realising its potential', *Physiotherapy*, 86(10): 517–22.

Cowan, J. (1999) *On becoming an innovative university teacher*, Buckingham: Open University.

Dewey, J. (1933) *How We Think. A restatement of the relation of reflective thinking to the educative process* (revised edn.), Boston: D. C. Heath.

Fade, S. (2005) *Learning and Assessing through Reflection*, *http://www.practicebasedlearning.org/resources/materials/docs/RoyalBromptonV3.pdf*

Finger, M. and Asún, M. (2000) *Adult Education at the Crossroads. Learning our way out*, London: Zed Books.

Hoyle, E. and John, P. (1995) *Professional Knowledge and Professional Practice*, London: Cassell.

Johns, C. (1995) 'The value of reflective practice for nursing', *Journal of Clinical Nursing*, 4: 23–60.

Kemmis, S. (1985) 'Action Research and the Politics of Reflection' in: Boud, D. *et al.* (1985) op. cit.

Kolb, D. A. (1984) *Experiential Learning: Experience as the source of learning and development*, Englewood Cliffs, N.J.: Prentice-Hall.

Moon, J. (1999) *Reflection in Learning and Professional Development: theory and practice,* London: Kogan Page.

Reid, B. (1993) '"But we're doing it already" Exploring a response to the concept of reflective practice in order to improve its facilitation', *Nurse Education Today,* 13: 305–9.

Schön, D. (1983) *The Reflective Practitioner. How professionals think in action,* London: Temple Smith.

Schön, D. (1987) *Educating the Reflective Practitioner,* San Francisco: Jossey-Bass.

Smith, M. K. (2001) 'Infed: ideas, thinkers, practice', *http://www.infed.org/thinkers/et-dewey.htm.*

Somerville, D. and Keeling, J. (2004) 'A practical approach to promote reflective practice within nursing', 100(12). *http://www.nursingtimes.net/nursing-practice-clinical-research/a-practical-approach-to-promote-reflective-practice-within-nursing/204502.article.*

Stenhouse, L. (1975) *An introduction to Curriculum Research and Development,* London: Heinemann.

Zwordiak-Myers, P. (2009) 'An enquiry into how reflective practice influenced the professional development of teachers as they engaged in action research to study their own teaching', London: Brunel University. PhD thesis quoted in Capel, S., Leask, M. and Turner, T. (2009) *Learning to teach in the secondary school* (5th edn), London: Routledge.

Chapter 3

Academic writing and reading

Learning outcomes

By the end of this chapter you will have an understanding of:

→ What academic writing is and what it is not

→ How to apply some basic grammatical rules, and practical tips to your writing

→ How to understand the requirements for your assignments

→ How to use feedback from your assignments to improve the quality of your work

→ Referencing and plagiarism and how it applies to your work

→ How to use peer-to-peer feedback to improve your work before you hand it in

Introduction

The aim of this chapter is to introduce you to the basics of academic writing for the purposes of your teacher training course and beyond. There are many books dedicated to academic writing alone, and you should use this chapter as a platform from which to seek additional detailed information in this area if you wish. The references at the end of the chapter point to further reading for this topic as required.

What academic writing is not

Just to be very clear on this: academic writing is not an informal writing style. It is not a chatty piece of prose. It is not an exclusively descriptive piece of work that details what you did and how you did it. For example, it is not solely a description of your experiences of teaching practice, or a verbatim reiteration of government or school policies and procedures in an essay. Academic writing is much more than that, and done in a very different style from what you might be used to, or in which you have very limited experience.

What academic writing is

There are many definitions of academic writing. If you type this phrase into Google, you may come up with are websites that do it for you! The idea behind this chapter is to enable you to do it confidently for yourself. Academic writing is not an easy skill to learn or practise – even experienced 'academics' agree that writing for journals and academic publishing is not an easy task.

From Google to Google Scholar the range of websites changes for the same search phrase, and from here you can find a range of texts available to students to introduce them to academic writing – examples of these texts and further references are given at the end of this chapter.

There are a myriad of text books on how to write grammatically correct English, however this is not necessarily the same as writing academically. From the wikipedia website academic writing is given as:

> 'Writing in academic forms or styles is usually serious, intended for a critical and informed audience, based on closely-investigated knowledge, and posits ideas or arguments. It usually circulates within the academic world ("the academy"), but the academic writer may also find an audience outside via journalism, speeches, pamphlets, etc.'
>
> (http://en.wikipedia.org/wiki/Academic_writing, 25.10.10)

As can be seen from the definition given above, academic writing can take on various forms; however, the style remains largely the same, independent of the form. Academic writing might, for example, include an essay, research paper, dissertation, thesis, conference paper, report, annotated bibliography, literature review, and so on.

Practical task

Make a list of what you have written in your academic career to date. Classify the different documents into academic and non-academic types of writing and identify the differences between them.

For the purposes of this book, academic writing will be taken as the type of formal writing that is specifically required for the assignments relating to your course. Academic writing involves an element of critical analysis and a synthesis of ideas in a constructively evaluative way. Thus, as an academic writer, you would be expected to critically evaluate and analyse the sources of your information. Subsequently you would construct your own arguments from the literature you have read about the research and scholarship of others, drawing on your own experiences and ideas, to produce an original piece of writing that demonstrates that you can constructively appraise the work of others in an informed manner, and can evidence this fact within your writing.

Stop and reflect

Think about how good your academic writing is. What are your weaknesses and strengths in relation to it? Is it critical and analytical? Can you sum it up in one paragraph?

Some key advice to support effective writing

You may feel that you do not need the advice in this section of the chapter, but only move on if you are very confident with your writing style. This part of the chapter covers some fundamental skills leading to writing grammatically acceptable English. If you start with these basics, before moving on to the more advanced skills of academic writing as defined above, you may find the transition between your current writing or more informal writing styles and academic writing easier to make.

Sentences – a sentence should normally describe a single idea. Academic papers rarely adhere to this rule, and as you become more experienced, you may find it better to link ideas within a single sentence using punctuation such as commas and semi colons. To start with, and to make your writing achieve an acceptable level of clarity, aim to have only a single idea per sentence. You should not accept an essay, assignment or report that has been written badly. Even if the relevant content is covered, poor writing skills will undermine this, confuse the message and present a less than professional impression. At all times be clear about what you are trying to say.

Sentences should, in line with the advice given above, rarely exceed 20 words. You should read a sentence aloud in your head to determine where the punctuation should go. Where you naturally take a pause is where commas and other punctuation should be placed. Again, academic writing rarely adheres to this, and the papers you will read will tend to have long, punctuated sentences. This is something you can aspire to, but is not advisable when you are inexperienced in this type of writing. As a starting point think about mixing short and longer sentences. This provides variety for the reader.

A paragraph should contain a linked set of ideas. Look at the paragraph above that describes the use of sentences. It contains seven sentences of differing length, but all are about the same theme. Having different-themed sentences within one paragraph can be confusing. It is often better in terms of clarity of writing to have several smaller paragraphs than one large one that contains many different ideas or themes.

Having covered what academic writing is, and how to go about starting to construct your written work, the next part of the chapter moves on to applying this knowledge to your assignments.

How to use feedback from assignments

In this section there are two main messages to communicate to the reader, and these will be illustrated using real-life examples so as to give context to the topic being described (see also Chapter 9 Assessment and feedback).

The first message is to understand that there should be no such thing as negative feedback. No feedback is negative if you reflect on it and allow it to inform and improve your future writing. The text below gives some examples of feedback given to trainees for their Level 7 (Master's) assignments. This feedback was also accompanied by annotations in the text of the work handed in to support the feedback statements given.

Here are some examples of less than positive feedback:

The reflection and critical evaluation is not well supported by appropriate literature, the same would apply to the judgements made – there is no real synthesis of the literature to support the work done.

It is largely descriptive and not critically evaluative or analytical enough. The language is also too informal in places.

You do not draw together and synthesise the theories and issues around teaching and learning enough, and there is no real critical or analytical consideration of the statements you make or the reflection you have done, which is then, in effect, largely unsubstantiated.

As was mentioned earlier, and as you can see from the above statements, one of the most difficult aspects of academic writing is the linking of ideas, arguments and experiences with a critical, analytical appraisal of the appropriate literature for the work. Without this, it is unlikely that an assignment would meet the required standard for work at Master's level.

The message here, however, is for you *not* to dwell on feedback that criticises your work. This can be disheartening, disappointing and frustrating as you will have put a lot of effort into producing it. However, you must understand that any criticism is of the work, not of you as a person. Do not take it personally. Use it to learn new things, and to learn from others – see also the section on using the 'buddying system' later in this chapter. If you are confused with any feedback, the first point of call should be your tutor. Discuss your feedback with them and get a clear understanding of where you went wrong. This is particularly important if you feel you really tried and still did not manage to achieve the marks you had aimed or hoped for.

The second message is about your use of positive feedback. Here are some examples of this:

An excellent critical reflection and evaluation of your own progress as a teacher that is well supported by an excellent use of a wide range of appropriate literature.

Critical evaluation is apparent and judgements are informed using literature to support them.

A lot of thought has gone into how you teach and you have reflected well in a critically evaluative way on individual needs of students.

Having said not to regard any feedback as negative, the next message is to celebrate but also to use any positive feedback. If this is used properly, i.e. reflectively, you will be able to monitor how your feedback (often known as 'feeding forward' in this case) is helping you to produce better-quality work, and thus achieve better outcomes for it as your course progresses. Do not rest on your success. Concentrate on areas that have been pointed out as needing development (targets), but do not neglect your strengths. Keep working on these also.

Practical task

Design an action plan for using with any future assignment feedback. Create a simple table for each set of assessment criteria for the assignment. Have a column for your strengths and target areas, and an empty column for the action you are going to take against each one. Do this for all your assignments and use it when you receive feedback.

Stop and reflect

What is the most useful feedback you have ever had? Evaluate it in terms of usefulness. How did you use it to help your future work?

Understanding and writing assignments at Master's level

You need to ensure that you fully understand what is required of you in terms of assignments. This means being able to match what you intend to do against the assessment criteria for the assignment. If, after going through this in taught sessions or on-line, at university, reading it, and talking it through with your peers, you still do not understand what is expected, go and see your tutor and seek further clarification. Better to do this than to risk failure for the sake of a short tutorial.

Much of the Initial Teacher Training (ITT) in England now offers opportunities to study at Master's (M) level. Thus, a higher level of work, often referred to as Level 7 (L7) is required of you. The main terms used to describe the learning outcomes or assessment criteria at this level of work are: *critical, reflective, analytical* and *evaluative*. Possibly the most difficult task in meeting the required standard for trainees working at M level is that of critical engagement with the literature surrounding their subject, and using it to develop their own thoughts and arguments in relation to it and the context of their teaching (Wyse, 2007). The style of writing has to be more formal at this level, though this does not mean that you have to write in the third person all the time, and often you may actually be asked *not* to do this – especially if the work requires a more reflective account of your own experiences in school. It is the language you use which has to retain some formality, thus avoiding the more casual terms you might use when writing to friends. It certainly means avoiding the ever-popular text speak used with mobile phones. For example, you might state your opinion of a piece of writing using the first person: 'I think that . . .', but you would not veer into colloquial language, and speak of students as 'kids', or shorten your words to mimic text speak, such as 'u' or 'gr8'.

As with the requirement for becoming a reflective practitioner (see Chapter 2), it is not enough simply to describe; you need to illustrate/provide evidence that you have engaged with, possibly even challenged, appropriate sources of evidence and theory – 'appropriate' meaning recognised journals and books.

In order to do this, you will need to judge the literature you intend to use and cite in your work critically. This means you will have to demonstrate a clear appreciation of what your sources are saying, and this in relation both to what *you* think, and to what others think too, and then relate this to the context, or setting, for your work.

For example, you might think that the zone of proximal development as presented by Vygotsky (Vygotsky, 1978) is something that you can relate to in terms of your own teaching. Before you wax lyrical about the advantages of this theoretical viewpoint, however, stop and make sure you can answer the following questions:

1 Do you really understand what Vygotsky was trying to put forward as a theory for learning? *First you need to understand.*

2 Why do you think it is a useful theory? Are there any disadvantages or issues you can think of in relation to this theory? *Then you need to critically appraise it.*

3 How can you use it in the context of your own teaching and learning? *Finally, you need to be able to relate it to your own experiences.*

In doing so, you also need to be aware of the limitations of what you are trying to say, or the argument you are presenting. While it can be useful to go off on a tangent out of sheer interest in the topic, nonetheless, when exploring the literature, you do need to keep focused on your task and the assessment criteria linked to it. Having said this, however, it is always useful in any academic work – particularly at this level and above – to indicate things you might have read and discounted, and say why you did so.

If, for example, you are studying culture in relation to classroom behaviour and management strategies, you might become keenly interested in the literature and ideas of Bourdieu and his notions of cultural capital (Robbins, 2000; Webb, 2002). By all means, acknowledge your reading of it, but if using 500–1000 words out of a maximum of 3000 for the assignment takes you off focus and leaves you no room for words that meet the assessment criteria more clearly, then it is best to just state why you were not able to include it as fully as you might have liked. It is better to include some of what you have read in some small way, and show why you have discounted it, rather than not to acknowledge it at all. The latter leaves the reader often wondering why you had not explored certain topics or areas, and they might then question your breadth of reading.

An example, using the above topic might read something like:

'[. . .]Although the work of Bourdieu (Webb, 2002) provides some useful links to the context of this report, it was felt that including more detail in this area would not add to the overall arguments put forward here in terms of cultural change within the school[. . .].'

Whatever you do, if at any point you do not fully understand some or all of the assessment criteria, and feel like you are going off focus with the work, seek advice from your tutor – it's what they are there for. Get things clarified before you go too far.

Critical synthesis

While this chapter covers much of what is required to enable you to start writing at Master's level, it does not cover it in as much detail as you can find. Visit your local book shop or library (learning resource centre) and evaluate the books that are dedicated solely to academic writing. Critically analyse whether or not they can offer you much more insight into this topic in relation to your needs for your course.

In terms of the types of things that elevate written work from an undergraduate level 6 (L6,) to Master's level (L7), take a look at the following table. In it, expectations for each level are compared:

Table 3.1 Comparison of the characteristics of written work at Level 6 and Level 7

Level 6 writing has . . .	Level 7 writing has . . .
Some understanding and application of theoretical underpinning	Good understanding and application of theoretical underpinning
Good use of further reading	Good critical understanding of reading
Synthesis of ideas evident as is critical reflection on literature	Good synthesis of ideas evident and good critical analysis of range of literature sources
Methods clearly set out	Methodology selected and justified using literature
Data analysis evident and discussion informed by reference to sources	Systematic use and analysis of evidence and data, and use of framework for analysis evident
Good sense of focus – not necessarily sustained. Limited arguments	Clear focus is defined and linked throughout. Arguments expressed

The table is not exhaustive, and there are other characteristics that could be added to show how L7 work is not simply more of the same thing, but is also different – incorporating, as it does, the ability to synthesise ideas, analyse and reflect on work critically, and to demonstrate a level of understanding through the extensive and appropriate use of literature.

Practical tips for writing assignments

As with some of the other topics covered in this chapter, you can get whole books on this subject alone; the reference list at the end of the chapter gives you some examples of these if you feel you need more information on this particular area.

Some of the more obvious practical tips are given here to try to assist you when starting out on your assignments. One important aspect of assignment writing is the art of *staying focused* – too many students find a particular area of the work more interesting than another, and then spend reams (literally) on it losing sight of their original goal or requirement for the assignment. (This is also covered in the preceding section.) Always keep the assignment brief and the assessment criteria at the forefront of your mind when writing up the work. If, at the end of the writing, you can tick all the assignment requirement boxes and the assessment criteria boxes – as it were – then you should be fairly confident that you can meet the standard required for the work (see also the section on buddying later in this chapter).

Write when you can. Set aside quality time for writing and don't waste it on work you find easier to do – the so-called 'colouring activities' that we can all find if we need to avoid doing something we don't want to. For me, my colouring activity would be dealing with my email, which is infinitely easier than sitting down and writing or reading papers. Work out what yours is and avoid it – stay away from the crayons – and use the time you have set aside to get on with the writing. If you are stuck with writer's block, (conjuring up images of a pen in the shape of an axe and a head on a block), take a break and do something else; think and reflect, discuss it with peers and friends, and come back to it when you feel able to continue. Do not waste your precious time staring at a screen all day, feeling more and more frustrated with the work. Better to spend one or two really productive hours on writing after a break, than to waste seven or eight hours staring and literally going nowhere.

Get prepared to write. Do all the reading and note taking in blocks, get all your notes together in a well-organised system, have everything you need at your fingertips. Avoid suddenly, desperately, needing a reference from the library (learning resource centre) that is two kilometres away. Make sure you have all the references you need, either in a paper format or in a database (see also the next section on referencing). Project plan and structure the writing, using headings if this helps, giving yourself milestones for the larger assignments.

Whatever else you do, always leave time for proofreading, as this generally removes/ negates much of the more casual 'clumsy' errors in the text, and ensures that you understand what you have written (see also the section on buddying) and *always, always* make a back-up of your work – hard or electronic copy.

Some writers, both creative and academic, offer the valuable advice to budding writers – write, write, write. The point being that these professional writers produce many words as well as they can and then craft them later. By not trying to put down perfect ideas and sentences, immediately they free themselves from the pressure that can produce blocks.

While the above is useful advice for many people, for you as busy trainee teachers, you may need to incorporate some additional element of planning into your writing – in the form of a schedule, for example. One way to go about planning for an assignment is to

Be organised from the start. Don't be confused by the wide range of resources and catalogue your findings, including quotes and page numbers, as soon as you find them
Source: Education Photos

work backwards from the hand-in date, to create a timeline of activities for the assignment from the present to the deadline. You can do this using pen and paper or, if you prefer, you can use the many types of project-management software packages available to do this for you.

For example, if you have a large assignment that is due to be handed in on 20 May, and the date is now 4 January, you have approximately four months to plan and do the work for the assignment. Starting with 20 May as your deadline, work backwards to incorporate the following activities and timings for them, in order to arrive back at the current date – use the example below as a starting point:

1 *20 May –13 May* – Final proofing and editing.

2 *13 May – 29 April* – Swap to proof each other's work – buddy system.

3 *29 April – start of Easter Holidays* – Main write-up of assignment and checking for errors.

4 *Easter Holidays through March to early February* – data collection and analysis, further literature searches.

5 *Early February to 4 January* – draft structures of work, literature searches, notes and early preparations.

What you have, then, is a simple but effective timetable or schedule for doing the work, planning from the deadline backwards so that you do not miss it, and so that you leave plenty of time for proofing and final checking. This is the most effective way to eliminate errors and ensure that your work is readable and well-structured.

For your next assignment, produce a schedule or project plan for the work using the above as a guideline, and working from the hand-in date backwards.

Remember that, although your academic writing will be read from start to finish, it doesn't have to be written in this way. If you have some useful things to say as part of a conclusion then write it down, even if it is the very first thing you write. With word processing it is a simple matter to write chunks of work as you are ready (part of the conclusion, then sections of the methodology, followed by a section of the introduction, for example) and then cut and paste things in the order you want when you are ready. After all this is how feature films are made. However, to do this well you need a clear overall plan or structure for your work.

Referencing

As with many of the other topics, this too has whole tomes written about it – see the end-of-chapter references – and so once again the advice is to seek more detailed texts if required. While such books are very comprehensive and detailed, they can be quite daunting, if not a little overwhelming, and it may be easier for you to use a more general text such as this, in conjunction with whatever requirements your university or college has set out for you.

Referencing is an expected academic practice in which you cite the sources, ideas, data and evidence of others that you have used in your assignments, giving them as a full list at the back of the work. We reference because it acknowledges the work of others, and indicates to the reader a depth and breadth of reading for critical judgement in producing your own work at this (Master's) level.

In addition to this, referencing can help you structure your own arguments, and to find your own thoughts and ideas by 'literally' bouncing them off the (acknowledged) work of others. In referencing you are also forced down a path of reflecting on your own experiences and perceptions, particularly in relation to those of others, and this too can often help students prepare and formulate their own arguments and ideas. In doing so, they can also often become better critical analysts of their own work, and of the work of others.

Despite these evident advantages of referencing, it does tend to be one of the most stressful activities of a student's academic writing life. The simple advice would be to utilise an electronic database for your references. Many Higher Education Institutions (HEIs) now provide access to an on-line referencing system for students, such as RefWorks$^{©}$, or EndNote$^{©}$, and also provide the help and support you need to use such a system in your work. These systems enable you to 'cite as you write', which automatically creates a reference in the text as you insert it at the point of the mouse, and simultaneously builds a reference list at the end of the document as you do so. All this is done in whatever format you specify without you having to check it all manually.

The advantages of using such a system are:

- It builds the reference lists for you.
- It avoids the inaccuracies that occur when you write out references long hand from the source to your notes, and then from your notes typed up into the assignment document.
- It does all the formatting for you – automatically according to the system you specify, such as Harvard.
- It transfers references direct from the literature searches to your database.
- It can be used over and over again for different pieces of work.

For assignments with fewer than ten references, you might feel that this is a long-winded way of working, as you also have to learn how to use the software before you start referencing with it. (Such packages are fairly simple to use for the basic operations such as these.) As your work builds up, however, and as you are more than likely to be required to produce work that has reference lists of longer than ten entries, this might be the way forward. (As stated before, though – as with any electronic file – make sure you back it up.)

Practical task

- Describe your own approach to referencing prior to reading this chapter.
- How has this chapter changed your approach?
- Go and find out about referencing software, or come up with an alternative, well-organised, paper-based system that you can apply to your work on the course.

Referencing software is invaluable for long and complicated lists of references, particularly where the references are mixtures of different types: for example, books, journals, articles, conference papers, electronic serials, websites, official reports and so on, all of which require different formatting.

For those of you with an innate fear of information technology, however, or who do not have easy access to such systems (they can be purchased), you need to make sure you do all of the above, but using a paper-based system. It is vital that you keep an accurate record of the references you use, and can access them easily for multiple pieces of work, using either a file-card system, or a hardback notebook, or whatever suits you best.

Stop and reflect

Have you evaluated your skills at referencing since you were at school? Do you feel comfortable with this part of writing? If not, list why not and, if you do, describe why you do.

When you reference work within your assignment documents you need to ensure that you format the references correctly as you use them, and then immediately write them at the end of the document as you go along. It is all too easy to forget to put them in at the end if you do not do it this way, thus increasing the probability that there will be a mismatch between the references used in the text, and those in the list at the back of the document. Even if you do compile your references in this way, you will still need to check that the list and text references match – not too difficult for ten or fewer references, but much more arduous when there are many more.

Students often get references confused with a bibliography. Put simply, a bibliography is a list of books, articles or any other reading that you have done in relation to the work you are submitting. Your references and reference list refer to the reading you have *cited* within the work you are submitting. Any evidence, data, ideas and so on that you have used within in the main body of the assignment must be acknowledged in the text and in the references. Any reading you have done that you did not use in this way would go into a bibliography. It is not always necessary to submit both types of lists with an assignment: generally it is the references that are required, and you should check before doing so, rather than waste precious time doing both when only references are required.

If you get referencing right, you should be able to avoid many of the pitfalls associated with plagiarism – or cheating – and the ways to do this are discussed in the next section.

Plagiarism and how to avoid it

There are many definitions of plagiarism, many levels and types and many reasons for it. Accordingly, there is a wide range of detailed literature available on it – see the References section. The three main forms of plagiarism are:

1 Copying someone's work – including that of your peers on the course – and claiming it as your own;

2 Presenting arguments as a blend of yours and a significant proportion that is copied from the original author, without acknowledging the source;

3 Paraphrasing without giving due acknowledgement to the original writer (Neville, 2007).

Plagiarism is taken very seriously at HEIs and can often lead to a student being removed from a course or even the whole institution, depending on the seriousness and nature of the copying offence. Despite all this, plagiarism is easy to avoid, and this section is intended to give you some practical ways to do this.

Always ensure you acknowledge the source from which you have used material for your work – see the previous section. If something is your work, or your opinion, say so. Be clear when text is your own by stating it clearly as your own, for example, using phrases such as:

'In my opinion . . .'
'The evidence from my research suggests that . . .'
'I feel that . . .'
'As I understand it . . .'

and so on.

Be clear when the text is taken from a different source, cite the source, or quote from the original text using quotation marks – as specified by the referencing system required for your HEI.

Extensive use of the internet by students to research and locate references and materials lends itself more easily to plagiarism than if students had to go to libraries and use notes from books and journals longhand. It is far easier to forget to cite or acknowledge the source when you are cutting and pasting from electronic texts on-line. Make sure you have a system by which you can avoid forgetting references when you do this. Here are some ways to do this:

- Cut and paste from and to documents with differently coloured borders on the screen so you know which is which.
- Cut and paste selected words to a notes-type document from which you can paraphrase the text as you type it up into the main document.
- Always cut and paste the reference with the text you are going to use – keep it at the start or top of any paragraphs you make use of.

Another easy way to keep on top of referencing is to always cite as you write – lest you forget – whether this is by electronic or hand-written means, as long as you do it as you go along. This becomes more significant as reference lists get longer for more extensive pieces of work.

Many students find this next piece of advice uncomfortable, to say the least. However, the results of not taking the advice are far less pleasant than the advice itself.

- Do not lend your work – hard or electronic copy – especially in its final form, to anyone.

Case study

A trainee teacher was called in to university from placement to attend an Academic Conduct Panel. Unbeknown to the trainee, the work that he had lent to one of his housemates had been copied – it being very easy to email electronic copies of assignments to friends for them to look at.

The first third of his assignment had been copied word for word and used by his housemate, who was behind on the assignment and worried that she would miss the deadline for the work. A very nervous and horrified trainee was stunned when he discovered what had been done with his work.

It was only when the marker had looked at the references and seen that the wrong Ofsted report had been used by the copier, that the alarm was raised and the two assignments were then carefully checked to see what had been copied from where.

As a result of this, the guilty party was forced to resubmit and the work capped. The innocent trainee teacher never again let others see his work in this way.

Collaboration is to be encouraged but copying is not, and often there is a fine line between the two. In the next section the buddying system is discussed as an example of a effective collaborative method by which students can improve the quality of each other's assignment work prior to handing it in.

The buddying system

This short section is intended to be used in conjunction with the previous sections on referencing and plagiarism, as it describes a method by which you should be able to hand in work that is readable, legible, makes sense, is correctly referenced and is not copied from anyone else.

The buddying system is, quite simply, a method by which you and another student on your course, or a small group of peers, get together and agree to proofread each other's work prior to the hand-in. You act as critical friends. Many tutors encourage this type of system at both undergraduate and postgraduate level as it encourages peer-to-peer assessment (see Chapter 9 on Assessment and feedback). All you need to do is to agree to work with someone to proof each other's work – you read theirs and give constructive feedback, and they do the same for you. This type of proofing picks up many of the more clumsy errors that can occur, and gives guidance on readability – if your friend can't understand what you've written, then it is unlikely that your tutor will. It can also be used – if done thoroughly – to pick up any referencing errors, and to bounce your ideas and arguments off your peers before you test them on your tutor.

Stop and reflect

Critically assess the advantages and disadvantages of using this system for your work?

In this way many students find it useful, as it also opens their eyes to different writing styles within the group. It also helps to strengthen areas of weakness, and to do the same for others, since the best way to improve your own limitations or faults is to try to explain them to others.

Practical task

Decide how best to achieve a workable buddying system with someone on your course, and construct a plan for both of you for your assignments on the course.

Challenge your thinking

You will be keen to do the best academic assignments that you can. However – to be realistic – you have many other pressures on your time – preparing for lessons for one.

In the busy and hectic professional climate you occupy you find a few minutes to discuss an assignment with a group of colleagues from your course. One of the group states that he has managed to get a copy of a similar assignment from his mentor – who did the course four years ago. The person hasn't copied the whole assignment but it is clear from the conversation that he has used sections and the bibliography is almost identical.

This leaves you with a moral and professional dilemma.

Reflect on how you would react in this situation.

- What are the options open to you?
- What are the implications of following each option?
- What are the implications of ignoring the issue entirely?

Sometimes looking at an issue from different viewpoints can be helpful. What advice do you think each of the following people give to you:

- the course tutor
- your school mentor
- a friend not on the course
- a friend on the same course?

What would you do?

Summary

The purpose of this chapter is to give you a brief overview of academic writing as it applies to students of Master's-level-type assignments in education, specifically in teacher training. It covered practical ways to prepare and produce assignments with correctly used and formatted references, and to avoid the hazards of plagiarism. It also described ways to make the most of the feedback you receive, and also to make use of peer-to-peer assessment to improve the quality of your work.

References

Neville, C. (2007) *The Complete Guide to Referencing and Avoiding Plagiarism,* Maidenhead: OU Press.

Robbins, D. (2000) *Bourdieu and Culture,* London: Sage Publications.

Vygotsky, L. (1978) *Mind in Society. The Development of Higher Psychological Processes* (1st edn), London: Harvard University Press.

Webb, J. (2002) *Understanding Bourdieu,* London: Sage Publications.

Wyse, D. (2007) *The Good Writing Guide for Education Students* (2nd edn), London: Sage Publications.

Web resources

http://en.wikipedia.org/wiki/Academic_writing

Part 2

LEARNING AND TEACHING

Chapter 4

Every Child Matters: a holistic view of the school

Learning outcomes

By the end of this chapter, you will have an understanding of:

→ How a teacher is more than just a teacher of a specific subject

→ How teachers become more than teachers to their students

→ How to differentiate between being friendly and being a friend

→ The policies and issues linked to the *Every Child Matters* report

→ The different parties that work in schools and how they all interlink

→ Where the future of inclusion lies

Introduction

This chapter is intended to give you an overview of the roles you will carry out as a teacher that are over and above that of subject teacher. Being a teacher means taking on many different roles, and in fact there are days when it may feel like you are taking on too many. This chapter discusses the wider role of the teacher and your duty of care, especially in the light of legislation related to *Every Child Matters* (DfES 2003, 2004). It should be read in conjunction with Chapter 16 on Pastoral care and the role of the form tutor.

Why is the Every Child Matters agenda important?

Teaching is a complex and challenging role, not least because it involves a complex range of interactions with students, across a large age range, requiring subject specialist knowledge combined with a role of carer – *in loco parentis*. From the 1940s until the advent of comprehensive schools children were placed into three different types of schools. This typing of children was first described in the Norwood Report (1943) and enshrined in the Education Act of 1944 (HMSO, 1944). In this act three types of school were identified:

- Grammar
- Technical
- Secondary modern.

In this way children of different abilities were to be catered for (McCulloch, 1994). Since this type of tripartite system was set up there has been a wider recognition that every child has special interests and special needs and increasing drawbacks in the selection system used (the eleven-plus exam) have been highlighted. The Labour governments of the 1960s and 1970s pushed for the abolition of the eleven-plus and the creation of comprehensive schools. However, this has never been universally accepted, and grammar and independent schools exist alongside comprehensive schools in the current system. The Warnock Report (1978) was influential in stressing students' individual needs. This report, followed by the 1981 Education Act, introduced the idea of Special Educational Needs (SEN) and paved the way for what is now termed an 'inclusive' approach. This approach stressed common educational goals for children – regardless of their abilities or disabilities.

During the 1980s and 1990s there was an increase in the number of children with special educational needs in mainstream schools and a decline in the number of children in special schools. Further improvements in SEN provision came through the SEN and Disability Act (SENDA, 2001) and the 2004 SEN strategy, *Removing Barriers to Achievement'* (DfES, 2004). During this time investment in Social, emotional and behavioural needs (SEBN) rose from £2.8 billion to £4.1 billion.

Stop and reflect

Reflect on the type of school you attended.

- Did it have a selection policy or were all of the children in the area able to attend?
- Were the students streamed into ability groups or were classes mixed-ability?
- How were students looked after pastorally? If you had a problem who could you turn to?

It is from the educational developments since the comprehensive schools movement, and also from some tragic cases of child abuse and neglect, that our current greater understanding of student needs has arisen – culminating in the 'Every Child Matters' agenda (DEfS, 2003) As you will appreciate, students with problems often see teachers as key adults in their lives and turn to them for support. Also, well-trained and aware teachers can often spot signs of distress and abuse and can alert the proper authorities. This is one of the important reasons why your role as a teacher extends beyond that of subject teacher.

More than just a subject teacher?

Practical task

Critically reflect on a particular teacher who was influential in your life.

- Which subject did they teach?
- What other roles did this teacher play in the school?
- What personal skills and qualities made this teacher so effective in supporting you?
- Try to list the roles you think an effective teacher undertakes.

Most of you will have entered teaching in order to use your subject knowledge, to pass it on to others and watch how they learn, fascinated by all the things that drew you to this subject in the first place. You might be hoping to fire them with the same kind of passion for it that you have. This is laudable indeed, and yet, this is only part of what a teacher is in a school – as some of you may already be realising (You might on the other hand have come into teaching for the holidays – although I have yet to meet a trainee who owned up to this!).

A teacher is more than just a subject teacher, for a number of reasons. For example, they are given other official duties in schools and because they take on other roles in the care of their students. These two are intertwined and hard to separate so that you become a teacher incorporating a wide range of roles and developing new skills. It is hoped this chapter will help you to gain an insight into the holistic approach to the care and education of your students that is needed to be an effective professional teacher.

Practical task

Use your school experiences to reflect on the tasks below.

- Write a list of all the roles that you have carried out as or with a form tutor.
- Classify them as either
    a. related to administration
    b. related to academic work
    c. related to pastoral work
    d. solving care and safety issues.

Some of the roles you might be expected to undertake for your students are:

- *Social worker* – when they bring in their problems – and you have to decide where to refer them to
- *(Constructive) critic* – when they bring in work they have done at home, drawings, paintings, music and so on
- *Initial first aider* – triage – until you can get them to the appropriate person in school
- *Relationship advisor* – again until you can refer them on
- *Subject tutor* – for many different subjects not just your own
- *Mentor* or coach
- *Police officer* for control and discipline.

In all these things it is important to remember where the limits of these roles lie, and this is discussed in the next section.

Friend or friendly?

The purpose of this section is to ensure that you are fully aware of the differences between being a friend and being friendly, and where the boundaries lie, so that you are also sensitive to where both these things stop and where problems begin. Before reading any further try the next task.

Stop and reflect

Reflect on the teachers you knew at school. Evaluate them in terms of the following questions:

- Can you differentiate between the ones that were friendly and the ones that tried to be your friend?
- What were the differences?
- Which did you prefer and why?

It is important that your students respect you and retain that respect for the duration of your relationship with them and, ideally, for many years afterwards. Respect of course, has to be earned, and often it can take a lot of effort and time with students to build the relationship up to one of mutual respect. Conversely, it can take only a moment to destroy, and it is advice about avoiding this that forms a major focus of this chapter.

All students need friends, but what they need from a teacher is someone who can be friendly, but who also sets boundaries for them. Students of all ages – right through to Y12 and Y13, still require, to a greater or lesser extent, someone who is able to direct them, and to show them where the lines are drawn. This is achievable if you are friendly, but not when you become a friend.

The problems associated with being their friend include the following:

- Knowing when to stop
- Knowing when it has become something more for them
- Spending too much time with any one student
- Being seen to do the above by other students – favouritism
- Undermining other roles you wish to adopt, e.g. discipline and class management.

By all means be friendly with your students once you have earned their respect. As long as they know how far to take you and don't over step the mark, or as long as you can regain control if you lose it, this is fine. Avoid becoming a friend and doing the things that friends do, as it is difficult, if not impossible, to withdraw from this position and regain any sense of authority you might have had.

Building relationships with children is not easy, and is a very personal experience. It can be a way of learning to communicate with other people, and comprises three main characteristics: control, responsibility and concern (Pollard, 2002). It is up to you to determine how you interpret and apply these things as a teacher, and thus how you become more than just a subject teacher. Further information on this can be found in Chapter 16 Pastoral care and the role of the form tutor.

The pastoral system – being a form tutor

In the kingdom of the tutor group, the form tutor is king (or queen). You are the most important person within this system, however it is organised within your school. As a form tutor you have first-hand knowledge (possibly more than you might have wanted) of your students' home circumstances, and as such you are the first port of call for your students for personal issues, and any changes to their behaviour arising as a result of things that might have happened at home or even on the way to school.

In some respects, the tutor group can form a home from home for some students. For some it might be the most constant aspect of their lives. In a school, the tutor can be the one fixed point of stability for a student's academic life there (Cole, 1999). It is worth remembering this. It is a responsibility not to be taken lightly, but also one which brings many rewards for you and the students. (See also Chapter 16 on Pastoral care and the role of the form tutor.)

The main thing to remember is that you are not alone, and that there are systems in place to assist you with any issues that may arise. Being first port of call does not mean you are the only port of call, and you need to be aware of whom you can call on for specific things. Details of the pastoral care system in schools are given in Chapter 10 of this book and you should refer to this for more details than can be given here.

Challenge your thinking

Naresh is the form tutor for a Y10 group. He arrives at work on Monday, fresh from half-term. Walking into his form room he is greeted by a group of his students wanting to talk to him. They gather round excitedly and all try to speak together. Eventually he manages to calm them down and asks one to give him the information that they are so keen to impart.

'Sir, Karla has run away from home, and we think she is with Jason from Mrs Huddleston's group.'

The news isn't a complete shock to Naresh. He knows Karla is a lively but troubled girl in his group. There has been a history of abuse at home, and she had been bullied at school briefly two month previously, but he had hoped this was all resolved.

Naresh needs to act but first he ensures that the tutor group period is completed properly.

- What further information will Naresh need in order to act appropriately?
- Where are his best sources of information?
- Whom must Naresh alert and what further action must he undertake?
- If you were a form tutor in this situation, would you try to gather more information from members of the form group?

Every Child Matters

'Every Child Matters' (DfES, 2003) was a report written in response to Lord Laming's enquiry into the death of Victoria Climbié that proposed a range of measures to reform and improve the care of children by bringing services for children into one place and under one person. The full report (a Green Paper) is available from a number of sources (*http://publications.dcsf.gov.uk* or *http://publications.teachernet.gov.uk*) and it contains a useful executive summary that gives you a brief overview of the full report.

The aim of the Green Paper was to address the problem of children falling through the cracks between different services, emphasising that child protection cannot be separated from policies to improve children's lives as a whole. The document looks at the progress towards a framework of services which aims to support every child, using this as a context in which to consider the specific needs of children at risk. Particular attention is paid to children who are in care, come from impoverished backgrounds or suffer from abuse. The document identifies the broad concerns which have been shown to matter most to children and young people, presenting plans to develop the roles of the voluntary and community sectors, schools and health bodies in fulfilling these needs. It stresses the importance of information sharing between different government agencies and of a higher level of

Within a busy school it isn't easy to spot those children who are particularly vulnerable or at risk. However, it is essential we all take great care in monitoring the health and wellbeing of the children in our care

Source: Education Photos

accountability (DfES, 2003). There is now also a website dedicated to this report and the issues surrounding it at *http://www.everychildmatters.gov.uk/*.

The report itself spawned a whole series of linked and related papers and reports which can be accessed from the above sites, and the website mentioned above, which is dedicated to this subject, is very useful in this respect with a wealth of information and downloadable resources on this and related topics. While it is not the intention of this chapter to describe in detail the full report and all its many implications for teachers, it is intended to give you an overview of the main outcomes/purposes of the report and also point the reader towards further reading. The report was followed by the Children Act (2004) and a report setting out the national framework for local change programmes (DfES, 2004).

Practical task

Spend some time researching the websites given above.

- Evaluate and make notes on what you think are the most important aspects of the Every Child Matters agenda.
- How are you likely to realise that some of the children you work with in schools might be regarded as vulnerable?

The main aim of the ECM agenda, then, was to:

'[. . .] ensure that every child has the chance to fulfil their potential by reducing levels of educational failure, ill health, substance misuse, teenage pregnancy, abuse and neglect, crime and anti-social behaviour among children and young people.'

(DfES, 2003)

This was to be done through the implementation of five outcomes, which were identified as those that mattered most to children and young people:

1 *Being healthy* – to include both physical and mental health and a healthy lifestyle.

2 *Staying safe* – being protected from harm and neglect.

3 *Enjoying and achieving* – getting the most out of life and developing the skills needed for adulthood.

4 *Making a positive contribution* – to include being involved with their community and with society, and not engaging in antisocial or offensive behaviour.

5 *Economic well-being* – not being prevented from achieving their full potential in life through economic disadvantage.

Stop and reflect

Consider the impact of the ECM agenda on you as a teacher in a school. Use the following to guide you in this:

- Evaluate what ECM issues might arise daily in your class. What are they and how will you deal with them? Use the list above to help you with this.
- In terms of teaching and learning, what influence has the ECM agenda had in your classroom? Which particular students does it affect, if any?
- Reflect on what inclusion means to you, and whether this is different now than what it was before you started teaching.

Action intended to achieve this was focused on four main areas: supporting parents and carers; early intervention and effective protection; accountability and integration (at local, regional and national levels); and workforce reform. These were enshrined in the Children Act (2004).

Supporting parents and carers

Extra funding was channelled into putting support for parents and carers at the heart of the approach to improving children's lives, including funding for universal services, targeted and specialist support, and compulsory action.

Early intervention and effective protection

The key to this area of improvement was to ensure that those children who required extra support would get it at the first onset of problems, with the hope that none would slip through the net, thanks to improving information sharing, developing a common assessment framework, the introduction of a lead professional for each case, and the development of on-the-spot service delivery.

Accountability and integration

Services for children were reorganised around their needs, and the key to these changes was the introduction of a single person responsible for improving the lives of children. Consequently, there now exists a Director of Children's Services, accountable for local authority education and children's social services. There is also legislation that enabled a lead council member for children to be created, and a much more integrated service approach to the care and education of children. There is also a Minister for Children, Young People and Families who is responsible for coordinating policies across government. Thus integration is being implemented at local, regional and national levels.

Workforce reform

As with the changes described above, changes under this heading are far reaching and very long term, although they might arguably be seen as depending more on reflecting current political priorities than being truly independent of then. The myriad workforce proposals are the responsibility of the Children's Workforce Unit which works with the relevant employers, staff and government departments to establish a Sector Skills Council (SSC) for Children and Young People's Services to deliver key parts of the strategy. There is not the space here to give details of all workforce reform policies and strategies; however, you can find more detail about them at the websites mentioned above. The Teachernet site is particularly user friendly for this type of topic. As a teacher you will wish to enhance your understanding of these issues.

Case study

A highly visible case that reflects on the ECM agenda is that of Doncaster Council children's services, for which a major overhaul was ordered by the government on 12 March 2009 after inspectors identified 'serious weaknesses' in performance. In addition to this, the then Children's Secretary, Ed Balls, ordered the appointment of a new senior management team, overseen by an external improvement board reporting directly to ministers. Referring to an on-site assessment of services by officials from the Department for Children, Schools and Families, Balls said: 'Despite significant investment over the past year and some progress, the review has concluded that urgent improvement is still required.'

The DCSF had carried out a 'diagnostic review' of safeguarding in Doncaster, after a damning annual performance assessment, published in December 2008, in which Ofsted graded Doncaster as inadequate both for safeguarding and also overall in children's services. Ofsted had found that, although the number of children subject to a child protection plan was significantly higher than in similar authorities, one in four of those cases was not allocated to a social worker. Safeguarding in Doncaster was found to be sadly lacking:

● The local safeguarding children board had not ensured effective implementation of procedures and practice to support the management of child protection allegations.

- The number of children subject to a child protection plan was significantly higher than in similar authorities.
- One in four child protection cases was not allocated to a social worker.
- The number of looked-after children with an allocated social worker had declined significantly.
- The proportion of initial and core assessments completed within target timescales was low and significantly worse than in similar authorities.

The *DCSF diagnostic review*, which was published in April 2009, echoed a number of these criticisms. It was still unclear whether child protection cases were allocated, and the local safeguarding children board was not working effectively.

Further details about the failure of Doncaster Council children's services to ensure the safety of the children in its care can be found at *http://www.communitycare.co.uk/Articles/2009/07/08/110417/doncaster-childrens-services.htm* and also at: *http://www.cypnow.co.uk/news/ByDiscipline/Social-Care/982367/Problems-remain-Doncastors-childrens-services/* (both accessed on 8.2.2010).

In the latter document are the following three criticisms:

- The electronic recording system is still 'underdeveloped' with no audit trail of decisions.
- Quality-checking procedures are in place but not linked to the area's Local Safeguarding Children Board.
- Some staff were not receiving formal supervision and support. Poor performance was not being identified and challenged.

What do you think of the way Doncaster Council children's services have *not* implemented the Every Child Matters agenda as it was intended to be done?

For each of the three criticisms above identify:

- How failings might impact on the health and safety of children
- One development or improvement that would help to address the criticism
- One lesson you can learn as a teacher from each fault identified above.

The team that is a school

A school is more than just the teachers that teach there. It comprises a number of different people and professional's who work together to ensure that students get the best education possible. All contribute in some way to this. Some of the various people involved in the running of a school that you will have to find out about and work with at some point are to be found in:

- *Finance* – this department is usually run by a bursar or business manager (with support staff), who might also be part of the senior management team. Finance are responsible for monies associated with school trips, purchases, and so on, for all acquisitions and payments, and most important, for your salary and expenses.
- *Exams* – not a small department in a school. In some large schools there are exams taking place in some form or other every single month of the academic year. This

department is responsible for all public exams, resits, and possibly some or all internal exams, such as mocks. They process all entries and results – through information given by teachers – and are responsible for all amendments made to exam entries, for example, when you decide that a student could be entered for a higher level than was previously thought.

- *Administration* – for this department it would be easier to say what they do not do. This forms the central hub of the school, and tends to be aware of everything going on, situated, as it normally is, in the reception area. Administration can be responsible for room changes, typing, phones, messages, first aid, school trips, bulletins, stationery, lost property, newsletters, SIMS student data, and on and on . . .

- *Caretaking/cleaning* – as well as the more obvious duties, they might also be the people who set up rooms for presentations, meetings and exams and so on. They are usually in school early, and it might be worth remembering that if you ever need a room setting up in a particular way for your teaching. They also like chocolate biscuits!

- *Medical* – this area includes the school nurse, who may attend a number of schools in the area. In a pyramid system, the school nurse may also attend feeder primary and middle schools as well as the high school. School nurses no longer do first aid for students as this is the responsibility of specific non medical personnel. It also includes the first aiders.

- *Catering* – this incorporates food for staff and students during the school day, for meetings and visitors (you yourself might be bringing some in) and for off-site and out-of-hours activities.

- *Cover/supply* – these two responsibilities are often covered by the same person, who may be responsible for seeing that there is cover for sickness and ad hoc absences, and also for ensuring that long-term supply teachers are provided where necessary. The person responsible, often a member of the senior management team – has to make sure there is a teacher present for every registration and class during the school day. They might also be responsible for recruiting supply teachers on a long- and short-term basis, and possibly also for exam cover.

- *Systems support* – this is an ever-increasing area now, with many activities being done through the use of ICT rather than longhand. In many schools, academic and administration systems are separate and maintained by different people. Schools often require a 'data manager' to look after these systems, and there may be certain functions delegated to specific people in the school, all of which link to each other, For example, timetabling, exams, attendance, finance, cover, and so on, all have different management systems, and require specialist personnel to perform the duties required of those using them.

- *Attendance* – as stated above this is usually done via electronic means such as BromCom, and SIMS systems. These are the people who know where your students should be at any one time. Registers are usually submitted to the attendance personnel after registration, and any students not attending without reason (according to the registers) would be contacted by the school. They can also produce reports on attendance, and are often required to do so for legislative reasons, on a weekly, monthly, termly and yearly basis. These can form very useful reference document for teachers for parents' evenings and reports.

This list is not exhaustive and is different in all schools. For a more detailed view of how the various teams of staff within schools are managed see Chapter 12 School structure, leadership and management.

A key issue to remember is that you have to be able to work professionally with all these people and departments, as there is likely to be a time when you will have to interact with them at some point in supporting your students. To do this effectively, it is important to appreciate the various roles that these people play within the school.

So, do these areas all fit together? Yes and no, depending on the school, is the most realistic answer. There can be a gap – perceived or otherwise in schools between teaching staff and the 'other' staff. This is not helpful, and you should make it your job to bridge that gap if there is one – after all, it should be a single team in a school, shouldn't it?

An example of how these different areas might interlink is with the running of an external examination. For this you would need:

- Caretaking staff to help set up rooms
- Cover/supply – for invigilation and class cover
- Administration – to provide information for all students on room changes, and to ensure that Parcelforce bring the exam papers and return the completed ones
- Finance staff – to collect and process any exam fees
- Academic staff – subject specialists to start the exams, to ensure that all instructions are understood by all students and invigilators. For example, as a music teacher, would you be comfortable setting off a physics practical exam?
- The exams office itself – to sort out the papers, the entries, collate the papers, parcel them up for collection, and deal with any queries with the exam boards.

Practical task

- List the different departments that exist in your schools.
- Do you think they all work well together?
- How many have you worked with?
- How would you interact with the different departments and people within the school if a student in your Y8 tutor group told you he was being bullied?

Every Child Matters and inclusion

It is arguable that despite progress in inclusive education since Warnock (1978) we should perhaps examine where we have progressed to and think about how we might move on from this position. This should in fact now be more possible than ever, given what we know about the subject. This might be particularly important given the Every Child Matters agenda. If every child matters, then it is imperative that we look to ways of providing effective access to education for all. Instead of continuing with the more traditional regimes of special education, which tend to rely on the views of exceptionality, we should perhaps be more inclined to embrace the more recent models of learning that emphasise the importance of identity in a community (Thomas and Loxley, 2007).

Rather than accentuating the distinctive differences of students with special educational needs, should we not be more inclined to embrace them as members of a whole school community? Current discussions on the consequences of difference also illuminates factors that disadvantage students at school – and we should heed them if we are to progress.

A new insight into the means by which inequality, relative poverty and contrastive judgement construct learning difficulties, is emerging from the research currently going on in various inter-related social scientific disciplines, leading to the definition of a new 'psychology of difference' (Thomas and Loxley, 2007). If we are to progress with inclusion, we have to study the emerging findings of this type of research and to understand the ways in which differences lead to alienation from a community – particularly when that community is a school community in which the major members are themselves young and often inclined to further accentuate any perceived differences in their peers and thus alienate them. (Children can be cruel!)

Communities for learning are becoming increasingly important and many types of such communities have been defined within education arising from research into e-learning (McConnell, 2006). As inclusive educators we should be looking for ways in which we can 'exploit' these communities to achieve more for those students who need them. We need to move away from the ways in which a school abstains from encouraging community structure, and arguably, through its inherent routines such as those associated with assessment and comparison, actually does more harm than good (albeit unintentionally) for the development of such communities of learning (Thomas and Loxley, 2007). The future lies in such communities. Ensuring that all students feel part of them will develop and enhance their self-esteem through this inclusion.

Critical synthesis

The Safeguarding Vulnerable Groups Act 2006 came in to effect in 2008, and introduced a new vetting and barring scheme for all those working with children and young people. As part of the new scheme, the DCSF announced the tightening of existing regulations and issued guidance on the implications of this legislation. Further information on this can be found on the Teachernet website and also the Every Child Matters website (full references can be found at the end of the chapter).

In the light of the very visible cases in the media regarding the safety of children in education – for example, the cases of Baby P (http://www.timesonline.co.uk/tol/news/uk/crime/article5140511.ece accessed on 8.2.2010) and the Soham murders (http://news.bbc.co.uk/1/hi/uk/3312551.stm accessed on 8.2.2010) evaluate how such cases have had an effect on you as a trainee teacher in school. Try to critically analyse how different media coverage might have resulted in different consequences for the education system.

Stop and reflect

- Reflect on the different communities that you belong to and compare them with the community that you belong to as part of your role as a teacher in a school.
- Evaluate how you can ensure that all members of this school community feel valued and part of the whole.
- Analyse how you can modify your teaching and learning in classrooms, your planning and preparation, the way you construct resources, the way you ensure learners meet their objectives and achieve the best that they can, and so on, to ensure that every child really does matter.

Summary

The intention of this chapter was to introduce you to your role beyond that of subject teacher and how your roles fit within the wider school community. In addition to this, a brief overview of the changes brought to education following the Every Child Matters report was also covered, with some indications of where we might go to from here in terms of inclusive education. Further reading on the subjects covered in this chapter is given below the References for those of you who wish to take this subject further. There are educational research journals dedicated solely to this subject, and it might be worth you searching your library databases for these if you would like to read the latest research on the subject.

References

Briggs, S. (2005) *Inclusion and how to do it: Meeting SEN in Secondary Classrooms*, London: David Fulton Publishers.

Cole, M. (ed.) (1999) *Professional Issues for Teachers and Student Teachers*, London: David Fulton Publishers.

DfES (2003) 'Every Child Matters'. Retrieved March 2008 from *http://publications.teachernet.gov.uk*

DfES (2004) 'Change for Children', London DfES. Available on-line at *www.everychildmatters.gov.uk/aims*. Accessed October 2010.

DfES (2004) The Children Act, London DfES. Available on-line at *www.dcsf.gov.uk/childrenactreport*. Accessed October 2010.

DfES (2004) *Removing Barriers to Achievement*, DfES at *http://www.dfes.gov.uk/*

McConnell, D. (2006) *E-Learning Groups and Communities*, Maidenhead: Open University Press.

McCulloch, G. (1994) *Educational Reconstruction – The 1944 Education Act and the Twenty-first Century, I*, llford: The Woburn Press.

Pollard, A. (ed.) (2002) *Readings for reflective teaching*, London: Continuum.

Thomas, G. and Loxley, A. (2007) *Deconstructing Special Education and Constructing Inclusion*, Maidenhead: OU Press.

Warnock Report (1978) HMSO at *http://sen.ttrb.ac.uk/*. Accessed February 2010.

Further reading

Broadhead, P., Meleady, C. and Delgado, M. (2007) *Children, Families and Communities Developing Integrated Services,* Maidenhead: OU Press.

Casey, L., Davies, P., Kalambouka, A., Nelson, N. and Boyle, B. (2006) 'The influence of schooling on the aspirations of young people with special education needs', *British Educational Research Journal (BERJ),* 32(2): 273–90.

Williams, R. and Pritchard, C. (2006) *Breaking the Cycle of Educational Alienation: A Multiprofessional Approach,* Maidenhead: OU Press.

Web resources

http://www.dfes.gov.uk/

http://www.dcfs.gov.uk/

http://www.everychildmatters.gov.uk/

http://www.teachernet.gov.uk

http://www.dcsf.gov.uk/everychildmatters/safeguardingandsocialcare/

Chapter 5

Engaging learners

Learning outcomes

By the end of this chapter, you will have an understanding of:

→ How learning approaches can be classified

→ The factors that contribute to effective learner outcomes

→ The different cognitive styles used by learners and ideas about the cognitive development of children

→ How ideas about multiple intelligences are impacting on learning and teaching

→ How to identify the preferred learning styles of students

→ Some key aspects of active, student-centred learning and teaching

Introduction

In this chapter we will look at some of the theories that underpin why we do what we do in the classroom. The school curriculum hasn't happened by accident, but is the result of many years of development and modification. There would be a whole chapter's worth of work on the political and social influences on this development, but here we will concentrate on the psychological ideas that have impacted on what teachers do and when they do it.

Stop and reflect

During you reading of the chapter it would be useful if you could bear in mind some key questions:

- How does your approach to teaching have an effect on student's learning?
- Why is it important for you to know about the cognitive development of those you teach?
- Are there different types of learner that you should be aware of when planning and teaching?
- How important are language and social interactions in your classroom?
- Which strategies might you adopt to encourage students to understand as well as recall?
- How do you read and reflect on your practice critically?

Audit of your learning experiences

There is a wide range of learning and teaching strategies in use in classrooms today – here you will gain an opportunity to reflect on those you are aware of already and be introduced to some that will be new to you. Ideally, you will also use many in the classroom yourself. When you do use them it is vital that you select them wisely and this chapter will help in this process.

Remember to reflect critically on your experiences of planning and using them – Chapter 2 will help with this vital process. It is this critical reflection that will aid your development as a teacher.

If you are motivated enough to read this chapter it is clear that at the moment you are concentrating on improving your role as a teacher. This is understandable, as your main focus will be on how you will work with students in the classroom. However, as you will appreciate, you are also very much in a learning situation. This is true for teachers throughout their careers as they continue with their professional development. Many teachers also believe that they learn from the students as they are teaching them.

In what ways do you think that even very experienced teachers can learn from students during lessons? What can our work with learners tell us about our teaching, their learning and the effectiveness of assessment strategies used?

Learners bring to each situation their past experiences and existing skills and knowledge. As a first step it is useful to consider these – in other words carry out an audit to attempt to understand the stage the learner is at before moving on. This is especially true if the learner is bringing into the new situation 'alternative conceptions' or 'misunderstandings' from previous learning. This may be referred to by using the metaphor (always powerful in teaching) as 'trying to build a building on shaky foundations'.

As a teacher you will wish to determine the level of understanding and awareness of your students before moving on – this will help you to identify any 'alternative conceptions' and aid you in addressing them, as well as providing evidence to inform you of the likely pace, content and approaches adopted in the lesson. Let us begin this learning situation by auditing your prior knowledge and experiences as a learner. You may wish to reflect on assessment experiences you have had. You will learn more about 'assessment for learning' later but you can audit your understanding of this now.

Practical task

Audit of personal learning experiences

Where?	Examples of when you have learnt by instruction from a teacher (indirect experiences)	Examples of when you have learnt by trying things yourself (direct experiences)
During your time at school		
During your time at university		
As part of the rest of your life		

Stop and reflect

Reflect on the experiences above. Select one example of learning by indirect experience and one example of learning by direct experiences.

● What did the approaches have in common, and in what ways were they different?

● Which did you find most useful?

● How were you assessed?

Come back to these questions having thought about the next section.

Classification of learning approaches

It is a stereotypical view of the teacher held by many that the teacher stands at the front of rows of pupils and talks to them – often using a board to write on – and gives the pupils new information to learn. Teaching is taking place, therefore learning is taking place. This **didactic** approach relies on the notion that direct instruction is the appropriate strategy to adopt. You may note that the term 'pupil' has been used here, whereas elsewhere in the book the term 'student' is preferred. This isn't simple semantics. A student is someone who 'directs zeal or enthusiasms towards something' – someone who quests to learn. A pupil is regarded as someone learning under the close supervision of a teacher. You can reflect on the differences between a pupil and a student as you develop as a teacher.

In contrast **heuristic** strategies encourage students to find things out for themselves through discovery. One of the main proponents of the heuristic approach was John Dewey (1963). Dewey started a school in the late nineteenth century that was dedicated to a pragmatic approach to learning. All learning was directed towards the practical skills needed by the community, and any other learning grew out of this. This approach developed into the progressive education movement of the twentieth century.

It will be clear to you that, rather than being two poles, these philosophies occupy two ends of a spectrum. It is unlikely that learning experiences will be solely didactic or solely heuristic and it is difficult to imagine that any teacher, irrespective of their personal philosophy, will rely totally on one or the other. Each has its own advantages and disadvantages (Cotton, 1995).

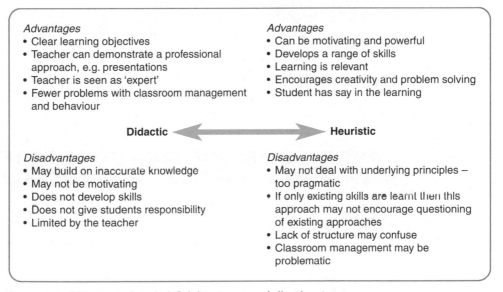

Advantages
- Clear learning objectives
- Teacher can demonstrate a professional approach, e.g. presentations
- Teacher is seen as 'expert'
- Fewer problems with classroom management and behaviour

Advantages
- Can be motivating and powerful
- Develops a range of skills
- Learning is relevant
- Encourages creativity and problem solving
- Student has say in the learning

Didactic ⟵⟶ **Heuristic**

Disadvantages
- May build on inaccurate knowledge
- May not be motivating
- Does not develop skills
- Does not give students responsibility
- Limited by the teacher

Disadvantages
- May not deal with underlying principles – too pragmatic
- If only existing skills are learnt then this approach may not encourage questioning of existing approaches
- Lack of structure may confuse
- Classroom management may be problematic

Figure 5.1 Didactic or heuristic? Advantages and disadvantages

Classrooms used to be set out formally to support didactic approaches. How is your classroom arranged and what does this say about your teaching style?

Source: David Savill/Getty Images

Stop and reflect

Think back to your personal learning audit.

- Do any of the examples fall into the category of didactic teaching?
- Are your examples of direct experiences truly heuristic?

Critically reflect on some of the barriers to heuristic approaches in schools.

Some theory

With the time, energy and money spent on schools it would be an understandable assumption that there must be a great deal of research that tells us which approaches to use in the classroom and which to avoid. Should we be didactic or heuristic? It is true that there is a great deal of educational research undertaken, but surprisingly little on how best to teach. Miijs and Reynolds (2005) state that 'the UK historically has had a very small research base' focusing on teaching, so it isn't going to be as simple as looking up the literature and being told what to do. Where research does exist it can be contradictory. Bennet (1976) did attempt to explore whether 'traditional' or 'progressive' primary school teachers were more effective in terms of 'achievement gain' of their students. Little variation in achievement based on teaching style was observed. Pollard *et al.* (1994) pointed out that in reviews of curriculum projects it was clear that what emerged was the amount of time students actually spent on task. Students spent much more time on task in whole-class and group work than they did during individualised work.

Mortimore *et al.* (1988) also found that teachers in primary schools were spending more time with individual students than undertaking whole-class instruction or group work. During this individual work much time was spent on routine tasks rather than encouraging higher-level thinking. The factors identified by Mortimer *et al.* (1988) that contribute to effective student outcomes were:

- Structured lessons
- Intellectually challenging teaching
- A work-oriented environment
- Communication between teacher and students
- A limited focus within lessons.

Stop and reflect

Analyse and critique the work of Mortimer and colleagues.

- How close towards the didactic end of the spectrum would you place the type of teaching indicated by the research of Mortimer and colleagues?
- How does the teaching you experiences at school match up to the factors above?

It is clear that there is a spectrum of philosophy from didactic to heuristic and that each in their extreme has advantages and disadvantages. What is also clear is that the time students spend on tasks is crucial to learning. In addition, some research would indicate that structure, limited focus and challenge are at the core of good learning. We will now consider this further; with a brief look at some of the theories of learning that have influenced teachers.

How children learn – some underpinning theories

Cognitive style

'Cognitive style is an individual's preferred and habitual approach to organising and representing information.'

(Riding and Raynor, 1998: p. 8)

This, as Riding (2003) states, reflects the fundamental make-up of a person. This means that the way a person sees the world and responds to it is influenced by their cognitive style. Surely then, learning must also be affected?

It has been concluded by some authors (Riding and Cheema, 1991; Riding and Raynor, 1998) that cognitive styles can be categorised within two dimensions.

1 *The wholist-analytic dimension.* Does a person organise information in wholes or parts?

2 *The verbal-imagery dimension.* Does a person represent information verbally or in pictures?

The dimensions represent continuums but Riding (2002) argues that it is useful to group them:

Wholist ←——————→ Analyst

Verbalist ←——————→ Imager

This is a useful model to help us to understand that some learners will tend to see the whole picture when studying an issue, whereas others will be more comfortable when able to study only one or two aspects of an issue or topic.

Verbalisers think in words or through verbal associations. Imagers experience mental pictures when they are introduced to information. These styles would appear to have a major impact on the processing of information (Rider, 2002)

Stop and reflect

- Do you think you are a wholist or an analyst?
- Are you a verbalist or an imager?

If you are a verbalist try to explain what you know about children's learning by drawing a diagram, cartoon or flow chart. If you are an imager then try to describe in words how a bicycle pump works.

Thinking back to the didactic-heuristic approaches mentioned earlier, which approach do you think would favour:

- Wholists?
- Analysts?
- Imagers?
- Verbalists?

It would appear that it is vital to be aware of the possible cognitive styles of our learners and to ensure that our approach does not demand an excess of one style to the detriment of another. For example, verbalisers use social relationships and social groupings to discuss their ideas to aid learning so would benefit from group discussion work. Imagers appear less dependent on talking to aid understanding.

This links to the Multiple Intelligences Theory of Howard Gardner (1983) which has similarities to the simpler, but more quoted use of the Visual, Auditory, Kinaesthetic (VAK) Learning Styles model developed since the 1920s. Gardner identified seven multiple intelligence types and the use of this model has had a key impact on teaching.

The seven are:

1 Linguistic – words and language

2 Logical-Mathematical – logic and numbers

3 Musical – music, sound, rhythm

4 Bodily-Kinaesthetic – body movement control

5 Spatial-Visual – images and space

6 Interpersonal – other people's feelings

7 Intrapersonal – self-awareness.

Gardner argued that the intelligence type would influence preferred learning styles. For example, a person who is very logical and mathematical but weak linguistically could develop linguistic skills by being encouraged to talk and write about mathematics and number.

The VAK model accepts that people learn in different ways. According to the model most people possess a dominant learning style, but many can be a mixture of two or all three. The styles are:

● Visual – seeing and reading

● Auditory – listening and speaking

● Kinaesthetic – touching and doing.

It is clear that if we accept this model then our lessons must include aspects of each preferred style. A student who has a visual preferred learning style would be hindered, and perhaps de-motivated, by listening for long periods of time. Likewise a kinaesthetic learner would prefer to be doing things instead of watching or listening.

Critical synthesis

Some researchers claim that the work of Gardner has been largely misunderstood and corrupted in schools and simplified to a dilution that makes it less valuable. Draw on current research criticism of multiple intelligences, and especially VAK, and arrive at an informed judgement about the value of multiple intelligence models on your teaching.

Other models of preferred learning styles include that of David Kolb (1984). Kolb highlights four learning styles based on two choices between conflicting models.

● Concrete experiences or abstract concepts

● Active experimentation or reflective observation.

Knowing a student's learning style allows the teacher to organise learning experiences that reflect the preferred method. However, in reality it is important to understand that people can be a mix of the styles and that learners benefit from engagement with other styles, so ensuring a mix of activities across the styles seems sensible.

The four learning styles are:

1 **Diverging.** Learners with this preferred style prefer to watch rather than do and use imagination to solve problems. Kolb called this style 'Diverging' because the learners do better at generating ideas. Group work is preferred by such learners.

2 **Assimilating**. Learners with this preferred style prefer a logical approach. Less good with people, these learners deal with ideas and prefer thinking problems through, readings, lectures and analytical models.

3 **Converging.** Learners with this preferred style prefer technical tasks and finding practical solutions for any theories encountered. They enjoy experimenting and simulating the real world.

4 **Accommodating.** Learners with this preferred style prefer a 'hands-on' and practical approach to their learning. They often act on instinct, set targets and enjoy working in teams.

A similar model has been proposed by Honey and Mumford (1986). In this the learning styles can be seen as a four-stage cycle. Many learners are more comfortable within one style, but can perform effectively within other styles.

1 'Having an Experience' (stage 1), and Activists (style 1): having the experience through active participation allows deeper understanding and an opportunity to try things out at first hand.

2 'Reviewing the Experience' (stage 2) and Reflectors (style 2): reviewing and reflecting provides an opportunity to step back and think about the experience

3 'Concluding from the Experience' (stage 3) and Theorists (style 3): analysing the experience enables conclusions to be drawn, generalisations to be made and provides a chance to put forward models.

4 'Planning the next steps' (stage 4) and Pragmatists (style 4): examining the experience to determine its practical value allows the relevance to be demonstrated to the learner.

There is a similarity between the Honey and Mumford's model and the corresponding Kolb learning styles:

● Activist = Accommodating
● Reflector = Diverging
● Theorist = Assimilating
● Pragmatist = Converging.

Stop and reflect

Give two examples from your subject area when students could be given an opportunity to learn in a kinaesthetic way.

• How can learners who prefer a theoretical/assimilating style be encouraged within your lessons?

Critically analyse any papers or articles you have read concerning learning styles.

• Do you recognise learning styles within your own learning and school experiences?

Piaget and stages

Jean Piaget (1896–1980) is credited with linking cognitive development to a series of stages that are approximately related to age, and these ideas had a profound effect on curriculum design (Piaget, 1971). The stages are:

1 The **sensory-motor** period (0–2 years old): movement and the senses are being combined in an attempt to make sense of the world.

2 The **pre-operational** period (2–7 years old): language is developed and symbols can be used. The concept of now, the future and the past are formed.

3 The period of **concrete operation** (7–11 years old): using direct observation the children in this period can draw conclusions from what they see and form ideas.

4 The period of **formal operation**: during this period logical reasoning develops, as does the ability to form abstract ideas.

Movement and the senses are being combined in an attempt to make sense of the world
Source: Pearson Education Ltd/Jules Selmes

Case study

Are learners ready for the formal operational stage?

Believed to commence about age 11, learners begin to think abstractly and reason more logically. The learner can start taking information from one source and apply it in new situations. Between the ages of 11 and 18 the learner starts to think in a more 'problem solver' fashion and is able to understand and use abstract models to explain the world around them. They are able to use deductive reasoning.

Many of the decisions taken by curriculum developers rely on the fact that many learners in secondary schools will be moving into, or already be in, this formal operational stage. Reflect on the complex concepts covered within the curriculum for your subject area. Consider how many rely on the abilities described in the definition of the formal operational stage above.

Though Piaget's ideas are open to debate in terms of whether or not movement from stage to stage is a smooth process or more haphazard and complex and whether the theory takes account of the unique individual progress of young people and the impact of their background and environment, it is still clear that stage theory underpins much curriculum design. We teach concepts to learners when we regard them as able to understand, and this is related to their age in years. The mathematics taught to 11-year-old learners commonly isn't as complicated as the mathematics taught to 16-year-old learners.

However, some research (Shayer and Adey, 1981) indicates that there is a serious overestimation of the number of young people who enter the formal operational stage between the ages of 11 and 18. It could be that we are not taking account of the learners' ability to understand the concepts presented to them. This might encourage learning in a shallow way – facts, figures and processes such as calculations done in rote fashion with no long-term understanding or recall.

Age of learner	Estimated % at formal operational stage
10	1
11	5
12	12
13	20
14	20
15	31
16	31
16–17	31
17–18	34

There has also been evidence from early but important research on brain activity that shows that the brain appears to develop in spurts (Shuttleworth, 1939: Epstein, 1986). There are growth spurts between the ages 2–4, 6–8, 10–12 and 14–16. However, there appears to be a slowing down of brain development between the ages of 4–6, 8–10 and 12–14. The latter is particularly important in developing concepts at the start of secondary schooling. Indeed, there have been calls for radically different schooling for youngsters within this age range, including development of middle (junior high) schools and more experiential learning.

- Study the schemes of work you are teaching to your Y7–Y11 groups. List the concepts you feel require complex reasoning skills as outlined in the definition of the formal operational stage above.

- What implications are there for you in terms of teaching these complex concepts to learners who may not yet have developed the reasoning skills to cope with them?

- How might knowledge of brain growth influence your thinking about your teaching?

You may wish to research publications related to **cognitive acceleration**. As well as searching the original articles below you will also find useful summaries of cognitive acceleration in science education (CASE) at *http://www.edu.dudley.gov.uk/science/CASE2.html* and cognitive acceleration in mathematics education (CAME) at *http://www.bsrlm.org.uk/ IPs/ip17-3/BSRLM-IP-17-3-5.pdf.*

The ideas proposed by Piaget, influential though they were, have been challenged by a number of writers, most notably by Bruner, an American psychologist. As well as stressing that, contrary to Piaget's stages, very young children were capable of forming abstract ideas and hypotheses, Bruner argued that language was a great aid to thinking, but was not essential (Bruner, 1966).

Another psychologist who challenged Piaget's work was Lev Vygotsky, a Russian psychologist. Vygotsky (1962) highlighted the importance of language in child development and the importance of social and cultural factors. Significantly, Vygotsky stressed the importance of social relationships between the teacher and learners and learners and other learners. Language and discussion work were key to development.

In the 1950s B. S. Bloom (1956) proposed an 'educational taxonomy' identifying different learning 'domains'.

- Cognitive (knowledge)
- Affective (attitudes)
- Psychomotor (skills).

It is Bloom's ideas about the cognitive domain that have influenced teachers and teaching so dramatically. The domain is made up of a ladder that starts with remembering and proceeds to more complex tasks such as analysing. This gives us a clue as to the progression of complexity for our activities and questions.

- Recall data
- Understand
- Apply (use)
- Analyse
- Synthesise
- Evaluate.

This ladder has helped teachers to devise tasks, sequences of tasks and questions appropriate to the level of thinking of their students. The reflective tasks in this book are aimed at encouraging you to think at the upper reaches of Bloom's taxonomy. You will find that Master's Level (level 7) assessment criteria also feature these key words!

Practical task

Consider a topic from your own teaching. Use Bloom's ladder to help you to devise a list or string of questions that start with recall but move towards encouraging students to analyse, synthesise and evaluate. One question from each of the six 'rungs' will suffice.

What is clear from these psychologists, and ones that followed such as Kolb (1984, 1985) and De Bono (1995), is that lessons and activities must be planned with good understanding of:

- The cognitive style of the teacher
- The preferred learning style of the learner
- The cognitive stage of the learner.

Active learning

Active learning approaches are designed to encourage learners to engage with tasks and to develop skills that are less likely to develop during teacher-led, didactic lessons. In a sense, active learning is a generic term that welds together a number of models of teaching growing out of 'discovery learning' ideas. Brandes and Ginnis (1986) suggest a range of differences between teacher-centred (passive) learning and student-centred (active) learning. These are summarised in Williams *et al.* (1992) and quoted in Table 5.1 below. Note that 'pupil' is used instead of 'student', indicating some interesting changes in approach since publication.

Table 5.1 **Teacher-centred and Pupil-centred learning**

Teacher-centred learning	Pupil-centred learning
Teacher exposition	Group work
Accent on competition	Accent on cooperation
Whole class teaching	Resource-based learning
Teacher responsible for learning	Pupil takes responsibility for learning
Teacher providing knowledge	Teacher as guide/facilitator
Pupils seen as empty vessels which need filling	Pupils have ownership of ideas and work
Subject knowledge valued	Process skills are valued
Teacher-imposed discipline	Self-discipline
Teacher and pupil roles stressed	Pupils seen as source of knowledge and ideas
Teacher decides the curriculum	Pupils involved in curriculum planning
Passive pupil roles	Pupils actively involved in learning
Limited range of learning styles and activities	Wide range of learning styles employed

Source: Williams *et al.*, 1992.

It is important to note that the table above does **not** indicate poor teaching on the left (teacher-centred) and good teaching on the right (student-centred). As has been mentioned earlier in this chapter, there is some evidence to suggest that whole-class instruction can be more effective than individual instruction, especially in terms of the time students spend on task. The key to effective teaching is the appropriate selection of approaches at any particular time and with any particular group. The most appropriate phrase might be 'fitness for purpose'.

However, it would be incorrect to assume that active, student-centred approaches cannot be used within more structured, whole-class settings, nor should one assume that active learning approaches encourage unstructured, unguided situations which leave learners confused (Kirscher *et al.*, 2006).

An appropriate lesson planning approach is to ensure that clear objectives are set by the teacher and shared by the students, that lessons have a clear structure and students are clear about expectations, **but** that lessons include a range of tasks that allow students to discuss issues and are encouraged to engage in higher-order thinking tasks such as analysis, synthesis, evaluation and reflection. Hudson (1992) argues that no intellectual or cognitive skill is required to cope with 'chunks' of knowledge. Though stressing that at times memorising diverse pieces of information might not be a bad thing, he argues that understanding could be said to occur only when the information is used for a wider purpose. By applying any new knowledge and having to synthesise it the learner will be helped to understand and appreciate its relevance.

Stop and reflect

Reflect on one of the lesson you have observed or taught. Critically analyse the lesson – what you did and what the learners did.

● How much of the lesson demanded that students memorise facts and information?

● How much of the lesson demanded that students analyse, synthesise and evaluate?

Do you think that this balance was appropriate?

Some active learning strategies

There is a wide range of strategies that may be included under the umbrella term of 'active learning'. However, it is vital to appreciate that the organ that must be most active with any learning situation is the brain of the learner. Though many activities require movement of the body, it is essential to realise that the learner's thinking is paramount and that this is often helped by discussion with the teacher and/or other learners.

One key to success is the careful use of questions before, during and after the activities. These should be used to probe prior knowledge, monitor activities and evaluate learning and increased understanding. For obvious reasons they should not simply require factual recall but should also encourage learners to reflect on the work they are doing. In other words they should include open-ended questions that encourage higher-order thinking skills.

List of possible active learning strategies

- Group discussion (talking and listening)
- Active reading
- Active writing
- Presentation
- Role play and drama
- Information technology
- Visits, visitors and field trips
- Data handling
- Problem solving
- Video and audio tape records
- Games and simulations.

It is not possible to go through each strategy in details. For more information about the strategies and some practical hints about how to introduce those to your classes see Williams *et al.* (1992). Though written for Science teachers, there is much in the book of generic, cross-subject interest.

What is important is to realise that different strategies are suited to different learning objectives. For example, learning definitions of key terms, factual information, rules and symbols may require a range of strategies that encourage long-term memory – such as games, poems, repetition and mnemonics – but will not involve detailed group discussion, problem solving or debating issues. Conversely, encouraging students to reflect on and consider complex ideas and issues will involve longer-term student discussions, investigations, research, problem solving and debate. You may wish to try to link each example of a strategy above to at least one learning objective that would match the approach.

Practical task

Think about a topic you have taught recently, or are about to teach. Select one of the strategies from the list above that you are not very familiar with. Research the strategy through books, the internet or discussing it with other teachers and then write down how you might integrate it into the lesson.

- What new skills will you need to develop in order to make the strategy effective?
- What new skills might the students need to develop?
- What particular classroom management issues might you need to bear in mind?
- How might you measure how effective the new strategy was?

Challenge your thinking

Read the newspaper extract shown below.

'Under the new system children are considered to have different "learning styles" and instead of being taught by the conventional method of listening to a teacher, they should be allowed to wander around, listen to music and even play with balls in the classroom.

But now Baroness Greenfield, the director of the Royal Institute and a professor of pharmacology at Oxford University, has dismissed as "nonsense" the view that students prefer to receive information either by sight, sound or touch.

She said that the method of classifying students on the basis of "learning styles" is a waste of valuable time and resources.'

(Henry, J., *Daily Telegraph,* 29 July 2007)

You may wish to find and analyse the whole article. The web page is: *www.telegraph.co.uk/news/uknews/1558822/Professor-pans-learning-style-teaching-method.html*

Many schools use VAK to underpin their approaches to lesson planning and teaching. Many thousands of teachers, and trainee teachers, are being encouraged to plan lessons that cater for visual learners, auditory learners and kinaesthetic learners. If the research basis for this is non-existent then this effort by teachers is misguided. Critically reflect on the article and your understanding of VAK.

- How much credibility are you going to give the author of the article, the original research and the newspaper source in questioning VAK as an approach?
- How much credibility are you going to give the sources that have resulted in your current understanding of VAK? Have you read any of Gardner's work, for example?
- As a professional teacher what skills and approaches should you develop in order to stay in touch with current developments in education but not be led and influenced by the latest 'fashion'?

Summary

The intention of this chapter was to introduce the reader to some of the key theories that underpin our ideas about how students learn. These theories span education, psychology and sociology. In the chapter we have considered how children develop in terms of their ideas and ability to handle concepts and how they each may prefer different styles of learning. The chapter has stressed that through knowing about these theories and ideas the teacher can ensure that learning experiences are effective and motivating for all students.

References

Bennet, N. (1976) *Teaching Styles and Pupil Progress,* London: Open Books.

Bloom, B.S. (ed.) (1956) *Taxonomy of Educational Objectives. Handbook 1; Cognitive Domain,* London: Longman.

Brandes, D. and Ginnis, P.M. (1986) *A Guide to Pupil-centred Learning,* Oxford. Blackwell.

Bruner, J.S. (1966) *Towards a Theory of Instruction,* Cambridge Mass: Harvard University Press.

Cotton, J., (1995) *The theory of learning – an introduction,* London: Kogan Page.

De Bono, E. (1995) *Parallel Thinking: from Socrates to De Bono,* Harmondsworth: Penguin Books.

Dewey, J. (1963) *Experience and Education,* London: Collier Macmillan.

Epstein, H.T. (1986) 'Stages in Human Brain Development', *Developmental Brain Research,* 30, 114–19.

Gardner, H. (1983) *Frames of Mind,* New York: Basic Books.

Henry, J. (2007) 'Professor pans "learning style" teaching method', *Daily Telegraph,* 29 July.

Honey, P. and Mumford, A. (1986) *Manual of Learning Styles,* London: P. Honey.

Hudson, T. (1992) 'Developing pupil's skills', in Atlay, M., Bennet, S., Dutch, S., Levinson, R., Taylor, P. and West, D. (eds) *Open Chemistry,* London: Hodder and Stoughton.

Kirschner, P.A., Sweller, J. and Clark, R.E. (2006) 'Why minimal guidance during instruction does not work: an analysis of the failure of constructivist, discovery, problem-based, experimental and enquiry-based teaching', *Educational Psychologist* 41(2): 75–86.

Kolb, D. (1984) *Experiential Learning,* Englewood Cliffs: Prentice Hall.

Kolb, D. (1985) *Learning Style Inventory* (rev. edn), Boston: McBer.

Miijs, D. and Reynolds, D. (2005) *Effective Teaching: evidence and practice* (2nd edn), London: Sage Publications.

Mortimore, P., Sammons, P., Stoll, L., Lewis, D. and Ecob, R.(1988) *School Matters,* Wells: Somerset, Open Books.

Piaget, J. (1971) *Psychology and Epistemology,* New York: Grossman.

Pollard, A., Broadfoot, P., Osborne, N. and Abbott, D. (1994) *Changing English Primary Schools?,* London: Cassell.

Riding, R. J. (2002) *School Learning and Cognitive Style,* London: David Fulton.

Riding, R. J. (2003) *School learning and cognitive style,* London: David Fulton.

Riding, R.J. and Cheema, I. (1991) 'Cognitive styles – an overview and integration', *Educational Psychology,* 11: 193–215.

Riding, R. J. and Raynor, S. (1998) *Cognitive Styles and Learning Strategies,* London: David Fulton Publishers.

Shayer, M. and Adey, P. (1981) *Towards a Science of Science Teaching,* Heinemann: London.

Shuttleworth, F.K. (1939) 'The physical and mental growth of girls and boys age six to nineteen in relation to age at maximum growth', *Monographs of the Society for Research in Child Development,* 4 (Serial No. 22).

Vygotsky, L.S. (1962) *Thought and Language,* Mass: Massachusetts Institute of Technology Press.

Williams, S., Hudson, T. and Green, D. (eds) (1992) *Active Teaching and Learning Approaches in Science,* London: Collins Educational.

Chapter 6

Individual needs

Learning outcomes

By the end of this chapter you will be able to:

→ Critically discuss the individual needs of your students

→ Locate and synthesise information on your students within your school

→ Evaluate the use of Individual Education Plans in your planning

→ Analyse how to utilise new technologies for supporting individual needs

→ State how to differentiate your teaching to support individual needs

Introduction

Every student you teach is an individual, and as a professional teacher I am sure you respect this and ensure you plan for the individuals in your lessons and create a climate of learning where each individual student can achieve his/her maximum potential. With Every Child Matters, which you have already become familiar with in Chapter 4, personalised learning, underpinned by the needs of each individual student, has been placed very firmly at the forefront of the current educational agenda. As you will appreciate, the goals may be similar for each student in a class, but the way each individual will achieve them and the support they will require, in terms of encouragement, target setting, resources and assessment will be different. This is appropriate in a cultural climate where we are encouraged to respect the individual.

This chapter sets out to give you the knowledge, skills and understanding you will need as a professional teacher to help you to become a teacher who plans for inclusiveness, and supports and guides your students to reach their potential and achieve their very best in your lessons. It will examine the different needs of your students and discuss strategies to support them, concluding with further reading that will help to develop your understanding of the various issues discussed.

In the first paragraph two phrases have been introduced: 'personalised learning' and 'individual learning'. There are many definitions of these terms, but for the purposes of this chapter they shall be defined as follows:

Individual learning is about knowing your student's learning style, being sensitive to their needs and their pace of learning, knowing what they need to know, the barriers to their learning, and the best way for them to learn by creating the right climate for them through high-quality teaching and an emphasis on learning how to learn.

Personalised learning is about identifying your student's prior learning, what their targets are, and how they are going to achieve them; it may involve e-learning and will include elements of individual learning, but will also include group, and whole-class learning with a greater focus on the learner taking control of their learning. It may also involve tailoring the curriculum to meet your student's needs.

Stop and reflect

Think about some recent lessons you have planned and taught:

- How did you identify the individual needs of your students?
- Where in your school did you locate information on your students?
- How did Individual Education Plans help you with your lesson planning?
- How did you utilise new technologies for supporting the individual needs of your students?
- How did you differentiate your teaching to support individual needs?

If your critical reflections have resulted in the feeling that you didn't address the points above in any great detail, don't worry. Identifying this is a very important step in your professional development. Meeting individuals' needs is a challenge for even the most experienced and skilled teachers. This chapter and the other support available to you from mentors, tutors and colleagues will help you to develop in this respect.

The curriculum

Much has been done, led by the government and advisors, to design a curriculum that provides for individual needs: there is a variety of subjects, some of which are optional, there are levels within each National Curriculum to reflect the different abilities of the students, the assessment processes are becoming more diverse with teachers now able to encourage students to use a format of work to suit their individual needs and abilities, vocational programmes have been introduced and redeveloped to recognise and reflect individual pathways and aspirations, students can now mix school, college and work from Key Stage 4, and take qualifications when they are ready to do so.

There has also been much debate about the need to retain coursework within some subjects, which appeals to different types of learners, and schools are increasingly being encouraged to make greater use of information technology not only to access information on individual learners and their needs, but also in planning and delivering increasingly individual learning to provide more opportunity for students to learn in their own way, at their own pace, and when they want to learn.

Stop and reflect

Critically reflect on your own learning experience at school. Think of one subject that you did not excel at:

- What were the barriers to learning in this subject?
- How could the teacher have altered your learning experience to ensure it met your needs and raised your attainment?

How to identify individual needs in your students

Reference is made in Chapter 9, Assessment and feedback, to accessing and using baseline and predictive data on your students. This is an excellent place to start building up a picture of the individual students in your class.

Although it may seem daunting at first, it is well worth while seeking information about your learners from key staff in the school. This might involve talking to your Head of Department, Year Tutor and pastoral team to gain information about any barriers to learning and progress that may be linked to changes in a student's home life, or difficulties in their personal circumstances. There is also vital information on the special-needs register and the gifted-and-talented register that colleagues can share with you. An important point to remember is that a student may be gifted or talented in a subject that is different from the one you will be teaching, or may have special needs that will not impact greatly on the subject you are teaching.

As you gather information about learners you will wish to keep it close to your planning documents. Chapter 9 suggests that you create columns in your recording document for each class for SEN, G&T, etc. so that you have this information at a glance when planning. Once you have accessed the information and identified the students you will be teaching from each register, you will need to access their IEPs (see below). A talk to the SENCO and gifted-and-talented coordinator to find out what specialised planning you need to do to support these students to reach their potential in your lessons will be time well spent.

Teachers are becoming increasingly aware of the different learning styles of students, so you should be able to access information centrally from your school's system. There is information in Chapter 7 on how to recognise individual learning styles and use these in planning. Also, try to learn what their strengths and weaknesses are in terms of learning and assessment strategies, ensure you plan so that they can achieve rather than put up barriers to their progression, and know what their career aspirations are.

Alongside the importance of knowing their educational needs, learning styles, targets, talents and abilities is the need to know what their interests are both at school and at home, and to use these interests to motivate and actively help them to learn. Added to this is the need to be aware of any cultural influences that may affect their learning. This is all fundamental to helping your students to be motivated, providing for their individual success and progression to achieve their full potential, and is also essential to good planning and preparation.

The section above has focused on accessing information that is available within the school. However, we must not forget the importance of having dialogue with your students to get to know their individual needs, expectations, interests and motivations. This is equally crucial to being successful in your teaching and in engaging your students in their learning. The impact this can have on the individual students can help them to achieve and maximise their potential as well as improving their interest and motivation.

Practical task

Make a list of the sources of information about individual learners that are available to you in your school:

● Which are best for letting you know of any learning needs?
● Which are best for letting you know about any emotional or behaviour issues?
● Which are best for letting you know about the people that are your learners?

Did you automatically include the students in your list of sources of information? Be honest!

Students with special needs

As a teacher you will already have experienced teaching students with wide-ranging abilities and disabilities. The above section has provided information on how to identify the varying learning needs of different types of students, but it is important to pause and consider how you can access information on how to support these students so that they can reach their potential.

The Education Act 1996 describes children with special educational needs as:

● Having a much greater difficulty in learning than most children
● Possibly needing some special arrangements to be made in school.

Following on from the Education Act 1996 the Department for Education and Skills (DfES), now the Department for Education (DfE) issued a guidance document entitled the 'Special Educational Needs Code of Practice' (DfES, 2001). This outlined in detail how schools, local authorities and other services should work together to make suitable educational arrangements for children with special educational needs. Some key points identified in the Code of Practice were:

- Most children with SEN will be able to have their needs met in mainstream school.
- Schools, local authorities (LAs) including Children and Young People's Services, and other agencies, such as Health, should work together to meet the needs of children with SEN.
- There are a wide range of special educational needs and a wide variety of ways to meet those needs.
- Parents should be fully involved in their child's education, along with the children themselves.

Since the Code of Practice the government has issued a number of other documents that focus on the provision that needs to be made for students with special educational needs. These can be downloaded from the Department for Children, Schools and Families website. These are still available however the DCSF is now part of the DFE. They include:

- **Removing Barriers to Achievement.** This focuses on raising educational achievement for children with SEN.
- **Every Child Matters.** This proposes a joined-up approach in the way that services are provided to children, young people and their families. As a consequence, what were formerly separate education and social services departments have now been brought together as Children's and Young People's Services.
- **Every Parent Matters.** This outlines the importance of parents' involvement in their child's education and emphasises the need for schools and parents to work in equal partnerships.
- **The Children's Plan.** This is a ten-year strategy for improving the lives of all children, but which indicates that funding would be made available to improve the quality of teaching of children with SEN, the way their progress is monitored and to provide specialist dyslexia support.

Where students do not make adequate progress schools may decide to give additional support and intervention as follows:

- **School Action.** Where differentiation strategies have not helped a student to progress, the school may wish to use School Action to intervene to provide more structured support. This may be due to a disability, behaviour difficulties, difficulties with literacy/numeracy, and so on. School Action will be made in consultation with the parents/carers and the SENCO will take a lead in the assessment of a child moving to this additional support.
- **School Action Plus.** Where the student has continued not to make adequate progress. At this stage an Individual Education Plan will be written (see below) and external agencies will normally be consulted. This may include social workers, educational psychologists, speech therapists, etc., depending on the needs of the student.

- **Individual Education Plans (IEPs)**. Students who are identified by the school as having a special learning need will generally have an IEP. This document is very useful as it is focused on the individual student; you need to access the IEPs of your students and keep them with your planning documents. As they are individual to the student, there will be information about their learning difficulty(ies), and advice on how to support the student in class with learning and teaching strategies, targets for achievement, success criteria, and so on. More information on these can be found at *http://www.teachernet.gov.uk/*

Case study

To reinforce the importance of accessing and following the information on these sheets I will share an observation of a lesson I carried out for a student teacher. The student teacher had prepared a good lesson, she had clearly thought about the learning styles of the students in the group, had prepared a variety of activities, set clear learning objectives, differentiated the learning outcomes which were linked to appropriate assessment strategies, and had provided a range of resources to support the lesson.

She began by issuing a starter activity which she had differentiated to take into account the different levels and learning styles of her students, and chosen a topic which reflected the interests of the group. The task was challenging, stimulating and linked closely to the learning outcomes. Most of the group engaged immediately with the task, but one female student was off task for most of the activity and became disruptive to those sitting close to her. The student teacher moved into an explanation of the topic for the lesson, shared her learning outcomes and linked these to the different levels of the national curriculum so the students had clear targets for achievement in the lesson. During this input the female student listened attentively. The student teacher then gave out the first task for the lesson. The female student again quickly became disruptive and the noise level increased in the area where she was sitting. I walked over to the female student and asked if she needed any help.

After a short supportive dialogue with her she told me that she was dyslexic and was unable to read anything printed in black on white.

Despite planning the lesson in great detail and working hard to meet the needs of the students there had been an oversight.

- What could the student teacher have done to help the student with dyslexia?
- What lessons can you draw from the case study?
- Is there anything you can do as part of your planning process to minimise the chance that you would make a similar mistake as the student teacher above?

Gifted and talented students

There are many definitions of what it means to be gifted or talented. The DfE define 'gifted' children as those showing exceptional ability in any national curriculum subject except art, PE or music. They define 'talented' as children who excel in the three latter subjects.

(Becta, 2008)

The Department for Children, Schools and Families website (2008) defines gifted and talented as:

*'**Gifted** describes learners who have the ability to excel academically in one or more subjects such as English, drama, technology; **Talented** describes learners who have the ability to excel in practical skills such as sport, leadership, artistic performance, or in an applied skill.'*

(www.dcsf.gov.uk)

These abilities can be general, such as the ability for extraordinary creative thinking, or a particular ability in a subject. It is the school's responsibility to recognise students that are gifted or talented. It is possible that a student may fulfil many of the criteria for giftedness yet not perform well at school, or may be gifted and talented in areas that are not reflected in your subject.

The previous labour government developed a national strategy for the education of gifted and talented (G&T) children as part of its Excellence in Cities (EiC) initiative, which is available at *www.becta.org.uk*. The 2005 White Paper, 'Higher Standards, Better Schools for All' (available from *http://publications.dcsf.gov.uk/*) sets out the government's ambition that every student – including the gifted and talented – should have the right to personalised support to reach the limits of their capabilities. The 2007 Children's Plan builds on this commitment (*http://www.dcsf.gov.uk/childrensplan/*). For gifted and talented students this means:

- Stretch and challenge in every classroom and in every school
- Opportunities to further their particular abilities outside school.

The EiC initiative plans to:

- Ensure that all national education policies include a focus on the needs of G&T children
- Develop effective ways to identify, educate and support them
- Ensure that these methods are taken up and used in every school and LA.

Your school will provide a list of the students in each class who are deemed by the school to be gifted and talented. You may want to put forward a student who is gifted or talented in your subject. The DCSF provided guidelines for schools in identifying and supporting gifted and talented students, which is available from their website: 'Identifying Gifted and Talented Learners: Getting Started' (May 2008). It is your responsibility to provide support for G&T children to ensure that they are challenged and able to achieve their full potential. There are indications that G&T students can receive peer pressure if they are singled out for 'special' provision. It is important therefore that you carefully balance your support when you are planning your lessons and develop systems of assessment that provide an opportunity for rapid progress and immediate feedback so that these students can progress quickly and, when appropriate, independently. Your school should provide you with support in planning for students who are gifted and talented.

Further support is available from the National Association for Able Children in Education (NACE), the Support Society for Children of Higher Intelligence (CHI), and the National Association for Gifted Children (NAGC) websites. There are also links on these websites to projects and resources dedicated to G&T children. These all provide communication, ideas, practical material and information to support teachers working in this area. Some offer regional conferences, provide CPD for teachers, produce book-lets, and maintain a database of contacts. Most recently the Excellence in Cities (EiC) programme led to the development of Xcalibre, an on-line resource database for students, parents and teachers to access materials, events and experts from across the curriculum to stimulate and challenge G&T students of all ages. There is also a hub of the DCSF website that provides links to support and information on the Excellence Hubs which are run with Regional Partners and provide support and opportunities for gifted and talented students.

A home–school network link can also provide a valuable method of communication between teachers, students, parents and carers via your school's MLE/VLE. Liaison about home computer use between teachers and parents can also be helpful. ICT can assist with parental/carer involvement in a variety of ways. The ability for a student to log in to their school network and continue work at home is a powerful facility to help satisfy those students for whom the limitations of timetabled lessons are frustrating. The development of an ICT-rich learning environment both at home and in school can lead to 'anytime, any-where learning', which is often more appropriate and satisfying for many G&T students. Such facilities can be helpful to relationships within the family and between home and school. Cooperative assistance by parents and teachers can be given to the children much more easily using ICT as a means of communication. The internet can provide a link with other families all over the world via specialised sites such as penpal exchanges for the children, educational links generally, parent and carer chat rooms, and message boards which help to solve isolation problems for children, parents and carers of both G&T children and those with special needs.

There is a changing focus on the education of G&T students, enabling more freedom of communication and development, much of it enhanced by the developing use of ICT. Technological advances in mobile internet and communications technologies are creating exciting opportunities for providing flexible learning opportunities. In addition, the more flexible educational environment both in school and in society generally has given the opportunity to identify and assist children's particular needs. All this is focusing the attention of educational establishments, parents and carers, and society in general, on the needs of G&T children.

Students for whom English is a second language

The number of children who have English as a second language (EAL) is increasing. Their level of the English language may be fairly good, but it may also be very poor. It is not unknown for students to arrive in Britain as a refugee and be placed within a few days in a school with little or no grasp of the language.

As a teacher it is important that you:

- Ensure you are aware of the level of support children who have English as an additional language will need;

- Find out if they have a teaching assistant with them;

- Work closely with the teaching assistant to ensure the student is being challenged and has targets for development, and that the assistant may also be able to help with creating resources, assessment and monitoring;

- Plan for the learning of these students in your lessons and provide the support they will need in order to achieve;

- Quickly assess their ability to ensure you are providing sufficient challenge and opportunity for them to maximise their achievement (just because they don't speak English does not mean they are weak in your subject);

- Carry out the usual steps of gaining as much information about them as possible (however, if they are refugees, or travellers, it may take a while for their data to arrive in the school);

- Try to ascertain their prior learning and ability by having a dialogue with them (but if they don't speak the language it may be difficult for you to ascertain their level);

- Set tasks that challenge them, and support them to achieve their potential;

- Consider different assessment strategies until they are more fluent, such as video, diagrams, working in a group, or through dialogue. It is possible for students who are recognised as EAL to have assessments in their first or other language(s); you will need to liaise with your Head of Department.

You may find it necessary to provide 'jargon' terminology relevant to your subject in their language, translated into English, so that they are able to engage with the lesson. You could set these to be learnt for homework with rewards for achievement to develop their motivation to learn more. There are numerous translation websites available on the internet, some of which will translate a complete lesson resource into a specific language – but do be wary of the student becoming reliant on your resources being translated; it is a fine balance between providing the scaffolding for them to access your lesson, and encouragement to learn the English language. There is also good advice to support you in planning, preparation and assessment for students who have EAL, provided by QCA Guidelines for assessing English as an additional language; the National Curriculum for your subject available from the Standards website will provide information on teaching your subject to EAL students; and there is a series of booklets on 'Access and Engagement in [your subject]', produced by the DfES that provides useful information. Becta also has excellent information, support and guidance on teaching EAL students, (available from *nationalstrategies.standards.dcsf.gov.uk*).

Differentiation

Differentiation has been referred to throughout this book. When planning for learning and assessing individuals, differentiation forms an essential aspect. As a professional you need to ensure you challenge all students to reach their potential. This may require different challenges for the more able students in your group, and scaffolding through support for the less able or those with special learning needs or EAL. This chapter is about being aware of the individual needs of your students, recognising that they arrive with different knowledge, skills, abilities and interests, and that they will learn in different ways and at different speeds and will need different levels of support. This is a good start to differentiation. However, what you need to do now is use all of that information in your planning and preparation.

In Chapter 8, Planning and preparation, we discuss the main aspects of planning your lessons – the aim(s), learning objectives, differentiating learning outcomes into 'all will …', 'most will …', and 'some will …' and linking these to assessment. To develop this further you also need to consider other strategies that you can use in your lesson to support your students. For example:

- Preparing writing frames to support the less able who lack language development to progress and meet your learning objectives;
- Translating subject jargon into the first language of your EAL students;
- Providing handouts on different-coloured paper for your dyslexic students;
- Providing handouts in larger font to support those with sight difficulties;
- In your questioning section(s) devising some simple questions and some questions that will search more deeply into the knowledge of learners;
- Producing an assignment or case study that reflects various levels of the national curriculum enabling each student to achieve their potential;
- Differentiating the homework that you set, possibly in the amount as well as the level;
- Producing some resources which include step-by-step guidance for some students to refer to during more independent learning sections of your lessons, or using screen-capture software to record a VLE/MLE for students who find it hard to follow a demonstration;

Teaching assistants can offer valuable support to children in your class, but independent learning should also be encouraged
Source: Pearson Education Ltd/Studio 8

- Providing differentiation in the format in which you expect work to be completed, aiming to be flexible and accepting video, voice recordings, written work, spider diagrams, etc.

The support you will receive from the teaching assistants (TAs) is very important both in your planning and teaching of your lesson. Ideally you will meet with TAs prior to your lessons to ensure they know what you will be covering, have familiarity with any activities, and understand your expectations of their role. They are normally an excellent source of information on individual students they are supporting and are generally well trained and professional in their role. It is important you develop skills in working with these support staff and make use of their expertise both in your planning and classroom organisation, as well as in your reflections following the lesson.

It important to remember that, while you use these strategies and provide differentiation, you also need to support your students in becoming independent learners, so you need to gradually reduce the amount and level of support when each student is ready for this next step.

Personalising learning

The Every Child Matters agenda supports the notion of personalised learning. As teachers you need to develop an ethos that supports and recognises personalised learning within your classrooms. To do this it is important to know your students, what they are capable of, their levels of attainment and previous learning in your subject when they arrive in your classroom, their interests, learning style and aspirations, and their short- and long-term targets. You then need to design your lessons so that each individual student is able to progress in a way that manages their pace, challenges, motivates and engages them and enables them to move towards their targets. Personalised learning does not necessarily mean students sitting on their own, possibly with computers, and working through their learning on their own – it is important to remember that students need to vary their mode of learning, and this should include collaborative group work as well as a balance of individual learning.

> 'Perhaps the choice we need to consider is less about choice between institutions, and more about choice in what students learn and how they learn it.'

> (Leadbetter, 2004: 10)

In Chapter 8, Planning and preparation, we discuss in detail how to set out your lesson plan, but it is important to revisit this briefly when discussing individual needs and personalised learning. Within personalised learning there will still be a general aim for the learning experience in your lesson, learning objectives will need to be stated from the outset of the lesson, but these will also need to be linked to individual learners and targets as part of the personalisation process. This doesn't mean that you will give out 30 individual learning objectives, but you will need to break each objective down into learning outcomes which are differentiated and, ideally, linked to national curriculum levels or exam board grades so that your students know what they need to do. You then need to structure the learning activities so that they are differentiated. You may have some gifted or talented students who may require different activities to ensure they are challenged and able to achieve their targets. Students will also have individual targets that they have received from you as part of an ongoing dialogue, or as part of assessment feedback. As technology develops, it will become increasingly simpler to give more individualised targets based on your lesson aims, student progress and achievement.

If your school has a VLE/MLE this can ease the preparation of differentiated resources and learning objectives by uploading the learning activities onto the VLE and giving differentiated routes of progress which balance individual targets, progress and achievement. This can also help you to change quickly the learning activities to reflect individual interests, and can enable negotiation of learning through the choices you provide. Most VLEs also have useful tools for assessment, again enabling a quick and easy system of creating differentiated quizzes with results and feedback becoming automated, thus providing individuals with progress more quickly.

Practical task

Consider three students that you teach, ideally from different key stages, that you find difficult to engage in their own learning. Now research into their individual needs using some of the strategies you have read so far in this chapter and critically reflect on the way you prepare for their learning in your lessons.

- What changes would you make to your planning to encourage and motivate these students to learn in your lessons?

Reflecting on progress

For individual learning to work well in your classroom, and to develop learning to learn skills in your students, you need to ensure that opportunity is provided for students to reflect on their progress and achievements. This will then help them to become autonomous learners.

- This reflection would commonly take place during the plenary.
- You may want to vary individual reflection and balance this with peer support and review.
- You may also want to provide an opportunity for your students to reflect on how they have learnt, their preferred learning style, what motivated them most, what they found most challenging, and so on.
- You may want to include in this reflection the support they received and how this could be developed. Using this information in future planning will increase your planning and support of individual needs and help you to provide opportunities for their preferred way of learning, such as individually, in groups, through reading, researching on the internet, rote learning, problem solving and so on.
- Encourage your students to consider the way they managed their time, and whether they were effective in making use of additional resources, such as the library or internet.

It is important in these reflection sessions that they are encouraged to acknowledge what they are good at, and what they need to work harder at – this needs to be linked to their individual targets for future lessons. This is an opportunity to celebrate success.

Awareness of cultural issues

We live and work in a multi-ethnic, multi-faith and multilingual environment. You do need to develop an awareness of the different cultures, faiths and first languages that are in each class and ensure you plan to support and respect them.

It is important to remember that part of your role is to motivate students. This can be more difficult with some ethnic minority groups where employment levels are still low, and there are few role models. Also, some groups of students may feel marginalised by the school system.

Stop and reflect

There has been research carried out into minority groups in schools. This has found that students identify racism in schools as a great barrier to their school experience. Consider how a school you have been into recently develops an environment that is free of racism. If possible obtain a copy of their equal opportunity policy and read it prior to starting this reflective activity

Blair (2001) identifies a number of aspects that students from ethnic minority groups may experience:

- **Unfair treatment.** Research, such as Mortimore *et al.* (1998), and Tizard *et al.* (1988) both quoted in Blair (2001), shows that children from ethnic minorities can receive less praise than white children. Children in primary school can experience situations where they feel 'picked on', and can arrive at secondary school with a poor experience.

  It is important that you treat all students in the same way. Have clear discipline policies and ensure all the students in your class know what the boundaries are, and that they are the same for all students – if you expect poor behaviour you will get it.

- **Respect.** Your students need guidance on what is acceptable behaviour and you need to set the example. In a survey of Y10 students reported by Blair (*ibid:* 79) the students listed the teacher's attitude towards them, through body and verbal language, as the greatest cause of conflict. It is important that you show respect to your students and in your turn gain their respect.

- **Stereotypes.** Some ethnic minorities, particularly black men, are sometimes represented by the media as violent, aggressive and engaged in illicit activities such as mugging and drug pushing. Some students perceive teachers to believe these stereotypes.

- **Racism.** Students may differentiate between teachers who are blatantly racist, those who seem ignorant of what racism is, and those who are racist at an unconscious level

(Blair, 2001). If children do experience racism, this is going to affect their ability to concentrate and participate in the classroom. It is essential you ensure that your students feel psychologically safe, comfortable and supported in your classroom.

● **Gender and culture.** The way some ethnic minority students can be perceived by teachers affected by media stereotyping often differs between boys and girls.

Boys from some ethnic minority groups feel they are expected to be 'cool' and develop a façade of being 'hard'.

It is essential that you make the time to build relationships with individual students. However, the experience a student receives in school will stay with him/her always and it is important you ensure this is a positive experience.

Critical synthesis

Reflect back on lessons you have taught or observed that were particularly well differentiated. Try to analyse what the consequences of those lessons would have been for both students and teacher if there had been no differentiation at all.

Look up the word 'differentiation' and try to determine where else in life you might come across it being used.

Many classes comprise boys and girls. Teachers need to be aware of any gender differences that might impact on learning.

Source: Pearson Education Ltd/Ian Wedgewood

Gender issues

Traditionally boys and girls learn in different ways which will have been reinforced at home and in primary school. For example, in using a computer males have traditionally had greater access and displayed more confidence (Broos, 2005). Although research by Imhof and colleagues has shown the gender gap to be closing, there are still some fundamental differences in the way that males and females use computer technologies (Imhof *et al.*, 2007). In addition, research by Becta has shown that boys are more often given computers by parents, or take over the family computer. These early experiences have a lasting effect. Similar differences can be seen in primary and secondary classrooms – i.e. boys will tend to take over the computer and girls are often quite happy for this to happen.

Gender and achievement

The DfES produced a report based on findings from four pilot secondary schools (available from the DCSF website). The four pilot schools were located in rural East Anglia, a deprived inner urban authority in north-east England, a new town in southern England and a northern mill town.

All four pilot schools were characterised by rising levels of achievement for both girls and boys, with boys starting from a lower base and making relatively greater gains. In each school the initial concern was with raising achievement for all; as this was addressed, so boys emerged as needing more support for their learning, and approaches became more targeted towards boys. However, teaching and learning strategies developed to support boys often have a positive effect upon girls too, such that the gap in performance between girls and boys might not necessarily narrow as a result of initiatives which are implemented. Attempts to establish a school culture where achievement is seen as desirable for all students, and is accepted as the norm, is something to be celebrated. This was important in all pilot schools and is probably a pre-condition for success in raising achievement.

However, there are subjects where strategies need to be employed to encourage girls. For example, in ICT schools are taking steps to actively encourage girls to develop higher-level skills equal to the boys, and often have 'girls only' after-school computer clubs.

Research published in 'Gender and Education: the evidence of students in England' (DCSF, 2007) identified some strategies that can be successful in increasing boys' attainment and, as stated earlier in this section can, when used equally with girls, also improve their attainment:

- A variety of interactive classroom activities are adopted, with a 'fitness for purpose', so that both short, specifically focused activities and more sustained, ongoing activities are used, as and when appropriate.

- Acknowledgement is given to the central importance of talk, to speaking and listening as a means of supporting writing.

- Teachers are prepared to take risks to bring more creativity and variety to literacy.

- More integrated use is made of ICT so that high-quality presentation of work can be more easily achieved, and drafts amended more simply.

This report also stated that, although there was little evidence that boys and girls had different learning styles from each other, they did find that it was helpful to discuss different learning styles (without simply encouraging a preferred learning style) and to develop an understanding with their students that, to be effective learners, they must be able to access different learning styles at different times and that teachers should plan for different learning styles in lessons.

It is important you gain an awareness of the differences in the ways the boys and girls in your groups learn and use these to your advantage. For example, if you are using computers to support your lesson, you may want to experiment with a seating plan which places them in girl-boy-girl order.

Stop and reflect

Consider the reading you have just done relating to gender differences in education. Reflect on any other wider reading you have undertaken that claimed gender differences in educational performance, learning or attainment. Now, think about your own experiences as a learner and as a teacher:

- Do you think there is sufficient evidence to argue significant differences in how males and females learn and how they perform in school?
- How did you experience gender differences in attainment as a learner?
- Have you any evidence of differences in what males and females enjoy doing in your lessons or any noticeable difference in aptitudes, skills or attitudes?
- Synthesise all of this information and try to arrive at your own thesis regarding gender and education.

Study skills

Developing good study skills is a life-long skill that requires development throughout the education of students. Universities often provide group and individual support for study skill development, but this is not always the case in secondary school. You need to be aware that in your expectations of your students in the learning you provide, and the assessments you set, that you have ensured they have the necessary skills and understanding. For example, if you are expecting your students to carry out an internet search on a specific topic for homework, have you ensured that they know how to do this correctly, that they know how to recognise an appropriate, reliable site, that they know how to précis the information they find and structure it correctly to answer the question you have set, and are they able to cite sources correctly? Another example is setting revision for homework with a Y7 group – what does this mean to them? Have they been taught the different methods of revising? There is greater detail on this topic in Chapter 3 on Academic writing and reading. This short section links academic writing to individual needs.

When you set any task, consider the language that you are using. Help your students to learn to break down projects and activities and plan the stages they will need to go through. Help them to break down assignment titles and essay questions so that they are able to recognise key words and know what the expectations of these are. Help them to understand that if an exam question gives two marks, they need to analyse how they will get the two marks: e.g. do they need to give an example for one mark, and an advantage for the second mark?

A part of developing study skills is developing time-management skills. Students will need different levels of help with this, and you will need to keep careful monitoring records of progress in order to ensure you are providing adequate support to students who find this difficult. I have sat in many meetings where staff have complained that a student has produced no work for an assignment which they have been working on for the past month in class – these students need targets, timescales, and help in planning their work as well as support in monitoring their progress; it is your responsibility to monitor their progress and ensure they are completing work and meeting their individual targets.

As part of study-skills development students need to develop skills in assessing what and why they are doing something. They need support, initially, in revisiting the assignment brief, or essay title, to ensure they are following it rather than going off at a tangent. They need to learn how to be logical in their approach to solving problems, and know the steps you expect them to take. It is useful to provide opportunities for students to share and work collaboratively in identifying what is expected of them so that they become increasingly independent learners. They also need clear signposts of where to go for support and resources to help them to complete their work.

Using new technologies

Some discussion of using computers to support individual learning has already been given above. While this book is not focused specifically on new technologies, a chapter on individual needs cannot be complete without a brief examination of how new technologies can be utilised to engage learners. Further reading focusing on new technologies in teaching is given at the end of this chapter. By using new technologies you can provide new ways for students to work as individuals: at their own pace, in their preferred way, linking to their own interests, working collaboratively as and when appropriate, and continuing with their learning out of school as and when they are able to or want to. This enables learners to take control of their own learning.

Mobile technologies are increasingly being used in schools for areas such as homework, class activities, revision, and so on. Becta has carried out some useful research into the use of mobile technologies and how these can be used, and the Institute of Education has published Mobile Learning: Towards a Research Agenda, which addresses a range of mobile technologies and how these are being used in teaching and learning. PDAs and PSPs are being utilised for students to download materials from the school VLE/MLE, making learning more engaging for students who may not be particularly motivated or engaged in their own learning.

You can make voice recordings quickly and easily using voice recording software such as Audacity (which is freely downloadable from Sourceforge) or within software such as PowerPoint. This can be used to record homework, explain difficult concepts, used for revision, etc. and can be uploaded to the school's VLE/MLE and accessed by students. If they are stored in a format such as MP3, the students can download them to their iPods or MP3 players and listen to them when they are away from their computer, which will lead to more flexible learning and the individual student taking more control of their learning.

E-learning is increasingly being used in schools. This was first introduced several years ago and supported in its development by the government through curriculum driven initiatives and e-learning Credits. However, there are still aspects that need to be developed, including CPD for teachers, skills in becoming e-learning users for students (Boulton, 2008), and access to computers for all subjects. However, if you are creating your own class resources using IT, it doesn't take very many steps before you have these uploaded to your VLE/MLE, with differentiated pathways for your different learners, thus creating some e-learning materials of your own that can be accessed from home, and can lead to the development of greater home–school links. It is important to ensure you don't buy an e-text book, add a few quizzes and expect your students to work through this at their own pace and call it e-learning. There is much more to e-learning than this as Gillespie, *et al.* (2007) and Salmon (2004) discuss, and students will become quickly demotivated and bored – they need lots of different activities and for their learning to be individualised, as this chapter has already discussed.

The use of weblogs (blogs) can be excellent for students to start to develop their own diaries of progress, or evaluation of projects. They can maintain these as private blogs or open them up to their class and yourself. Blogs can also be used for group projects, to record progress in projects, to share experiences such as visits, field trips, etc. and these can be shared with others including parents/carers and other groups of students. One of the advantages of blogs, which are normally available free of charge over the internet, is that they can support text, video and audio, thus encouraging all abilities and learning styles. Blogs can also be used for other developmental and support strategies, such as putting together a group of children who lack self-esteem – by setting up a blog, which is private to them, you can encourage them to support each other and share their experiences.

Wikis are an excellent way of encouraging collaborative work and, as they can be accessed via the internet, students can continue to collaborate outside the school day. For a teacher a wiki enables you to look at the history of the contributions so that you can encourage students who are 'lurking' rather than contributing to join in. You can also use their contribution to inform your assessment. An example of using a wiki is to set up a group wiki at the start of a new project and encourage your students to break down the tasks, create a glossary of key terms, plan targets for completion related to criteria, and so on. Another example is to give a piece of homework, such as a poem, and ask each group member to put his/her ideas on the wiki – these can then form part of the next lesson.

There are numerous examples of blogs and wikis on the internet; some links and references are given at the end of this chapter.

You may also want to introduce your students to social bookmarking. This enables sharing useful internet sites which can be divided into topics. An example of this is *www.delicious.com*. YouTube.com has some excellent short video clips that are tagged so they are simple to find and not only make a good change of activity in class, but can be linked to your VLE/MLE so that students can review them if/when they want to; they also appeal to your visual learners. There is an excellent video clip on YouTube that you may want to watch on 'Wikis In Plain English', which explains very quickly what a wiki is and how it works. There are also shared sites for images that you may want to use – when you were at school you probably made use of the free ClipArt available in MicroSoft packages, which has now moved on to sharing images through sites such as *www.flickr.com*. Some of the images are copyrighted, but most are available to use and you can upload your own/your groups' images and store them so that they are available for your students to access from home.

Hints and tips

- Make sure your lessons are well planned, interesting and differentiated. Students will become disruptive if they are bored. Try to find out what matters to the students, the issues that affect their lives, their interests, etc. and use these in planning for your lessons.
- Make sure your students are motivated and challenged: nurture a desire to learn, understand how they learn, with the thrill of acquiring new skills and knowledge.
- Use baseline and predicted data in your planning and ensure you have accessed IEPs and the G&T register. Keep records of your groups up-to-date.
- Treat all students as individuals and consider their personal identities when planning your lessons.
- Listen to and value all students and treat them with respect.
- Make sure you instill in students the notion that learning is something desirable, enjoyable, rewarding and for life.
- Acknowledge that not all students will go on to university or into jobs/further training, and ensure they understand how your subject will fit into their future life and experiences.
- Adopt positive learning approaches that encourage pro-social behaviour and avoid power struggles with students.
- Create a caring environment where you demonstrate an interest in students' ideas, experiences and personal lives. Acknowledge that students do arrive in your lesson with 'personal baggage' and you need to develop an understanding of their experiences.
- Don't shout at or humiliate students. Listen to their concerns and help them to learn to respect their input to lessons. Praise and positive feedback is more effective than reprimands.
- Ensure your students know you don't subscribe to stereotyped views.
- Avoid cultural stereotyping.
- Reinforce positive messages about minority ethnic groups and cultures.
- Value the experiences students bring from their lives outside the classroom, including linguistic and cultural differences.
- Encourage the use of home and shared languages to support learning.
- Provide a range of texts and teaching materials that avoid cultural stereotyping and reinforce positive messages.

- Reflect on whom you praised and whom you reprimanded in your lessons.
- Make sure your students feel safe, comfortable and supported in your lessons.
- Be aware of your students' aspirations, abilities and learning styles.
- Encourage students to review their learning and progress, and provide them with the skills to set their own realistic learning targets.
- Monitor the progress of your students carefully.

'Teachers that utilise a sense of humour, well-timed smile, setting high expectations, respect and praise students can affect their learning.'

(Pickering, 1997, in Majors, 2001)

Stop and reflect

Consider a group you have taught recently or have observed being taught. Critically reflect on how you would now change your teaching to better meet the individual needs of your students.

Challenge your thinking

Many refer to a 'hidden curriculum', a way of filtering out students through the structures and practices of schools such as the middle-class values that schools uphold and propound, the practices of setting and streaming children, the content of the school syllabus and the system of examination. As early as 1964 John Holt in *How Children Fail* stated that children's failings were not despite the efforts of schools but actually because of schools. He reasoned that the main reason children did not learn in the school environment was fear: fear of getting the wrong answers, fear of being ridiculed by the teacher and classmates, fear of not being good enough. Holt argued that this was made worse as children were forced to 'learn' things that they were not interested in. John Holt became convinced that schools were as they are because of the needs of society not because of the needs of learners.

Holt also said:

'The most important thing any teacher has to learn, not to be learned in any school of education I ever heard of, can be expressed in seven words: learning is not the product of teaching. Learning is the product of the activity of learners.'

In the preface to *How Children Fail*, Holt states:

'But there is a more important sense in which almost all children fail. Except for a handful, who may or may not be good students, they fail to develop more that a tiny part of the tremendous capacity for learning, understanding and creating with which they were born and of which they made full use during the first two or three years of their lives.
Why do they fail?
They fail because they are afraid, bored and confused.'

Critically reflect on how true you feel John Holt's views are from your experience of school.

● What do you think Holt would say about your role as a professional teacher in meeting the needs of learners?

● Do you think any recent changes in the curriculum may help to make schools more appropriate for learners?

● In terms of your own philosophy, what do you think is the purpose of schools?

John Holt (1964) *How Children Fail,* Pitman Publishing Company, New York.

Summary

The intention of this chapter was to introduce you to the requirement, as a professional teacher, to ensure you are meeting the needs of individual children and personalising the learning experience of your students. This requirement has been linked to current government advice and the current government agenda. We have examined the needs of individual students including those with special education needs, those who are gifted and talented, those for whom English is an additional language, as well as exploring gender issues. We have looked at different ways to motivate your students. We have examined where to find the information within your school to help with your planning and assessment, and you now have knowledge on where you can find further support and guidance. We have also examined how to utilise new technologies in supporting individual needs and in personalising your lessons and assessment. The 'Stop and reflect' sections have provided an opportunity for you to critically consider your current teaching situation and strategies for applying your new knowledge. This chapter has stressed the importance of having all information available on your students before you start planning your lessons and assessments.

References

Blair, M. (2001) *Why Pick on Me? School Exclusion and Black Youth,* Stoke on Trent: Trentham Books Ltd.

Boulton, H. (2008) 'Managing e-Learning: what are the real implications for schools?', *Electronic Journal of e-Learning,* 6(1).

Broos, A. (2005) 'Gender and Information and Communication Technologies (ICT)anxiety: male self-assurance and female hesitation', *CyperPsychology and Behaviour,* 8: 21–31.

DCSF (2007) 'Gender and Education: the evidence of pupils in England', available from *http:// www.standards.dfes.gov.uk*

DfES (2001) 'Special Educational Needs Code of Practice'. Available on-line at *www.teachernet. gov.uk/wholeschool/sen.* Accessed November 2010.

Gillespie, H. Boulton, H. Mramiah, A. and Williamson, R. (2007) *Learning and Teaching with Virtual Learning Environments,* Exeter: Learning Matters.

Imhof, M., Vollmeyer, R. and Beierlein, C. (2007) 'Computer use and the gender gap: The issue of access, motivation and performance, *Computers in Human Behaviour,* 23(6): 2823–37 (November).

DfE (2010) 'Gifted and Talented Learners', available on-line at *www.education.gov.uk/schools.* Accessed November 2010.

Leadbetter, C. (2004) 'Learning about personalisation: how can we put the learner at the heart of the education system?', *http://www.standards.dfes.gov.uk/innovation-unit/pdf/Learningabout personalisation.pdf?version=1*

Majors, R. (ed.) (2001) *Educating our Black Children*, London: Routledge Falmer.

Salmon, G. (2002) *E-Tivities: the key to active on-line learning*, London: Kogan Page.

Salmon, G. (2004) *E-Moderating: the key to teaching and learning on-line*, London: Routledge Falmer.

Further reading

Davitt, J. (2005) *New Tools for Learning: Accelerated learning meets ICT*, Stafford: Network Education Press.

Ofsted (2001) 'Managing Support for the Attainment of Pupils from Minority Ethnic Groups', available from *www.ofsted.gov.uk*

Pachler, N. (ed.) (2007) *Mobile Learning, Towards a Research Agenda*, London: Institute of Education.

Potts, P. Armstrong, F. and Masterton, M. (eds) (2000) *Equality and Diversity in Education: Learning, Teaching and Managing in Schools*, London: Routledge.

QCA 'A language in common – assessing English as an additional language', available from *www.qca.org.uk*.

Warlick D.F. (2004) *Redefining literacy for the 21st century*, Worthington, Ohio: Linworth Publishers.

Warlick, D. (2005) *Classroom blogging: A teacher's guide to the Blogosphere*, Raleigh: The Landmark Project.

Web resources

http://audacity.sourceforge.net/ – to download voice recording software

http://elgg.net/

http://www.becta.org.uk/

http://www.blog.com/

http://www.blogger.com

http://www.delicious.com

http://www.dcsf.gov.uk

http://www.edublogs.org

http://www.flickr.com

http://www.livejournal.com

http://www.nace.co.uk – National Association for Able Children in Education (NACE).

http://www.pbwiki.co.uk

http://www.qca.org.uk/ca/5-14/afl/ – Assessment for Learning website.

http://www.rmplc.co.uk – National Association for Gifted Children (NAGC).

http://www.standards.dfes.gov.uk

http://www.teachernet.gov.uk

http://www.users.dircon.co.uk – Support Society for Children of Higher Intelligence (CHI).

http://www.youtube.com

http://www.Xcalibre.co.uk

http://www.ygt.dcsf.gov.uk – Young, Gifted and Talented portal.

Chapter 7

Raising achievement

Learning outcomes

By the end of this chapter, you will have an understanding of:

→ What motivates learners to learn

→ How you can increase motivation in learners

→ How achievement links to assessment

→ The effect on teachers and students of testing linked to achievement in schools

Introduction

This chapter is intended to give you an overview of motivation theory and what might motivate students in school. The underpinning theories and ideas on motivation are generally drawn from wider psychological studies rather than educational research. These theories are applied to school situations and linked to how students learn. Traditional schooling relies heavily on a behaviourist approach to motivation – mainly extrinsic. These can be summarised as *rewards* and *punishment*. More modern ideas about motivation relate more to intrinsic motivation – that which comes from within the person. This approach draws on a person's natural curiosity, feelings of self-esteem at a job well done and a desire to enjoy activities. Making lessons relevant and enjoyable is a major step towards motivating learners.

It is now being understood that children in UK schools have faced an over-burden of assessment, and the teaching-testing approach enshrined in the Key Stage tests has been challenged. There may be more freedom to plan lessons with motivation and engagement in mind, and you may wish to take some of the ideas in this chapter and the background reading and use them in your own teaching in order to best prepare your students for the wealth of learning and testing they will be presented with during their school careers.

Defining motivation is not an easy task. However it has been usefully described as:

'… an internal state or condition (sometimes described as a need, desire, or want) that serves to activate or energize behaviour and give it direction'.

(Kleinginna and Kleinginna, 1981)

Franken (1994) adds arousal, direction and persistence of behaviour to his definition.

Self-discipline and achievement

Everything in life requires effort – despite what your students say. Becoming an expert is often simply through working harder (at something) than anyone else has been willing to work. You can go a long way in life if you just will not (or do not) give up. So when you look at your most able students, much of it is down to the time and effort they invest in their work – it is down to sheer practice time (Jensen, 2006).

There is a strong body of research on expertise that indicates that domain-specific knowledge (that is, working harder at acquiring it) is the most important single component in effective learning. Those students with the highest grades study more than their under-performing peers (Jensen, 2006).

In a study on self-discipline and academic achievement by Duckworth and Seligman (2005) self-discipline accounted for more than twice as much variance as IQ in the final grades, high school selection, school attendance and hours spent on homework, indicating that pure effort and self-discipline matter more than natural 'talent' (Duckworth and Seligman, 2005).

There is, therefore, plenty of evidence that working hard is important and it is this message that you should try to get across to your students. The value of self-discipline comprehensively surpasses intelligence and other components. Becoming an expert, becoming better, is *not* based on how smart or clever you are, but on how hard you work at getting better.

Stop and reflect

Reflect on the different ways you could get the message across to your students about the value of hard work and self-discipline.

What role models from sport, science, history, for example, could you use to illustrate the point for them?

Motivational theories and ideas

Motivation is generally not a single driving force. It is usually a complex of interlinked desires or intentions – some of which may even be competing, and it is, consequently, not easy to define motivation simply or concisely. Through the ages, however, a number of people have tried, and some of these efforts are summarised briefly below. You should refer to the Critical synthesis section or References at the end of this chapter for more detail in these areas, though general psychology textbooks would usually have the information you need for your course.

Stop and reflect

Think about your own situation. You have a number of different needs which you wish to satisfy.

- Which are most important to you?
- How do you prioritise?
- Do your needs change over time and in different circumstances?

In the nineteenth century Freud proposed his instinct theory that human behaviour is motivated by two instincts. The first of these is the life instinct (Eros) which leads to sexual motivation. The second is the death instinct (Thanatos) which leads to aggressive behaviour. Typically Freud regarded these instincts as an integral part of an individual's unconscious. This seems to indicate a lack of any conscious control – an idea that would alarm many educationalists.

Hull (1943) presented the theory of Neo-behaviourism in which the probability of a given behaviour was based on:

- *Drive* – determined by need
- *Incentive* – as the perceived capacity of the external stimulus to reduce the need
- *Habit* – the extent of an individual's experience in performing the behaviour.

Hertzberg's dual factor theory (Herzberg *et al.* 1959; Hertzberg, 1966) explores the notion that there are two types of motivators. One type leads to satisfaction with the job, situation or task in hand (motivators). The other type does not act in a positive way but simply prevents dissatisfaction (hygienes). If hygienes are absent then dissatisfaction occurs.

Motivators, what we might now call 'motivating factors', include:

- Achievement
- Recognition
- The interest level of the work itself
- Responsibility
- Advancement.

Hygienes include:

- Working conditions
- Work policies
- Supervision
- Interpersonal relations
- Money
- Status
- Security.

You will note that the motivators relate very closely to what Maslow (1943) describes as esteem and self-actualisation – see below.

Skinner (1953) expanded on existing ideas and developed a theory of motivation that became well known as 'behaviourism'. In this theory Skinner argues that living things, including humans, respond to stimuli, and that these responses can be conditioned or ingrained so behaviour is altered. This theory appears to make evolutionary common sense. If eating a food provides a pleasant taste the animal is more likely to eat that substance again. Conversely, a foul-tasting food is less likely to be eaten and so behaviour is learned. In a classroom setting it is generally understood that praise and rewards (positive reinforcement) increase the motivation of learners.

The Attribution Theory is one example of a cognitive model or theory. Weiner (1972) concentrated on factors such as thought, intention and expectation (even though these are difficult to observe and study) in an attempt to understand actions and relate these to thought processes – cognition (Chambers, 2001). An elegant description of the importance of this theory, and its possible impact on learning, is outlined by Huitt (2001). Huitt explains that:

'. . . every individual tries to explain success or failure of self and others by offering certain "attributions". These attributions are either internal or external and are either under control or not under control'.

(Huitt, 2001)

Huitt (*ibid.*) goes on to state:

'In a teaching/learning environment, it is important to assist the learner to develop a self-attribution explanation of effort (internal, control). If the person has an attribution of ability (internal, no control) as soon as the individual experiences some difficulties in the learning process, he or she will decrease appropriate learning behaviour (e.g., I'm not good at this). If the person has an external attribution, then nothing the person can do will help that individual in a learning situation (i.e., responsibility for demonstrating what has been *learned is completely outside the person). In this case, there is nothing to be done by the individual when learning problems occur.'*

(Huitt, 2001)

Clearly, the notion of learners giving up as soon as they perceive something to be difficult will be familiar to many teachers. An understanding of aspects of Attribution Theory can help us to understand this and apply solutions.

Critical synthesis

Attribution Theory is only one example of a cognitive theory of motivation. Read Huitt's (2001) paper (link below) and reflect on other cognitive theories.

- *From your reading of Huitt, what are the main differences between Attribution Theory and Expectancy Theory?*
- *Do these two theories overlap or contradict Cognitive Dissonance Theory?*
- *How might your knowledge of these theories help you to motivate learners?*

Huitt also summarises aspects of intrinsic and extrinsic motivation.

- *What are the sources of motivational need highlighted by Huitt?*
- *Which do you recognise from your own experiences as a teacher and as a learner?*

http://www.edpsycinteractive.org/col/motivation/motivate.html

David McClelland (1961) linked motivation to the need for achievement. This is sometimes referred to as *Achievement Motivation*. McClelland argued that a person's needs are shaped over time and influenced by life experiences. These needs can be described as achievement, affiliation or power.

McClelland states that a person's motivation, and how effective they are, is influenced by these three needs. No two people are alike and some people have a higher need than others for achievement. Those with a high need (defined as n-ach) enjoy taking on responsibility and thrive on problem solving. This allows them to show their skills and competence but also it acts to challenge them into developing new skills. These n-ach people set moderately high goals for themselves that provide appropriate challenge but are achievable. Lack of success would be de-motivating, but so would lack of challenge. Another group of people identified by McClelland are those motivated by affiliation needs (n-affil). These people enjoy and need relationships with colleagues. They need to feel wanted and respected and thrive on interpersonal relationships and network building. Finally, those motivated by a need for power, described as n-pow by McClelland, are motivated by positions of authority and the ability to direct the work of others. Role prestige is vital and there is a genuine need to be in charge and to own problems.

A major influence of motivation theory has been Abraham Maslow (1943). In his work Maslow proposes that human beings are motivated by needs. The most basic needs involve those things we need to remain alive, warm, comfortable and safe. These needs are often shown as a diagram – a triangle or pyramid of needs (see Figure 7.1). The lowest four layers of the triangle represent, according to Maslow, the 'deficiency needs'. Once these have been met a person will work towards meeting the needs of a higher level.

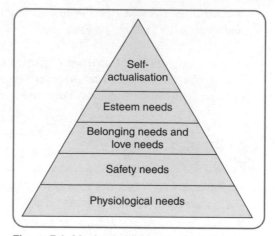

Figure 7.1 **Maslow's hierarchy of needs**

The impact Maslow has had on motivation theory involving education is in the realisation that learners will only concern themselves with higher-order activities such as creativity and problem solving once their more fundamental needs have been met. A hungry child facing abuse and loneliness cannot be expected to be motivated to concentrate on their school work.

In addition, if a person is happily operating at the self-actualisation level of the hierarchy, but then becomes seriously ill or is involved in an accident then they quickly return to the 'deficiency needs'. You may have witnessed this in your classroom. An otherwise hard-working and successful student suddenly becomes unmotivated – occasionally linked to poorer behaviour. On enquiring, you may find this student has had some serious upset in their home life and is now focused on trying to meet deficiency needs which were until recently well met.

Case study

The following passage is from a report of the House of Commons Education and Skills Committee (2003). If you wish to study this further, the full reference is at the bottom of the box.

'During this inquiry we have been told repeatedly that poor children are, on average, less likely than others to flourish at school. This is a major concern of the Government and has inspired strategies such as Excellence in Cities and the Ethnic Minority Achievement Grant. Education can provide children with the skills they need to succeed and we are aware that those who have left school with few or no qualifications are statistically more likely to live below the poverty line. Poor education is one of the main reasons for poverty continuing from one generation to the next. Professor David Gillborn told us that "if you want to predict how well a student will do, find out their social class. That is the best single predictor, not their gender, not their ethnicity".

Nevertheless, this relationship between poverty and educational outcomes is not inevitable. Now, as in the past, many children from poor socio-economic backgrounds excel in school. In evaluating policy designed to help children from poor backgrounds, it has to be borne in mind that child poverty is not exclusively about income. Poverty impacts on children through lack of opportunities and of social capital in the form of the support available to families in better circumstances.

'House of Commons (2003) p. 19

Consider the quote, then reflect on your growing knowledge of motivation theory.

● Do you believe that a child's attainment is predetermined by its social class?

● What needs, in Maslow's hierarchy, do you think children from poor socio-economic backgrounds may be lacking in comparison to children from more affluent backgrounds?

Elsewhere in the report there is a statement relating to the impact of parental interest on a child's attainment. Reflect on this and then suggest effective ways that schools might motivate parents to be more involved and supportive of their child's education.

House of Commons (2003) Education and Skills Committee, *Secondary Education: Pupil Achievement Seventh Report of Session 2002–03,* London: The Stationery Office Limited.

Hopefully this level of poverty does not exist today but there are still many disadvantaged children in the country
Source: Getty Images

Maslow's work has not been without its critics and its developers. For example, Alderfer (1972) has a related hierarchy that defines the level of need as one of these three:

● Growth

● Relatedness

● Existence.

Later researchers, such as Wahba and Bridgewell (1976), have reported no evidence of a hierarchy of needs but as a mental model Maslow's theory remains influential.

Four common attributes for success are thought to be:

- Ability
- Effort (which links back to the previous section on self-determination)
- Luck
- The complexity of the job or task being undertaken.

Ability and effort are internal and are therefore the responsibility of the individual. The latter two, luck and task complexity, are external and therefore cannot be influenced in the same way by an individual (Chambers, 2001).

Other motivational theories to consider as teachers include Rosenthal and Jacobson's Expectancy Theory (1968) which stresses that learners pick up a series of signals or cues from teachers, which influence their motivation. For example, if a teacher is always expecting low standards from a class then there is a strong likelihood that this will happen. The learners will pick up this message of low expectation and react accordingly. This is sometimes known as the 'self-fulfilling prophecy'. It is important to always expect high standards from learners and encourage them to do their best.

If you have any experience of management, or of being managed at work, you may recognise McGregor's (1960) analysis of motivation. McGregor asserts that there are two types of manager (or teacher?) – Theory X and Theory Y.

- The Theory X manager arrives at work with the assumption that everyone there is lazy and will be trying to get away with things. The workers will not react well to change and the manager assumes they have little ability.
- The Theory Y manager holds the opposite views. Workers are regarded as being talented and motivated – keen to take responsibility. The manager sees potential in the workforce.

Though related to management McGregor's ideas should be of great interest to the teacher. Our work with learners can be clouded by a pessimistic view their attitudes, abilities and potential. This may say more about us than them.

Ideally, we should try to take a more holistic view of motivation, given that at the start of this section it was stated that motivation is not a single entity but a multitude of inter-linked factors. It is more likely that an eclectic stance on motivation is arguably the most appropriate to take given its propensity for multiplicity.

Stop and reflect

- Having read the above, which do you think most applies to what motivates you? Read around the subject more and see if your ideas change.
- Are you a Theory X or a Theory Y teacher?
- What evidence do you have to support your judgement?

Motivation and why we want to learn

There are a number of reasons why people (not just students) want to learn. Some of them are linked to long-term motives, and some to far more short-term goals. Some of the reasons why we are motivated to learn are given below (Petty, 2004):

1 It is useful to us.

2 The qualification I am studying is useful to me.

3 It increases my self-esteem when I am successful – a main motivator for most people.

4 It is vital for the acceptance of my teacher and/or peers – which is linked to self-esteem.

5 The consequences of not doing it will not be agreeable and will probably be fairly immediate.

6 It is interesting and appeals to my curiosity.

7 Learning activities are fun.

Some of these learners appear to lack motivation and engagement
Source: Pearson Education Ltd/MindStudio

The first two in the list are long-term reasons for learning with long-terms goals in mind. The remainder are comparatively short term and generally linked to that piece of learning currently being undertaken. What you have to do as a teacher is to find ways to increase your student's desire to learn, by appealing to some or all of the above, in a variety of combinations depending on whom and what and how you are teaching. (See also Chapter 5 on engaging learners for further details on motivation.)

Once you have motivated your students to learn in your classes, you have to maintain this, and this can be done through positive approval of the work done. The recognition

These learners appear more enthusiastic and engaged
Source: Pearson Education Ltd/Gareth Boden

of achievement is one of the most powerful tools a teacher has. It is usually the single most effective way of improving motivation; learning and attainment. (See also Chapter 9 on Assessment and feedback, for more information on this topic.)

Stop and reflect

Why do you want to learn? Think about your motives to enter the teaching profession and consider which of the above most applies to you.

Practical task

- Chose one of the classes you have taught so far.
- Write down which of the reasons listed above applies to your students, and determine if it changes substantially when you change classes and subjects.
- Describe how it changes between pre- and post-16 learning.

How testing and performance have affected teaching and learning

A vast industry has arisen around the testing regimes currently being used in the schools of England, and this has arguably been the most significant aspect of recent reforms within education in the last few decades. This increase in testing and the reliance on it to indicate many different aspects of a child's performance and potential in schools has also arisen despite the reliability of such testing being constantly under question (Gardner, 2006). (For more detail on assessment see Chapter 9.)

The school students of English schools undergo more national assessments than any others in the world, and more than in any other previous period in education. In addition to national tests there are also optional and practice tests which they are likely to experience throughout their schools lives. This environment also reinforces the view that only those experiences that enhance test performance are important (Gardner, 2006).

In primary schools it is currently the trend to test all years at SATS times ostensibly so that the children undergoing them for real do not feel under as much pressure. Presumably this also gives the others a chance to practise them and so not feel so threatened by them when it is their turn. You could argue, however, that all this does is make the children feel the pressure all the time, and conditions them to associate school with testing rather than learning.

What this does, therefore, is to lead to a focus on teaching rather than on learning in order to cover a very busy curriculum in preparation for any given test along the way. Such an emphasis has a negative influence on learning.

When teachers concentrate on teaching rather than learning in this way their teaching can become defensive (Watkins *et al.*, 2007), since they are put under pressure to achieve the best results possible with their classes, to get the kind of results that improve positions in league tables – for example, giving all their attention to the D/C grade boundary rather than to the other grades within a class. This pressure increases year on year and lends itself to an increasing focus on teaching through classroom management as a way of achieving this goal, rather than a focus on the learning goals of the individuals within that class. This type of teaching also eliminates any holistic vision of teaching and learning, going beyond the bounds of the curriculum to teach students around and about the topic in hand to ensure that they get a more rounded view of it – such are my memories of school (pre-1990s) when it was felt to be important that we learned more than just the syllabus.

The response by teachers to external pressures, then, is often to control the classroom experience more, and to instinctively narrow the confines of what will be taught and (ideally) learned. In consequence, they adhere only to the lesson plan and scheme of work that details exactly what the objectives are for that specific point in time within the school year – in preparation for the next round of testing.

Control within the classroom is often imposed by fragmenting, simplifying or omitting complex aspects of what is to be learned. Knowledge is presented in more digestible forms and this limits the complexity of the learning process (Watkins *et al.*, 2007). Hence, you might hear the term 'spoon-fed' with reference to the type of teaching that goes on in schools today, as an indicator of the way teaching is perceived by members of its own profession and also by parents and politicians. The three- to four-part lesson that is currently in vogue in today's classrooms as a way of controlling pace and content of lessons is not so far removed from the five-part lesson of Johann Herbart in the early nineteenth century (Watkins *et al.*, 2007). How little things change! So little, in fact, that it can often seem as if we have not come so far in several centuries of teaching and learning. Cycles of reform are not uncommon within education and need to be understood within the broader historical framework to provide an unobstructed view (McCulloch, 1994).

When teachers teach defensively, pace (hurried and unrelenting) can often dominate the lesson, and can result in the more deliberate activities related to learning , such as discussion, sharing ideas, reviewing, and so on, being marginalised (Watkins *et al.*,

2007). Lessons then become a point in time whose sole purpose is to cover a portion of the curriculum. Rather than move students on when they are ready, it becomes a matter of necessity to move them on when the teacher is ready to move on to the next part of the curriculum. Such a focus on the teacher's agenda – set by external pressures – is not likely to prove effective for learning (and any enjoyment that should arise as a result of it).

Stop and reflect

- Do you feel under pressure to produce good test results with your classes?
- How do you think it has affected your teaching style and your own professional stance on teaching?
- Do you think your students like the way you teach when you and they are under pressure to perform?

Challenge your thinking

Motivating yourself to read about Maslow

Maslow work on the Hierarchy of Needs has had a major impact on ideas about motivation – both in education and management. The idea of a hierarchy has been criticised (as you will have seen above) but this was generally levelled at Maslow's model with five levels (psychological needs, safety needs, belongingness and love needs, esteem needs and self-actualisation).

In fact, in 1970 Maslow added two levels to his model:

- Cognitive (need to know, understand and explore) needs
- Aesthetic (desire for beauty, order and symmetry) needs.

These he placed just beneath self-actualisation. Indeed, Maslow assumed that some people rise above self-actualisation to reach transcendence. This means that just before his death in 1971 Maslow had developed an eight-level hierarchy.

In view of the criticisms of Maslow's model – with many researchers claiming that, not only is there no evidence that people pass through level of needs, but that his model has cultural bias (Wahba and Bridgewell, 1976: Eckins and Max-Neef, 1992) where do you now stand on the value of Maslow's Hierarchy of Need?

- Have you altered your views on the application of the model to learning, teaching and behaviour?
- Does the model help to explain what you see and experience within your professional work?
- Does the fact that Maslow was modifying his model up to his death make the model more pertinent or does it weaken it?

Summary

There is some research to suggest that those students who work hardest are the ones who achieve success. Of course, this does not answer the question – why do some students work harder than others? The answer to this is complex and draws on many areas, not least the social background and the school success, or otherwise, of parents and other significant adults. The answer is also related to some extent to our understanding of what motivates humans. Maslow suggests that humans will not prioritise learning activities such as problem solving and creativity until more basic human needs are met. A freezing person will be more concerned with getting warm than answering questions in class.

Other researchers highlight the responses humans have to external motivators such as punishment and reward. This idea underpins behaviourist answers to motivation and has influenced much of our schooling. Work hard and you will get rewards, do not work hard and you will be punished.

Good teachers pay attention to what motivates people internally or intrinsically. These factors come from within the individual – they form part of the value structure of the person and are not influenced by short-term rewards and punishments. Intrinsic factors include the desire to learn relevant material and skills, the satisfaction and self-esteem resulting from learning new things, longer-term self-esteem based on successful careers and the satisfaction of curiosity. Another important factor is that learning can be motivating because it is enjoyable. Bearing these factors in mind will help you to plan motivating activities and lessons.

Gee (2005) asks a very important question. How do computer game designers manage to get players to learn long, complex and difficult games (and pay for the privilege) when often the same people cannot be motivated to learn in school? The answer obviously lies in the different way that computer games designers engage the learner and structure the learning to encourage involvement. The learning becomes biologically motivating. It is important that as teachers we look for ways of 'hooking' young people on to learning rather than forcing them or making the work too simple.

The emphasis on testing in schools has had a detrimental effect on student motivation and recent moves to free up the curriculum, encourage more cross-curricular work and increased relevance through such things as 'how science works' and work-based learning can only be helpful.

References

Alderfer, C. (1972) *Existence, relatedness, & growth,* New York: Free Press.

Chambers, G. (ed.) (2001) *Reflections on motivations,* London: CILT Publications.

Duckworth, A. and Seligman, M. (2005) 'Self-Discipline Outdoes IQ in Predicting Academic Performance of Adolescents', *Psychological Science,* 16(12): 939–44.

Eckins, P. and Max-Neef, M. (eds) (1992) *Real Life Economics? Understanding Wealth Creation,* London: Routledge.

Franken, R. (1994) *Human motivation* (5th edn 2001), Pacific Grove, CA: Brooks/Cole.

Gardner, J. (ed.) (2006) *Assessment and Learning,* London: Sage Publications.

Gee, J.P. (2005) 'Learning by Design: good video games as learning machines.' *E-Learning,* 2(1): 5–16.

Herzberg, F., Mausner, B. and Snyderman, B.B. (1959) *The motivation to work,* New York: Wiley.

Herzberg, F. (1966) *Work and the nature of man,* Cleveland, OH: Holland.

Huitt, W. (2001) 'Motivation to learn: An overview', *Educational Psychology Interactive,* Valdosta, GA: Valdosta State University. Accessed November 2010 from www.edpsycinteractive.org/col/motivation/motivate.html

Hull, Clark L. (1943) *Principles of Behavior: An Introduction to Behavior Theory,* New York: Appleton Century Crofts.

Jensen, E. (2006) *Enriching the brain: How to maximise every learners potential,* San Francisco: Jossey-Bass.

Kleinginna, P., Jr. and Kleinginna, A. (1981) 'A categorized list of motivation definitions, with suggestions for a consensual definition', *Motivation and Emotion,* 5, 263–91.

Maslow, A.H. (1943) 'A Theory of Human Motivation', *Psychological Review,* 50(4): 370–96.

McClelland, D.C. (1961) *The Achieving Society,* Princeton, N. J: Van Norstrand.

McCulloch, G. (1994) *Educational Reconstruction – The 1944 Education Act and the Twenty-first Century, I,* llford: The Woburn Press.

McGregor, D. (1960) *The Human Side of Enterprise,* New York: McGraw-Hill.

Petty, G. (2004) *Teaching Today* (3rd edn), Cheltenham: Nelson Thornes.

Rosenthal, R. and Jacobson, L. (1968) *Pygmalion in the classroom: Teacher expectation and pupils' intellectual development,* New York: Holt, Rinehart and Winston.

Skinner, B. F. (1953) *Science and Human Behaviour,* New York: Macmillan.

Wahba, A. and Bridgewell, L. (1976) 'Maslow reconsidered: A review of research on the need hierarchy theory', *Organizational Behavior and Human Performance,* (15), 212–40.

Weiner, B.J. (1972) *Theories of Motivation,* Chicago, IL: Markham.

Watkins, C., Carnell, E. and Lodge, C. (2007) *Effective Learning in Classrooms,* London: Paul Chapman Publishing

Chapter 8

Planning and preparation

Learning Outcomes

By the end of this chapter you will be able to:

→ Plan for progression, including effective learning sequences, and evidence a range of teaching strategies

→ Design appropriate lesson structures, including transitions

→ Plan for the assessment of objectives

→ Plan homework and other out of class work to consolidate and extend learning

→ Develop a format for a scheme of work and lesson plans

→ Demonstrate ability to evaluate the impact of teaching

Introduction

To fail to plan is to plan to fail.

Good planning and preparation is an essential aspect of your professional development. Even the most experienced teachers carry out lesson planning and preparation. Planning can be broken down into two elements: long/medium-term planning – scheme of work; and short-term planning – lesson plans. This chapter will address both of these aspects.

Long- and medium-term planning

Your long/medium-term planning document, sometimes called a 'scheme of work (SOW)' is a written statement, which describes the work planned for students within a class or group over a specific period of time, i.e. it may last for a six-or 12-week module, or may last for the full two years of a GCSE/vocational Diploma course. This planning document is an essential element of your planning process. It should reflect whole-school approaches to teaching and learning, such as linking to cross-curricular themes – for example, literacy, numeracy and information-communications technology. It should be written in sufficient detail that, should you be off sick, cover teachers should have sufficient information to take the lesson(s). Each long/medium-term planning document/SOW is part of the 11–18 continuum and, taken with preceding and subsequent schemes, will describe the detailed curriculum structure for your subject for students across all the Key Stages. This planning document must clearly show progression for all students.

For Key Stages 3 and 4 you need to refer to the programmes of study and attainment targets from the National Curriculum for your subject – these can currently be found on websites such as *www.nationalcurriculumonline.gov.uk*, *www.ncaction.org.uk* and *www.teachnet.com*. You will find that some of these websites have schemes of work that you can use for reference. For post-16 and KS4 you need to refer to the examination specifications – these can be found on exam board websites.

Practical task

It would be sensible at this point to look at some existing schemes of work. Try to obtain a Key Stage 3 and a Key Stage 4 scheme of work from the school. Also, examine a variety of different ones from different sources. You can do this by looking at published schemes, checking on-line and sharing examples with colleagues on your course.

Critically evaluate the content and identify the common aspects.

- What do they have in common?
- How are they set out?
- How do they differ?

Make a list of the essential components you believe should be in a scheme of work.

Your long/medium-term planning document/SOW must ensure that all areas of exam board specifications or National Curriculum are experienced by learners, sometimes more than once. This is necessary to broaden experience by learners, and to ensure reinforcement of learning and progression to a higher level of achievement.

Where to start? For learning to be effective you need to consider how you will break down the learning for the students.

What should be included?

It would be very wrong to suggest there is a model way of doing this. Ideas and practices evolve very rapidly, and schools may have their own pro-forma that you will use when you start your full-time teaching post. You may be issued with a pro-forma to use during your teacher training that will link to providing evidence for the teaching standards. If not, start to build a list of different aspects that you identified in the Practical task above. An example of a pro-forma that you could use is shown at the end of the chapter; this is a very detailed example as it links to the teacher-training teaching standards; you may find the one used in your school is less detailed.

If you are designing your own long/medium-term planning document/SOW you should include:

- Information on the lessons – e.g. how many and for how long each week, who the teacher is, the room, etc.
- Information on the subject – key stage, examination specification being used.
- Assessment methods, both formative and summative – as you read through this chapter you will understand how important it is to consider assessment of students' achievement from the initial planning stages. An explanation of formative and summative assessment can be found in Chapter 9.
- Resources that are to be used – e.g. textbooks, specific software, school intranet or virtual learning environment, internet resources, etc.
- Prior experience of your students. This is very important as all schemes of work need to evidence clear progression of students from one year to the next, through each key stage.
- The aims relevant to the scheme of work – you can often locate general aims within the National Curriculum for your subject, or within examination board specifications.
- Which modules or programme of study will be encompassed within the scheme of work.
- The teaching styles you will be using. This will be further discussed in the next section of this chapter.
- The differentiation that you will be planning – i.e. how you will support and challenge all learners within the class. This will be further discussed in the 'Differentiation' section of this chapter.
- Links to areas such as literacy, numeracy and ICT.
- A break-down of each lesson to indicate what you will cover. This needs to include the subject content, the teaching and learning activities, differentiation activities, and the assessment strategies to be used.

You will need to consider:

- Continuity of experience across the 11–18 age range
- Interests of the students. Engaging with their interests in learning and teaching activities will help to engage them in learning
- Progression in ideas and in the skills and strategies used
- Differentiation (matching tasks to all students including those with special needs (SEN), balancing challenge with likelihood of success over the whole ability range)
- Providing maximum access for students, including those for whom English is a second language (EAL), SEN and gifted and talented students
- Gender considerations
- Minority ethnic considerations
- Assessment strategies
- Material which is not specified in the programmes of study and specification
- Procedures for review and evaluation
- Recording and reporting processes.

Examples of teaching and learning activities

Students need to experience a range of teaching and learning activities to reflect a range of learning styles. Chapter 7 offered a selection of possible activities, so you may wish to look back and refresh your memory of these. A balance of activities is needed in each lesson to ensure the students are engaged, stimulated and challenged.

Stop and reflect

Examine the four possible activities below:

- Creating a board game
- Digital photography
- Wikis
- Producing a newspaper.

For each example decide how you might incorporate the activity into your lessons. Consider the skills and knowledge you would have to develop to manage the activity effectively.

Finally, critically reflect on the value of including these activities in terms of:

- How the activity might motivate the learners and create interest
- The skills learners can develop through these activities
- Ways that the activities can help you to address individual learning needs.

Assessment

Your medium/long-term planning document/SOW will need to address which strategies you will use for assessment. These will be more detailed in your lesson plan, but it is important that you start to think about assessment in the initial planning stages. You will need to include both formative and summative assessment strategies. These will be further discussed in Chapter 9. When starting to think about your medium/long-term planning document/SOW, consider how assessment will remain an internal part of the learning process and how it can be used in a positive and supportive manner. This is both professionally challenging as well as positively stimulating.

When you have prepared your scheme of work you need to check:

- **Balance** in terms of content, context, teaching
- **Breadth** in terms of learning experience
- **Relevance** to the ability, age range and interests of the students.

Stop and reflect

Select a scheme of work you have planned, or modified, for a group you teach. Consider a block of six weeks or so. This will allow you to reflect on the development of objectives and ideas across a reasonable time span, rather than just a single lesson.

Critically reflect on your scheme of work in terms of:

- How do the objectives of one lesson link to those of subsequent lessons?
- Is there a variety of learning and teaching activities?
- How have you considered individual needs?
- Is there a range of formative and summative assessment opportunities?
- How do the learners know what is expected and how to do better?
- How do you know how well each learner understands the work?
- Is the work included in your scheme challenging, relevant and motivating?

Having carried out this exercise, what changes will you make to the scheme?

Short-term planning

The short-term planning document used in schools is a lesson plan. A lesson plan should:

- Meet the needs of the students
- Provide for student progression
- Enable variety
- Engage and motivate students
- Provide for different learning styles
- Build on prior knowledge

- Develop concepts and processes
- Enable learners to apply new knowledge, understanding and skills
- Meet learning objectives
- Identify timings.

Clear aims and objectives linked to assessment are at the heart of good lesson planning.

The **Teaching standards** state that you 'teach lessons and sequences of lessons across the age and ability range'. To do this you are advised to base your planning on your knowledge of:

- The students
- Evidence of their past and current achievements
- The expected standards for students of the relevant age range
- The range and content of work relevant to students in that age range.

Before you start to plan your lesson you need to gather essential information on your class. This might include:

- Individual Education Plans (IEPs). These are learning plans that are available for all students with a recognised learning difficulty.
- Base-line data. For Key Stage 3 this may include Key Stage 2 levels, CAT scores, etc.; for Key Stage 4 this may include end of Key Stage 3 levels; for post-16 classes this may include Key Stage 4 results for Year 12, and/or AS results for Year 13.
- What the group has covered before within the subject that impacts on the topic you are going to be teaching.
- Past and current achievements.
- Expected standards for students. This might include predicted grades and levels, e.g. Key Stage 3 levels, GCSE grades, Vocational Diploma results; or AS/A2 grades.
- Range and content of work relevant to students in that age range. A good source for this is the Key Stage 3 and 4 National Curriculum, textbooks designed for the subject/Key Stage programme of study/exam board specifications and age range you are going to be teaching.

Teachers used to use the National Strategy. This stated that:

'Good teaching fosters good learning. It stems from effective lesson design whatever the age of the learner, their level of ability, or the subject or skill being learned. Good teaching results when teachers:

- *focus and structure their teaching so that students are clear about what is to be learned and how, and how it fits with what they know already;*
- *actively engage students in their learning so that they make their own meaning from it;*
- *develop systematically students' learning skills so that their learning becomes increasingly independent;*
- *use assessment for learning to help students to reflect on what they already know, reinforce the learning being developed, and set targets for the future;*
- *have high expectations of the effort that students should make and what they can achieve;*

- *make the learning motivating by well-paced teaching using stimulating activities matched to a range of learning styles;*

- *create an environment that promotes learning in a settled and purposeful atmosphere.'*

(*www.nationalcurriculumonline.gov.uk*)

The Secondary National Strategy (*http://nationalstrategies.standards.dcsf.gov.uk/ secondary/*) focused on providing access to excellent teaching and engaging, purposeful learning.

Practical task

Research the impact of The National Strategy on schools. As sources you can use:

- *http://nationalstrategies.standards.dcsf.gov.uk/secondary/*
- Conversations with colleagues in schools
- Ofsted reports on the National Strategy (2005 and 2009) found at www.ofsted.gov.uk.

In your opinion, has the National Strategy made an impact in school?

What can you learn from the National Strategy?

Effective lesson design involves careful consideration of a number of factors. It starts from learning objectives, encompasses a 'climate for learning', and then focuses on pedagogic approaches, teaching and learning strategies and techniques, and classroom organisation.

Objectives

Before we look at what aims and objectives are in terms of planning for your teaching it is worth pausing to consider the different domains of learning. Bloom's Taxonomy (Bloom 1956), which is the taxonomy most frequently used by teachers in their planning, suggests three distinctive types of learning domains:

- The 'cognitive domain', which involves the intellectual capability of our students – that is, their ability to acquire new knowledge or to think;

- The 'affective domain', which relates to feelings, emotions and behaviour;

- The psychomotor domain, which relates to manual and physical skills.

More on the learning domains can be found in Chapters 6 together with further reading on this area of teaching as indicated in the References section for this chapter.

What are aims?

These are generalised statements of intentions, they are often difficult to completely evaluate in a single lesson as the students may only achieve them in the long term. An example might be to understand the various legislation affecting the use of computers.

In a one-hour lesson there would normally only be one main aim. This may increase if the lesson were extended to two or three hours or if you have a post-16 group who may progress through work more quickly.

Aims of a lesson are clear concise statements that describe what the teacher hopes to achieve. These statements of intent are usually expressed in a rather broad way:

To improve the students' ability to...
To develop an understanding of how...

Lesson aims are expressed from the students' point of view. Aims are rather like compass directions, which indicate the general direction in which students will travel. As an outline they are vital, but they are not specific enough to help the teacher identify appropriate learning activities, or to assess whether learning has taken place.

The problem then is that aims may point you in the right direction but they do not tell you how to get there, or when you have arrived. So intentions must be described in a more detailed way with objectives.

What are objectives?

These should relate to the overall aims of the scheme of work and be specific statements relating to learning. The question which prompts objectives is: what do you want the students in the class to learn? The National Strategy referred to this as WALT (We Are Learning To ... .)

Objectives indicate what you want your students to learn during the lesson and are often expressed by using active verbs. Teachers generally use verbs from Bloom's Taxonomy. Objectives are written in a form to demonstrate what the students will do and learn and are usually expressed as:

By the end of this lesson the students will be able to:

- *Explain ......*
- *Recall .....*
- *Produce ....*
- *List ......*
- *Examine and so on.*

(*www.nationalstrategies.standards.dcsf.gov.uk*)

When planning your lesson you must decide how you will assess that the students have achieved each of these objectives. You could use homework, observation, a test, case studies, mock exam papers, completion of coursework, and so on. The important aspect is that each **individual** student has understood them. Oral questioning can be used to help you to assess that the group understand the topic, but you cannot be sure that each individual has understood.

Objectives are testable statements describing the abilities to be learned. For example, the student should be able to:

- List the main principles of the Data Protection Act.
- State the role of the Data Protection Registrar.
- Explain the main difference between the 1984 and 1998 Acts.

Writing objectives does take practice. Some student teachers have difficulty in writing specific objectives or outcomes, at first tending to think in terms of what the teacher will do rather than what the student will learn.

Stop and reflect

Select three objectives you have produced for recent lesson plans.

- Critically evaluate the clarity and purpose of the objectives.
- Are they objectives or aims?
- Are they differentiated in any way?

Some teachers argue that telling the learners the objectives at the start of a lesson removes the mystery and discovery in lessons.

What would your response be to colleagues who hold this view?

Suggested areas for framing objectives

1 Knowledge

- Recall – facts, terminology, conventions, generalisations ...
- Be aware of ...
- Apply knowledge of ...
- Recognise ...

2 Comprehension

- Calculate, translate, interpret, extrapolate, make deductions ...
- Awareness of attitudes and values.

3 Application

- Apply knowledge and information in unfamiliar situations.
- Use a model.

4 Analysis

- Breakdown of material into constituents in order to establish relationship between it and rest of material – or between constituent parts.

5 Synthesis

- Putting together of constituents by rearranging or combining them.

6 Evaluation

- Make value judgements about materials, ideas, methods and so on. Examine quality of evidence.

Rephrasing objectives

The National Strategy provided useful words for defining lesson objectives and expected students' outcomes shown below. These are taken from the Key Stage 3 Framework, Standards and Assessment pack and are shown in Table 8.1.

Table 8.1 National Strategy Guidelines for defining lesson objectives and outcomes

Draw	State	Record	Recognise	Identify
Sort	Describe	Select	Present	Locate information from text
Decide	Discuss	Define	Classify	Explain how
Devise	Calculate	Interpret	Construct	Clarify
Plan	Predict	Conclude	Solve	Determine the key points from ...
Formulate	Explain why	Use the pattern to ...	Reorganise	Explain the differences between ...
Link/make connections between	Use the idea of ... to ...	Use a model of ... to ...	Provide evidence for	Evaluate the evidence for

General increase in demand →

Source: *http://www.nationalstrategies.standards.dcsf.gov.uk.*

What is an outcome?

Outcomes should indicate how the objectives will be met. Outcomes can be differentiated using 'All will ... Most will ... Some will'. ('All' is the learning that everyone in the group will achieve; 'most' is the learning that the majority will achieve; and 'some' is the planning for learners who will need additional challenge.

Defining specific learning outcomes has a number of advantages. It makes clear what students have to do. It makes lesson planning easier by suggesting learning activities. Also, if you know exactly what students should be able to do, it is much easier to assess whether or not they can do it. This enables you to evaluate how successful your lessons have been. This also puts the teacher language used in framing the objectives into 'student speak' for the outcomes.

The crucial point is that the outcomes precisely describe observable learner performance, shifting the focus on to what the students will be able to do as a result of their learning, and away from what the teacher will do.

The question which prompts outcomes is: *what are your expectations of students of different abilities and with different needs?* or *how do you expect students of differing abilities and with different needs to demonstrate what they have learned?*

This is often referred to as **WILF** (*What I'm Looking For ...*).

Practical task

Pause at this stage to put some of this theory into practice. Write two objectives that would be suitable for a lesson relating to a topic within your subject area for a group of Y11 GCSE students.

● Now write the learning outcomes for each of these objectives.

● Try to plan for differentiation by breaking each outcome into 'all will', 'most will', 'some will'.

Pedagogic approaches

To support effective lesson design, as a minimum, the National Strategy promoted the use of direct, inductive and exploratory approaches (National Strategy: Key Messages Pedagogy and Practice from: *http://www.nationalstrategies.standards.dcsf.gov.uk*). All teachers can benefit from proficiency in these teaching styles, varying and adding to their repertoire as they gain confidence and experience. They are not the only approaches, but they are a good foundation. The key elements of these three approaches are summarised in Table 8.2.

Engaging students in learning

Students are more likely to be engaged in their work when:

● They are clear about its purpose because the work has been well explained;

● The work builds on their prior attainment; they are able to do the work but find it challenging;

● They are emotionally, physically and intellectually involved by the tasks set;

● The presentation, variety and structure of the work and activities generate curiosity and interest;

● They have opportunities to ask questions and try out ideas;

● They can see what they have achieved and how they have made progress;

● They get a feeling of satisfaction and enjoyment from the work.

Literacy, numeracy and ICT

There is an increasing move by schools to require teachers to include planning for these core subjects in lesson plans. This is simple to do by referring to the national curriculum for each of the topics for the age range that you are planning for. The National Curriculum for numeracy, literacy, and ICT can be downloaded, or ordered free of

Table 8.2 **Pedagogic approaches**

	Direct	Inductive	Exploratory
Purpose	To acquire new knowledge or skills.	To develop a concept or process.	To use, consolidate or refine skills and understanding.
Key features	A structured sequence, often beginning with whole-class work with modelling, demonstration or illustration. Typically, this is followed by individual or group work. The sequence often ends with whole-class review.	A structured set of directed steps. Students collect and sift information, then examine data. They construct categories, and generate and test hypotheses.	Testing a prediction or hypothesis based on the understanding of a concept. Students decide what information to collect, obtain the data and analyse it.
Examples	Developing communication skills, such as using different writing text types; listening to argument; constructing sentences orally in French; in mathematics, drawing to scale; using a spreadsheet to model the impact of light intensity on plant growth.	Generating spelling rules, e.g. when to use -*sion* rather than –*tion*; collecting visual and other information in order to understand the use of materials and processes to make a sculpture; assessing the usefulness of portraits as sources of historical information.	Exploring the best method of making a light crispy batter; exploring the likely causes of flooding in a particular area; exploring the best method of removing grease from clothes.
Key questions	• How could you ...? • Why am I doing this?	• Can you group these? • Can you see any pattern?	• What might affect ...? • What possible reasons are there for ...?

Source: http://www.nationalstrategies.standards.dcsf.gov.uk

charge from: *http://publications.teachernet.gov.uk*. This document contains the framework for Key Stage 3 which you can use for your lesson planning. For Key Stage 4 and post-16 classes you can use the same frameworks but raise the level for your planning and preparation.

Prior knowledge of students

Make sure you have found out about the students you are going to teach. You can find out this information from their usual class teacher, Head of Department, SENCO or form tutor. They will be able to tell you the physical and emotional state of the student,

Stop and reflect

To create an effective climate for learning you need to think about a range of issues such as the physical state of the learner and their prior knowledge and attainment.

- What other factors should you reflect on when planning lessons for all of your students?
- Consider your teaching experiences to date. How have you tried to ensure that learners gain a feeling of satisfaction and enjoyment from their work?
- What have you actually done to try to ensure they are emotionally, physically and intellectually involved by the tasks set

Are these factors important to you? Where would you rank them alongside efficient and effective transmission of subject knowledge?

the student's prior attainment and knowledge in your subject area and, possibly, the learning style of each student. You need to know which students have IEPs; the SENCO will be able to provide copies of these. It is important to use these in your planning as they contain helpful learning and teaching strategies and some contain targets for behaviour. You also need to know who the high achievers are, and any 'problem' students. You should obtain relevant data for the group: for example, CATs, SATs, and so on – your colleagues will advise you on appropriate data (see also Chapter 9). Add this information to your class recording/planning sheet.

The lesson

Each lesson should be broken down into subsections. These should commonly include a lesson introduction with a starter activity, the main section of the lesson broken down into episodes with different activities to stimulate learning, and a plenary.

The lesson introduction

You need to consider what you are going to say to gain the attention of your students and stimulate them into engaging with the lesson and making progress. You need to plan a starter activity that links to the learning objectives, will stimulate learning and challenge them; you may need to differentiate this activity to enable all students to achieve. It is important you get feedback from this activity before progressing. There are some good ideas for starter activities on various websites – some of these are listed at the end of this chapter; you can also try an internet search on starter activity followed by your subject area. Try to use different activities rather than the same type at the start of every lesson. It is a good idea to have the starter activity ready on the students' desks when they arrive, or hand them out as they arrive; as they complete the activity you can hand out textbooks, pass back homework and take the register. This will help to reduce opportunity for breakdown in classroom behaviour. Make sure the starter activity is short and snappy – about five minutes, and consider using a timer displayed on the board to focus the students' attention. Timers can be downloaded free from the internet and displayed on the whiteboard, and are also available as part of the interactive whiteboard software.

At this point you need to link to prior learning to check the students' understanding of the topic before moving onto new aspects. Remember to move from the known to the unknown using Vygotsky's Zone of Proximal Development (ZPD) (Vygotsky, 1978). Think about key phrases and questions. As you become more confident you will find the introductions become easier, but to start with plan them carefully as they will set the scene for the rest of the lesson.

Remember to collect in any homework – by collecting it in at the start of the lesson you can check who has not handed in their homework and follow up using the school procedures.

Developing the lesson

Consider what teaching and learning activities you are going to use (see section above), how long each one will take, and what teaching/learning methods you are going to use.

Consider what instructions you are going to give. You will need to adapt your language to suit the students in your classes. This is particularly important when introducing new ideas and concepts, during explanations, questions, discussions, and so on. If you are not sure about the language level, look at textbooks for the age range and subject you are going to be teaching – they are based on good market research by the publishers covering the age group they are written for. Instructions and information must be clear and you may need to repeat them more than once. Check that the students have understood you. You may want to write these instructions on the whiteboard or put them on a handout for the students to refer to in the lesson.

Any handouts you are going to use must be in the room, as must all items for the lesson. You must *never* leave a group unsupervised. If you need any help, send a responsible student – do not go yourself. Remember to include the handouts/board work in your lesson plan.

Think about the activities the students will do. Try to plan different activities during the lesson. Remember that we all learn differently and it is therefore important to vary the way you impart information so that there is opportunity for them to all learn. See also Chapter 6.

You will need to include differentiation in your lesson plan. When you are planning you will need to plan for those students who may have special educational needs and refer to their IEPs, which will be available in your department. Remember when designing activities and resources to use a range of different types and also take account of diversity and promoting equality and inclusion. Some students may be 'exceptional' or gifted and talented and will need more challenging tasks. Always include differentiated material and always plan for students who may finish before others. Differentiated materials are needed for the

- Learners with learning difficulties
- The gifted and talented
- EAL students.

List all your resources carefully and make sure you have them all prior to entering the classroom.

Timing

Timing is an essential part of lesson planning. You need to be realistic about the amount of time you will spend on different sections of the lesson. There has to be some flexibility, but you should follow it as carefully as possible. The worst scenario is that you may run out of work for the students, so ensure you have an extension task that will further develop skills learnt in the lesson – just in case.

Table 8.3 gives an example.

Practical task

Using the internet search for lesson plans for your subject area – you can use some of the websites listed at the end of this chapter. The KS3 Framework includes lesson plans and resources for all KS3 lessons.

● Study the different sections of the lesson plans and reflect on the range of activities, the timings used, the resources needed, and so on.

● What are some of the serious drawbacks in using pre-prepared, downloaded lesson plans?

Transitions

You can see from the example given in Table 8.3 that there are different sections to the lesson. You need to move from one section to another smoothly, but at the same time making sure the students know that a transition is being made. This may be done by:

● Where you are standing
● Your use of visual aids
● Where you ask students to sit
● Starting a new activity
● Moving to the whiteboard, and so on.

Ending the lesson – the plenary

It is important to note that there may be several short plenaries during lessons, where the teacher draws the learning together at a point before introducing new learning. This section specifically refers to the final ending of the lesson: the planned time when you

Table 8.3 An example of part of a lesson plan showing timings for activities

Starter activity • Register • Collect homework • Feedback on starter activity • State objectives for lesson	10 mins
Introduction • What is a database? – question/answer session – electronic filing • What is an example of a d/base? – q/a session – police, school, hospital, holidays, etc. • Introduce the different aspects: field, record, file and give example on w/board – draw example from students, e.g. computer games, pop groups	10 mins
Episode 1 • Demonstration of setting up a simple d/base using Access – try to draw each step from students – have used Access at feeder schools • Practical – students to set up example from handout	15 mins
Episode 2 • Bring students together to explain a misunderstanding • Demonstrate new examples, brainteaser exercise, etc. • Continue with next stage of practical work • Extension work for any students that finish • Differentiated worksheets for gifted students and SEN to link with individual targets	15 mins
Plenary • Discuss difficulties, revise aspects of d/base and uses • Revisit objectives • Self-assessment on progress and understanding • Link to next lesson • Issue homework	10 mins

will draw the lesson to a conclusion, revisit the objectives, and provide an opportunity for your students to reflect on their learning and set targets for development.

This part of the lesson needs to be well planned and should last for between five and ten minutes. It is a very important part of the lesson, since it consolidates the learning, helps students to evaluate their own progress and sets targets for future development.

In starting to plan this section of the lesson consider how you are going to draw the lesson together. You need to go back to your objectives and check that the students have made progress on each objective. Also, check that they have all written down their homework and are clear when this needs to be handed in. In your planning and preparation consider suitable questions and indicate these on your lesson plan.

Plan an activity for students to evaluate their own learning and set targets for progression. This may be as simple as having a resource with learning outcomes designed for the student to write at the side of each one how they have achieved the outcome, which aspects they feel confident with, and which they would like more help and support with. Or it may be an opportunity to exchange work with another student, and assess the work against criteria, then set targets for development before passing back – this is called *peer assessment*; more information on this can be found in Chapter 9.

The ending of the lesson is very important, and can make the difference between students walking out saying they have learnt nothing, and walking out feeling delighted at the amount they have learnt and their new understanding, and looking forward to the next lesson.

Case study

A new teacher working in the English Department at a large secondary school in the West Midlands found the plenary section of her lessons challenging. The previous teacher had rewarded good behaviour during lessons with ten minutes on the internet at the end of the lesson with no guidance on websites. Most of the students in her group were therefore used to being allowed to go on Facebook and MSN. When she arrived and wanted to make use of this valuable time as a plenary with planned work focusing on aspects such as revisiting learning outcomes, self-assessment, target setting and homework, the students challenged her.

She discussed the problem with her Head of Department. It was agreed that, as she needed to have a plenary, she would work with the students by harnessing their use of the internet during the plenary time but in a way that would allow her to achieve what she needed to. She set up an evaluation of the lesson, including a self-assessment exercise linked to National Curriculum levels, using the free software on the Hot Potatoes website which she then linked to the school's VLE. She also uploaded the homework to the VLE and set it up so that the students uploaded the homework when it was completed enabling her to provide feedback including targets linked to levels, via the VLE that the group would be able to access at the start of the next lesson.

The next time she taught the group, ten minutes before the end of the lesson she told students to log onto the school VLE and work through the quiz; she then went through the homework with them to ensure they all understood what was required and how to upload their completed homework. Some of the students still challenged her but were not able to win the argument that they should be able to use the Internet, as this was exactly what she was allowing them to do, but in a structured way that linked to her learning outcomes for the lesson. The students became used to this way of working and the teacher found it a very useful way of monitoring progress and was able to use their evaluations when planning her next lesson.

- What lessons can you draw from this case study?
- Have any similar situations or scenarios arisen in your experience?

Differentiation

Throughout this chapter reference has been made to *differentiation*. Within each class you will have a range of students with different abilities. There will probably also be students with SEN, who are gifted and talented, and EAL. In planning your lesson it is important to consider how you are going to differentiate the activities to meet the needs to all learners. Remember that each student in your class must have a planned opportunity to make progress. Different types of differentiation are listed below building on information that can be found at *www.spartacus.schoolnet.co.uk/*

- *Differentiation by content.* The students use different materials at different language and ability levels, but all complete similar questions. You could also use different methods of presentation: for example, one group could be given a set of newspaper articles; another group could watch a video; and another group could view an on-line presentation, depending on their language and ability levels.

- *Differentiation by activities.* The students study the same content, then carry out a range of different activities aimed at the different levels they are working at, or aiming for.

- *Differentiation by negotiation.* The students study different materials within the same topic area and also do different activities. You might involve the students in selecting appropriate materials or you might engage the support of learning assistants and so on in the negotiation. It is important that the students know the level they are working at and their target level, so as to be able to make sensible and appropriate choices, and it is important for you to monitor those choices.

- *Differentiation by support.* The students study the same materials, perform the same activities, but receive different amounts of support from the teacher or from extra printed information. Remember to consider the students' language level as well as their ability level and, again, you need to take care to record the amount of support given to the students.

- *Differentiation by extension.* The students study the same materials and carry out the same activities. Extension work is given to some after they have finished the basic activities. Consider how appropriate this is – will they become bored and demotivated by completing tasks that are not challenging them until they can start the extension activity? You may want to set a different task using different strategies discussed above to engage, stimulate and challenge them while still reflecting your lesson objectives.

- *Differentiation by response.* The students are set open-ended assignments that can be interpreted at different levels. This can also reflect the response you elicit from them in question-and-answer sessions. When you are planning questions, it is sensible to consider the level of the students so you ensure that you aim questions at students with the ability to answer them. It is also important that you use deeper-level and more searching questions for the more able students.

- *Differentiation by group work.* The students work in mixed ability groups. Students help each other by working together and interpreting the tasks at different levels. Groups of the same ability can work equally well. Do plan groups carefully before the lesson. (See also Chapter 13 for group-work ideas.)

- *Differentiation by role*. The students carry out different activities depending on the role they are playing in a simulation. The roles are matched to the abilities, aptitudes and needs of the student. The worksheets are differentiated by content, activities, extension, response, support, gradation, group work and role. To help you maximise the potential of the students in the class, code all the worksheets. This coding should be based on the readability levels of the sources as well as the level descriptions addressed by the questions on the worksheets.

Homework

You should set homework following your school's policy. For example: KS3 once per week; KS4 twice per week; post-16 at least twice per week. Normally homework should last approximately 30 minutes.

Use homework:

- To sustain learners' progress
- To consolidate knowledge development from lessons
- To prepare for the next lesson
- To extend students' knowledge of the subject.

There are a wide variety of techniques you can use for homework such as: quizzes, preparation for tests/exams, word puzzles, finding data/preparing designs/background reading for the next lesson, reflective work to encourage the students to evaluate their work, writing frameworks. You can use textbooks, case studies, past exam papers, gapped handouts, intranet/internet-based work, etc.

Tips

- Endeavour to make homework as interesting, motivating and stimulating as your lessons.
- Ensure you give the students variety.
- Always set homework regularly.
- Don't turn it into a punishment.
- Always provide feedback and reward.
- Return homework in the next lesson and go over it where necessary.
- Use homework to inform planning.

When setting homework that will involve the use of computers, it is important to consider how much access to computers your students have. Most schools run computer clubs to provide access for students without access at home. It is sensible to find out from your group who does not have access at home and ensure they know when they can use the school's computers to complete this homework.

Practical task

Devise suitable homework for the following lessons for your subject area:

Year 7 class who have only been in school for one week.	
Year 8 class who have just started a new module.	
Year 10 class who have just started a new piece of coursework.	
Year 11 GCSE class who have just completed a piece of coursework.	
A 6th form group who are about to take their AS exam.	

When you have devised these, take time to critically reflect on the different language you are using and the way in which you have linked your homework tasks to the level of learning that the individual students are moving towards.

Professional development targets

While on teaching practice you will need to identify professional development targets; usually these will be agreed with your school mentor. For each target you need to consider a timescale for achievement. It is good practice to include these when it is appropriate in your lesson plan so that you remember to focus on them. Examples of PDTs are:

● Project and intonate the voice

● Maintain eye contact during demonstrations

● Make greater use of questioning techniques

● Use the interactive whiteboard to interact with the students

● Ensure all students remain on task

● Develop subject knowledge for this topic, etc.

When you have finished planning your lesson

When you have finished your lesson plan you need to consider whether you have met all of the requirements for a well-planned lesson. Some reflections you can make are:

● How will I settle the class?

● What methods will I use?

- How will I maintain the pace and move between sections of the lesson smoothly?
- How will I break up a mainly practical lesson, or an activity that is going to take up most of the lesson?
- What visual aids can I use?
- Have I provided materials for all the abilities in the lesson?
- Have I made provision for students who may work faster than planned?
- Have I checked my timings carefully?
- How will I assess my aims and objectives?
- How will I issue the textbooks, discs, paper, handouts, etc. with the least disruption?
- What range of activities will I use?
- How will I end the lesson?
- How will I ensure the students are challenged and motivated?
- What homework can I set that will support their learning?
- What materials do I need: handouts, board markers, book data projector, etc?

Critical synthesis

What does planning literally mean? Look up the definition of planning, then deconstruct the phrase at the start of the chapter about failing to plan (this could also be applied to preparation).

Reflecting on your own teaching, how often did that phrase fully or partially apply to you? Analyse which specific part of the lessons have the greatest effect on learning when planning has failed. Does, for example, poor planning in the starter activity have a greater effect on the whole lesson, than poor planning for differentiation?

Evaluating the lesson

When you have taught the lesson you need to reflect back and consider:

- What have the students learnt?
- Have I achieved my aims/objectives? How can I evidence this?
- What have I learnt from this lesson?
- How can I improve it next time?

Other areas you will want to consider include how you have made use of:

- Interventions, interactions and control
- Deployment, usage and quality of resources
- Pace and use of time
- Expectations and challenge

- Grouping
- Learner responsibility, autonomy, response and skills
- Questioning strategies and class discussion
- High- and low-order tasks
- Match and differentiation
- Specific planning/requirements for EAL students
- Problem solving and enquiry
- Assessment and target-setting
- Homework – was it used constructively to raise achievement?
- Supporting planning and preparation
- Teaching and learning styles used
- Creating an orderly and purposeful atmosphere
- High expectations for each student
- Noting which students asked for help and the response which they got
- Noting what kinds of help they asked for
- Room layout
- Clear instructions/guidelines
- The acknowledgement of the achievement by appropriate assessment methods.

You need to ensure that these end-of-lesson reflections are used to inform the planning and preparation for your next lesson with this group, or the next time you teach this topic. It is sensible, when you are a trainee teacher, or during your NQT year, to annotate your lesson plan to reflect your evaluation.

Hints and tips on taking control of your lesson through lesson planning

By spending time in lesson planning and preparation you can reduce the opportunity for students to become disruptive. Below are some hints and tips on this:

- Have well-planned lessons with smooth transitions, variety of teaching/learning methods and plenty of work to challenge and stretch all students – don't allow for any aspect of disorganisation.
- Have confidence in your subject.
- Ensure all equipment and materials are in the classroom prior to the start.
- **Never** leave your classroom.
- Don't turn your back on the class.
- When helping individuals always ensure you know what the rest of the class are doing.
- You choose where students are going to sit – use seating plans.
- If using group work, you decide on groups – split up difficult students.
- Make sure you arrive promptly.

- Establish a rule that the students do not enter your classroom until you tell them to.
- Develop strategies to gain their attention – without shouting.
- Have a copy of the students' passwords if you are using computers.
- Check access to any software/websites, etc. you may be using from the school network.
- Make sure there are no health and safety hazards and that you can walk round the room easily.
- Make sure students know what is expected of them at all times – behaviour and work.

A final note

A quick guide to each step in planning your lesson, taken from the National Strategy Key Messages Pedagogy and Practice, is given below:

Locate the lesson or sequence of lessons in the context of:

- The scheme of work-based learning
- The students' prior knowledge
- The students' preferred learning styles.

Identify clearly the essential objective(s) for students in terms of:

- Their knowledge, understanding, attitude and skills
- Their attitudes and personal development.

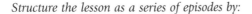

Structure the lesson as a series of episodes by:

- Separating the learning into distinct stages or steps.

Decide how to teach each episode, and then choose:

- The best pedagogic approach
- The most appropriate teaching and learning strategies
- The most effective organisation for each episode.

Ensure coherence by providing:

- A stimulating start to the lesson
- Transition between episodes which recapitulate and launch new episodes
- A final plenary that reviews learning. (From: *http://www.nationalstrategies.standards. dcsf.gov.uk*)

Challenge your thinking

There has been a great deal of emphasis on the 'three part lesson'. Ofsted certainly encourage the view that this formal structure will offer clarity for learners and will be looking out for it. Your mentor might also been encouraging this in your planning.

There is no doubt that a three-part structure is better than no structure at all, but there is no evidence that a three-part lesson is any better than any other way of structuring learning activities. In fact, with more lessons taking place in large spaces and with cross-curricular themes and groupings one might argue that the three-part lesson is out of date and unsuitable for flexible and innovative working.

To satisfy yourself, you may wish to search for any evidence supporting the three-part lesson structure over others.

- What are the advantages of a three-part lesson?
- What might some of the disadvantages be?
- Where does the three-part lesson fit into a longer series of learning activities, or one long learning activity such as planning and carrying out investigations, project work or drama production?

Summary

The intention of this chapter was to introduce you to some of the key aspects you need to be aware of when planning and preparing for your teaching. In the chapter we have stressed the importance of planning, both short-term (your lesson plan) and medium- and long-term planning, still referred to in some schools as a *scheme of work*. We have also considered the importance of good planning not only in terms of ensuring that all students make progress in your lessons, but also so that in your planning you are considering all aspects that will ensure a smooth lesson, and therefore reduce classroom management issues. We have also made links to assessment, which is discussed in more detail in Chapter 9, and the chapter ends with advice on how to evaluate your planning.

References

Anderson, L. W. and Krathwoln, D. (eds) (2001) *A Taxonomy for Learning, Teaching, and Assessing: A Revision of Bloom's Taxonomy of Educational Objectives*, New York: Longman.

Bloom, B.S., (1956), *Taxonomy of Educational Objectives, the classification of educational goals – Handbook I: Cognitive Domain*. New York: McKay.

Key Stage 3 Framework, Standards and Assessment pack available from the DCSF publications site: *http://www.dfefss.gov.uk/publications/*

The Numeracy Strategy Framework, ICT Strategy Framework and Literacy Strategy Framework (can be ordered or downloaded from *http://publications.teachernet.gov.uk*)

Vygotsky, L. (1978) *Mind in Society The Development of Higher Psychological Processes*, 1st edn., London: Harvard University Press.

Web resources

www.nationalcurriculumonline.gov.uk

http://www.nationalstrategies.standards.dcsf.gov.uk

www.ncaction.org.uk

www.teachnet.com

www.aqa.org.uk

www.edexcel.org.uk

www.ocr.org.uk

www.cityandguilds.com

www.lccieb.com

www.cambridgeassessment.org.uk

www.educationalresources.co.uk

www.support4learning.org.uk – links to information on learning styles.

http://hotpot.uvic.ca/ – hot potatoes website for creating on-line quizzes, etc.

Appendix 1   Planning pro-forma for schemes of work

Scheme of Work:		Subject:	

Syllabus:		Units:		Teacher:	

Time allocation:		Assessment/methods of evaluation:	

General resources used:	

Previous student experience:	
Aims:	
National Curriculum (NC) Programmes of Study to be addressed or GCSE/GCE/GNVQ level and module:	

Teaching styles:

Differentiation:

Cross-curricular links: e.g. literacy, numeracy, citizenship

Appendix 2   Alternative scheme of work planning sheet with examplar

Weeks		Content/Activities/ Extension Tasks	Resources	Subject Links	Homework
1	Subject Content	Introduction to Spreadsheets	Activity sheets 1–3 (attached). Demo notes. Handbook pages 3–6. Blank grids for homework. Writing framework for less able. Activity sheet 4 for more able. Homework sheets – differentiated	Mathematics – applying maths and solving problems; calculations – checking results. Literacy – key words.	Design a spread-sheet layout for recording data for the school tuck shop. Separate sheet to support less able.
	T&L Activities	Demonstration, group work, task-based			
	Differentiation: Less able	Complete all tasks on activity sheet 1. Writing framework for starter activity and plenary. Differentiated resource for activity sheet 1.			
	More able	Activity sheet 4 – different scenario to challenge more able. Don't need sheets 1–3.			
	Assessment	Completion of tasks: activity sheets, practical prints. Evaluation of progress in plenary and targets for development.			
2	Subject Content				
	T&L Activities				
	Differentiation: Less able				
	More able				
	Assessment				
3	Subject Content				
	T&L Activities				
	Differentiation: Less able				
	More able				
	Assessment				
4	Subject Content				
	T&L Activities				
	Differentiation: Less able, etc.				

Appendix 3   Lesson plan

Date:		Lesson:	1	of	

Class:		Topic:	

No of boys:		Duration:	mins	Link to National Curriculum:	

No of girls:		Ability:		Level:	

Total students:				GCSE/GNVQ/ AS/A2 Module:	

Professional development targets:	1
	2
	3

(Link these to the evaluation targets from your previous lesson)

Information used in planning:	

Aim:	

	Learning objectives: The students are learning to (WALT):	Learning outcomes: What I am looking for (WILF):	Assessment: I will assess this objective by:
1			
2			
3			

Key Skills:

Literacy,

Numeracy,

ICT

What resources do I need to remember to prepare?

Differentiation:	The less able will:
	The more able will:

Procedure:	Teaching and Learning	Time
Starter activity Register Share objectives		
Episode 1		
Episode 2		
Episode 3		
Plenary activity: Revisit objectives Link to next lesson		
	Total time:	

Questions: **My key questions are:**

1

2

3

4

5

6

7

8

9

10

**Possible
misconceptions:**

Board work:

Homework:

Date to
submit:

Deployment
of AOT, e.g. SEN/
technician/etc:

Risk
assessment:

Notes on

Lesson:

Chapter 9

Assessment and feedback

Learning outcomes

By the end of this chapter you will be able to:

→ Identify links between the role of the teacher and the need for assessment, feedback and target setting

→ Critically evaluate the purposes of assessment

→ Distinguish between the different types of assessment

→ Make effective use of a range of assessment strategies, including homework

→ Provide feedback on assessment, progress and future development

→ Develop appropriate monitoring and recording strategies

Introduction

'Assessment is an integral part of effective teaching and learning. It allows progress to be recognised and celebrated and it informs the next steps and priorities of both teachers and learners. It is inextricably linked to the curriculum, which provides the content and context of assessment.'

(*www.qca.org.uk*, 2008)

The Assessment for Learning (AfL) Strategy identifies assessment as a process through which

'every child knows how they are doing, and understands what they need to do to improve and how to get there. They get the support they need to be motivated, independent learners on an ambitious trajectory of improvement.'

(Assessment for Learning Strategy, 2008 available at *www.teachernet.gov.uk*)

This chapter is intended to introduce you to the purposes of assessment and different types of assessment. It will help you to gain in confidence in using a range of assessment methods to help you with your planning and to ensure you are considering a range of issues associated with assessment that are essential for qualified teachers. The chapter will then discuss feedback and target setting, how and when to give it, and discuss various methods that you can use. Throughout the chapter the importance of recognising that students have different learning styles and will therefore need a variety of assessment methods to help them to achieve is discussed. We will then discuss reporting to parents, and examine how to write reports as these are an important element of assessment and feedback.

There will be opportunity within the chapter to develop methods of recording and monitoring the progress of your students, with clear links to developing the use of data in ensuring that each individual student is making progress. It is important to remember when planning assessment strategies that the type of assessment you choose can influence both the quality of learning and the amount/depth of learning that takes place by individual students, as well as impact on the motivation of your students.

'To fail to assess is to fail to teach.'

(Best, 1992, quoted in Somers, 2000)

Every teacher should be 'equipped to make well-founded judgements about students' attainment, understand the concepts and principles of progression, and know how to use their assessment judgements to forward plan, particularly for students who are not fulfilling their potential' (*Assessment for Learning Strategy,* 2008, available at *teachernet.gov.uk*.) Assessment is an everyday process in a classroom, whether formal or informal. As new teachers it is important that you are able to discuss with colleagues not only the various characteristics of your students but also how they are doing. For example, which students find certain concepts more difficult than others? What do you know about how your students learn? Do you have to provide special help for some learners? How do you integrate your assessment processes with your planning? At the simple level, when you use questions in a classroom, you are checking whether students have understood a concept, which you then use as feedback, which in turn modifies your teaching. This kind of informal assessment is pervasive, and an essential part of the teaching process.

Assessment

Assessment is a key aspect for almost everybody involved in the process of learning. Within the school there will be interest shown by the learners, teachers, colleagues, curriculum leaders, other school managers and governors. Outside the school assessments will be of particular interest to parents, prospective parents, LA Advisors/Inspectors and Ofsted and may influence how others within the community view the school.

We must take a wide view of what is meant by assessment, its purposes and forms. In their highly influential article *Inside the Black Box*, Black and Wiliam (1998) state:

> 'the term "assessment" refers to all those activities undertaken by teachers, and by their students in assessing themselves, *which provide information to be used as feedback to modify the teaching and learning activities in which they are engaged.* Such assessment becomes "formative assessment" when the evidence is actually used to adapt the teaching work to meet the needs.'

> (Black and Wiliam, 1998: 2)

It is important to note the involvement of learners in this definition.

When used inappropriately or incorrectly, assessment can have a detrimental effect upon a child's future approach to learning. For this reason it must be carried out with fairness and sensitivity. To achieve this you must know what you are assessing and how to use the most appropriate method to do this. It is important that students understand what the basis of the assessment is, and thus know whether they have achieved what was intended.

Stop and reflect

Reflect on a recent example of an assessment that you have been involved in as a student. This might be a degree assignment, a diving qualification assessment, or your driving test. Critically evaluate whether you thought that this was a fair assessment of your skills/knowledge/understanding?

● If you think it was, what made it fair?

● If it wasn't, what needed to be changed to make it fair?

Every teacher needs to build in assessment as a natural part of lesson planning. Performance must be assessed and students must receive feedback and achievable targets to correct errors and enhance future performance. Students need to be aware of the assessment criteria and methods of assessment, which need to fit tightly with the methods of learning. Ongoing assessment provides students with a clear picture of their own progress and teachers with a means of evaluating the learning experiences that they are giving to a particular group of learners. By critically charting your students' progress you will be able to make improvements to your teaching for both present and future lessons.

The purposes of assessment

It is important to recognise that assessment is going on all the time between yourself and your students and between students themselves, since each can affect future performance.

According to Broadfoot (1996) (in Stobart and Gipps, 1997), assessment influences learning in four main ways, each of which was supported by Ofsted in its report 'Good Assessment in Secondary Schools' (2003):

1 Assessment provides motivation to learn:
   • By giving a sense of success in the subject (or demotivation through failure)
   • Through giving a sense of self-confidence as a learner.

2 Assessment helps students (and teachers) decide what to learn:
   • By highlighting what is important to learn from what is taught
   • By providing feedback on success so far.

3 Assessment helps students learn how to learn:
   • By encouraging an active or passive learning style
   • By influencing the choice of learning strategies
   • By inculcating self-monitoring skills
   • By developing the ability to retain and apply knowledge, skills and understanding in different contexts.

4 Assessment helps students learn to judge the effectiveness of their learning:
   • By evaluating existing learning
   • By consolidating or transforming existing learning
   • By reinforcing new learning.

These four areas link to those identified by the DCSF in the Assessment for Learning Strategy:

'Every child knows how they are doing, and understands what they need to do to improve and how to get there. They get the support they need to be motivated, independent learners on an ambitious trajectory of improvement.

Every teacher is equipped to make well-founded judgments about pupils' attainment, understands the concepts and principles of progression, and knows how to use their assessment judgments to forward plan, particularly for pupils who are not fulfilling their potential.'

In planning for assessment it is important to consider the impact it will have on the students' learning. According to Marton and Saljo (1984), there are two types of learning (Table 9.1).

In your planning you need to be aware of these approaches and, where possible, make sure that a deep-learning approach is followed and that students are provided with opportunities to link their new learning to existing learning, and have opportunity to try out new learning in different situations, thereby developing transferrable knowledge and skills.

MacIntosh and Hale (1976) use the following classification of the purposes of assessment (Table 9.2). While this reference is slightly dated, it is none the less very pertinent in today's education environment.

Table 9.1 **Approaches to learning**

Deep learning approach	Surface or shallow-learning approach
An intention to develop personal understanding	An intention to be able to reproduce content as required
Active interaction with the content, particularly in relating new ideas to previous knowledge and experience	Passive acceptance of ideas and information
Linking ideas together using integrating principles	Lack of recognition of guiding principles or patterns
Relating evidence to conclusions	Focusing learning on assessment requirements
	Example: rote learning

Source: Marton and Saljo, 1984

Table 9.2 **Purposes of assessment**

Diagnosis	To monitor progress and to find out how the student is assimilating what is being taught. Specific action may be instituted as a result of diagnostic assessment
Evaluation	To evaluate the effectiveness of the teaching which can lead to specific action
Guidance	To assist students in making decisions about the future, whether it concerns choice of a subject or a course, or whether it is to help in choosing a suitable career
Prediction	To discover potential abilities and aptitudes and to predict probable future successes whether in school or outside
Selection	To determine which are the most suitable candidates for a course, a class or a university
Grading	To assign students to a particular group, to discriminate between the individuals in a group

Source: MacIntosh and Hale, 1976

The first three areas are student related, while the remainders are society related, but all still provide feedback to the teacher.

Assessment may also be used for screening through the process of testing groups of students to identify individuals who may need special help: for example, tests are often carried out in Y7 to assess the language level of new students and CATs tests (cognitive-ability tests) are often used to put students into sets in Y7. The results may also be used for diagnosis following screening to identify particular strengths and weaknesses in individuals or groups of students.

Different types of assessment

Teacher assessment may be formal or informal, formative or summative. The National Strategy identifies formative assessment as being assessment **for** learning, and summative assessment as assessment **of** learning.

Formative assessment

Formative assessment is a student-centred process, which provides the teacher with a developing picture of each student's learning. It provides feedback to students and information for teachers to use in their planning. According to Lincolnshire County Council Curriculum Policy Statement (2008):

> 'The process of assessment cannot be separated from the teaching process since its prime purpose is to improve student performance by diagnosing students' strengths and weaknesses, matching the work to their capabilities, and guiding them into appropriate courses and groups.'

Everyday formative assessment in the classroom provides information, which enables the teacher to make judgments about how learning can be taken forward. It enables the teacher to give students definable targets and feedback about their achievements.

The National Strategy supported the involvement of students in their assessment

> 'by sharing expectations and targets with students, assessment for learning (formative) can contribute to assessment of learning (summative). For example, students can be given experience of marking and moderating, and also reviewing test papers in the light of performance.'

> (Standards and assessment, available at *www.standards.dfes.gov.uk*)

The following extract is from the Assessment for Learning website:

> 'Much recent research indicates that effective formative assessment is a key factor in raising students' standards of achievement.
>
>   Central to formative assessment, or "assessment for learning" is that it:

- is embedded in the teaching and learning process of which it is an essential part;
- shares learning goals with students;
- helps students to know and to recognise the standards to aim for;
- provides feedback which leads students to identify what they should do next to improve;
- has a commitment that every student can improve;
- involves both teacher and students reviewing and reflecting on students' performance and progress;
- involves students in self-assessment.

> Assessment for learning is the process of seeking and interpreting evidence for use by learners and their teachers to decide where the learners are in their learning, where they need to go and how best to get there.

> (Assessment Reform Group (2002))

Assessment for learning is using formative assessment, but involves more than marking and feedback – it involves identifying the next steps for learning and having a clear understanding of the errors students make and the difficulties they experience.

The Assessment for Learning Strategy (*ibid.*) states that good assessment for learning makes:

- *An accurate assessment* – knowing what the standards are, judging students' work correctly, and making accurate assessments linked to National Curriculum levels;

- A *fair assessment* – knowing the methods used are valid;
- A *reliable assessment* – ensuring that judgments are consistent and based on a range of evidence;
- A *useful assessment* – identifying barriers to student progress and using that information to plan and discuss the next steps in learning;
- A *focused assessment* – identifying areas of a child's learning where there are blocks to progression, which might, for example, benefit from the attention of one-to-one tuition;
- *Continuity of assessment,* enabling better transfer between years and schools.

The key message is that assessment for learning depends crucially on actually using the information gained. Gaining information about students is only valuable if teachers then go on to do something with it for the benefit of the students.

In a review of approximately 580 articles and chapters from numerous books and over 160 journals Black and Wiliam (1998) concluded that there was significant evidence to show that improving formative assessment raises standards. Many other studies show that significantly the learners who have a record of low attainment are most likely to benefit most from formative assessment strategies (Fuchs *et al.*, 1997).

Stop and reflect

Consider a unit of work you will be teaching or have taught and write down all the formative assessment strategies you have used.

- Look back over the list and critically analyse whether there is a good variety.
- Does the list consider the different learning styles of your group?

Summative assessment

Summative assessment provides information to parents, governors and others about the levels of attainment reached at certain points in time – i.e. at the end of the year, or key stage, and about progress made since the last reported assessment. This would include final assessments at the end of modules, GCSE exams, or coursework, AS/A2 module tests and so on. This is referred to as *Assessment of learning.*

The Assessment Reform Group (ARG), in its publication 'The Role of Teachers in the Assessment of Learning' available from the ARG website, identifies that the goals of summative assessment should be 'learning with understanding' and 'understanding learning'.

Research by the ARG identifies the negative impact that summative assessment can have on students:

- Test performance can become more highly valued than what is being learned.
- Testing can reduce the self-esteem of lower-achieving students and can make it harder to convince them that they can succeed in other tasks.
- Constant failure in practice tests demoralises some students and increases the gap between higher and lower achieving students.

Test anxiety can have a detrimental effect on students
Source: Education Photos

- Test anxiety affects girls more than boys.
- Teaching methods may be restricted to what is necessary for passing tests (e.g. neglect of practical work). ('Testing, Motivation and Learning', 2002, available on the ARG website: *http://k1.ioe.ac.uk/tlrp/arg/publications.html*.)

In 2008 the National Strategy team reviewed their assessment advice to schools. The materials are still currently on the DCSF (now DFE) website. You are encouraged to visit this website and download the new materials to support your subject. The subject materials include 'day-to-day' assessment which will be used to inform the next steps in planning and student development. 'Periodic' assessment will provide an opportunity for review of students' achievement across the subject and will be used to develop medium-term planning and targets for improvement. The summative assessment will become 'transitional' assessment.

Other types of assessment

1 **Self-assessment** is where students will evaluate their own work. Criteria are generally set by/agreed with the teacher at a language level that can be understood by the student. The result of the self-assessment will usually be in the form of targets following reflection. This system is aimed at developing independent learning (metacognition = being aware of your own learning) and encourages students not only to think about what they are learning, but also how they have learnt.

2 **Norm-referenced assessment.** Norm-referenced measures are generally used to rank students for selection, e.g. GCSEs. The use of norm referencing can make it difficult to judge whether standards have improved. There is a small fluctuation based on the examiners' considerations of the quality of the work. Each August when GCSE and AS/A2 (GCE) results are published, there is much discussion in the media about whether standards have improved or whether there has been a general easing of standards by the Examination Boards, who will not want future entries to be affected by poor results.

3 **Criterion-referenced assessment** is where there are clear criteria that have to be achieved to gain the award, and is not dependent on how others in the cohort perform. However, there is still some basis of norm referencing because the grades have to be set so that they are 'attainable by those for whom they are intended'. Using this method of assessment gives teachers a specific picture of students' attainment. Vocational qualifications generally use this method of assessment and candidates are provided with clear guidance of what they must achieve to gain the award.

4 **Ipsative assessment.** This process of assessment is self-referenced and research has shown it is particularly suitable for low achievers. Students are encouraged to pit themselves against their former achievements, rather than comparing themselves with others. It, therefore, individualises assessment and can be used alongside other forms of assessment in providing students with some choice in the way they go about achieving their objectives (Brooks, 2002).

The National Curriculum levels

Most National Curriculum (NC) subjects have ten levels, although some, such as ICT, have eight levels. These are clearly set out in the NC document for each subject and it is important you become familiar with the requirements for each level for your subject(s). As you progress through your teacher training and NQT year you will need to become confident with the NC and the different levels. You also need to know that the QCA expectations are:

- Level 2 represents expectations for the average 7 year-old
- Level 4 represents expectations for the average 11 year-old
- Level 5–6 represents expectations for the average 14 year-old.

Assessment strategies

In your teaching it is essential to make use of as many different assessment techniques as possible – you have already started to think about these in the reflective task above. Assessment techniques can be grouped into these three broad categories: 'product', 'observation' and 'dialogue'.

There are many factors, which may determine which type of assessment technique is appropriate in a given set of circumstances. You may be influenced by:

- The subject matter (content/practical/skill based)
- The nature of the activity or task
- The ability and potential of the class (differentiation)
- Resources – including teacher time
- Classroom management and organisation.

Assessment of product

With product a large number of students can be assessed simultaneously: i.e. by marking their work. 'Products' can be saved and reviewed over time, and the teacher can then engage in dialogue with the student as part of the feedback process. When designing activities that involve the marking of product you need to consider how they will be marked. You will need to do some of the marking, but you also might want to consider peer assessment and computer assessment using software within your school's MLE/VLE, or free software such as Hot Potato available at: *http://hotpot.uvic.ca/*.

However, the quality of the product could be influenced by the students' presentation skills and not always their understanding. Assessment of product can lead to whole-class teaching at a specific level with the setting of differentiated tasks and assessments. It is, therefore, important to consider different approaches students could have to the assessment of product – i.e. the range of products they can produce, such as video clips, a wiki for collaborative work, a voice recording, or a web blog as an alternative to a reflective diary.

Assessment through observation

Most teachers carry out assessment through observation as part of their informal classroom observation. Some teachers such as those working in ICT, Design and Technology, PE, Drama, Art, etc. may use focused observation as a form of formative assessment or diagnostic tool. This is an excellent opportunity to challenge your students to achieve greater improvement of their skills and knowledge. You may decide to observe students over a period of time and will need to log the observations carefully. As with any assessment process you must plan the activity and ensure a good level of match between strategy and purpose.

Assessment by observation takes place instantly in the classroom and does not involve the teacher in the storage of bulky evidence. It provides the opportunity for the teacher to recognise unexpected achievements and allows him/her to focus upon an individual within a normal classroom situation.

Stop and reflect

Critically evaluate whether or not there any problems with assessment by observation in your subject?

- How could you overcome these problems?

Assessment through dialogue

Talk is an invaluable classroom activity. Student–teacher interaction and teacher intervention are a natural part of classroom activities. For example:

- Teacher talk
- Question and answer
- One-to-one
- Feedback
- Praise
- Use of conversation to motivate and test understanding
- Humour and classroom 'atmosphere' to develop classroom relationships
- Peer group assessment.

It is possible to assess through dialogue in a variety of contexts, for example, individually, in groups or through presentations. Interaction through dialogue may be either formal or informal. Assessment may be through using question and answer.

Stop and reflect

Rank the following in order of importance and justify your choice. Student teacher dialogue will be most effective when:

- Questions are open-ended and probing
- Questions are pitched at a level which challenges the student
- Language is straightforward
- The teacher listens, but is sensitive to the moment for intervention
- The teacher asks the student to explain and make connections
- The teacher is able to focus upon individuals
- The teacher can create a good constructive classroom atmospheres
- The teacher can use dialogue to move on to the next stage of learning.

Now consider each of these and analyse them when you utilise these in your teaching.

Techniques of assessment

Assessment is **evaluative** as it can be used to make comparisons about students' achievements. It is also **informative** as it aids communications with parents, governing bodies, LAs and the wider community. Assessment is also helpful for professional development. It provides teachers with an understanding of the effects of recording and moderating outcomes, and provides the basis with which you can assess new thinking.

Access a copy of the NC for your subject. This should be available at
http://www.standards.dfes.gov.uk/

- Read through the Programme of Study and levels.
- Look particularly at the expectations for level 4 and level 5. Look at the language used for level 4.
- Critically analyse what your students need to learn to move from level 4 to level 5.
- Consider what form of assessment you could use for students to provide this evidence.

Assessment and planning

Chapter 8 on Planning and preparation referred to medium and long-term planning through schemes of work, and short-term planning through lesson plans. It is essential that when you are planning your lesson you consider how you are going to assess learning outcomes and plan for the progression of your students. A recommended way to do this is to align your learning outcomes and objectives with assessment within a table. An example is shown in Table 9.3.

Table 9.3 **Alignment of learning outcomes and objectives**

Learning objective	Learning outcome	Assessment method
Identify the responsibilities of data users	All – will define what a data user is Most – will understand that data users are required to register with the Data Protection Registrar Some – will identify what information data users must register	Plenary – self-marking computer test

Using Table 9.3 above reflect on a lesson you have recently taught or observed. Take one of the learning objectives you planned, write an appropriate learning outcome (these are explained in Chapter 8 on Planning and preparation), then consider the most appropriate assessment method.

- How would you mark and record this assessment to show individual progression in the lesson?

As you start to plan your lesson and learning objectives you need to consider a variety of opportunities for assessment and recording of progress, some of which have been discussed earlier in this chapter. You should discuss appropriate types for your subject area with your school mentor and university tutor.

A key element in your planning will be to decide on the assessment strategies you will use. For example, will you present the assessment in class or will some assessments form the basis for all or part of students' homework to extend their learning? Remember that assessment should support and promote school policies and initiatives as well as link to your scheme of work and curriculum subject needs.

It is important when you start teaching at a new school that you quickly familiarise yourself with the school's assessment policy. These will differ from school to school and students need to experience consistency across subjects and teachers. You must also make sure that you use assessment to add precision to your teaching. For example, assessment outcomes must be communicated to the student clearly and constructively.

In order to start to plan for progression you need access to data on your students – this can be provided by your Head of Department or the school office. It is important that you access this data to establish existing knowledge. The data will consist of base-line data – i.e. what level your students are currently working at – and predicted grades/levels that your students need to achieve by the end of a key stage, or year. Some schools also provide Value Added Data, which predicts a raised grade/level that teachers are expected to enable students to achieve.

Setting meaningful class work activities

It doesn't matter how old the students are – if they are not interested in the activity you give them they will find it difficult to feel motivated to complete it. It is important you relate to their prior knowledge and experiences in the tasks you set. You also need to build in differentiation so that all the students can feel a sense of achievement as well as challenged to develop their understanding/knowledge/skills.

Homework

Your school will have a homework policy which you need to follow. This may vary between subjects, but it needs to be set regularly and not be seen as a 'punishment'. Homework should extend and consolidate the students' learning, and should be an activity that forms part of your lesson planning. It might also be researching or preparing for the next lesson. It should not be finishing work students have not completed in class. Use a variety of homework strategies to stimulate their interest and learning: e.g. written work/short essays/literacy frameworks, question sheets, mock exam questions, case studies, quizzes, reading, and preparation for a test. As with all assessment tasks, ensure that the students understand the criteria and that the homework is accessible to all of them (i.e. is differentiated and written in a language that each student can understand).

If you are setting homework that requires the use of a computer, make sure that all students have access, or that provision is made via a lunchtime computer club or open computer facilities for those that don't have a computer at home. Try to avoid overuse of internet searches; when you do use these, ensure the students know they are expected to carry out research then put the information into their own words, rather than copying and pasting chunks of information they don't necessarily understand. Also, when students are using research encourage them to acknowledge sources.

You may want to post homework on the school's VLE or MLE and to consider making provision for students to email it to you.

Using school data to inform planning

There will be a number of documents within your school that you can use to inform your planning:

- **CATs** (cognitive ability tests) – baseline tests that some schools give to Year 7 students. These tests are normally specific to maths, English and science. If your subject is not one of these, you can still make good use of this data in your planning, and use it to ensure your students are working at an appropriate level. You will receive data from your primary feeder schools, which is the baseline data in addition to CATs data; the type of information will vary. At the moment local authorities are establishing systems of databanks available to all schools so that information will be shared electronically, but in most areas this is still reliant on information being received from the partner primary schools. These data will reflect the students' Key Stage 2 results and may not include all subjects. This will be translated by your school into predicted levels for Key Stages 3 and 4 and post-16 predicted results.

- **KS3 predicted levels** – these will be available to you and will provide you with information about whether your students are under-or over-achieving. There will be an expectation that your students will achieve these levels, so it is essential that you are aware of them and refer to them regularly as part of your professional role.

- **KS4 and post-16 predicted grades** – these will be available and will provide you with information about whether your students are under- or over-achieving. Again, there is a level of accountability as a teacher and you will be expected to ensure you plan opportunities and progression so that your students can achieve these grades.

Practical task

Start to use student assessment data in your lessons. It is useful to ask to see these data and record the data for your students on your monitoring record to gain an overview of what your students have already achieved. If you are taking KS4 or 5 you may want to record their prior KS level on your recording sheet – these will be discussed in more detail in the next section. This information can help you to motivate students and when setting individual targets for improvement and achievement.

Use of assessment to inform planning

It is essential that all of your assessments are recorded and then used to inform your planning for your next lesson. The process is:

- Plan your lesson objectives and ensure your students understand how the assessment task links to the objectives, National Curriculum levels or exam board criteria.

- Decide on suitable methods to assess whether your objectives have been achieved, develop criteria and share the criteria with your students – criteria for exam board courses can be accessed via the appropriate exam board's website.
- Mark the work using the criteria you have developed, provide feedback and set achievable targets for development.
- Record the assessment data – this will inform you which objectives have been met by which students, and where any gaps in knowledge, skills or understanding exist.
- Use the information relating to the gaps to inform the planning for your next lesson.

Stop and reflect

You have been giving an introductory lesson to a group of Year 10 students on creating forms in databases and have taken their printouts in for marking. You find that not all of the students have followed the criteria you had issued for the form design. You start to understand the gaps in their knowledge and therefore start the next lesson with an exercise that enables them to fill the gaps. The use of differentiation will enable those who did understand to move onto new aspects of form design.

- Critically evaluate the above example in terms of your own subject and determine how you would best use differentiation in the following lesson to ensure that all students learn something.

Recording students' progress

While on teaching practice you will need to keep records of students' attendance, marks, work they have handed in (or not), and homework. When you start as a teacher you will usually be issued with a Teacher's Organiser by your school. There is an example of how to record below. If you need to set up your own recording sheet you might want to consider using a spreadsheet software package such as Excel. The benefit of this is that you can include formula to highlight failing students, those working below or above their predicted grades/levels, and use colour coding to show other information such as yellow shading for students handing work in late, green shading for students who have received a detention, purple shading for students arriving late to your lesson, etc. This helps to build up a picture of your students and is very useful when talking to parents/carers, or writing reports. You could also develop this further with mail-merging facilities to produce a parental report. When you set up your recording sheet, remember that you need to be able to show progress of students, so you will need space for information at the top of each column to show at a glance what was being assessed, together with information about the lesson as a cross-reference to your lesson plan.

You need to communicate the assessment outcomes to students in a way that your students understand your expectations. These need to link to the National Curriculum or the exam board criteria, whichever is appropriate to the class you are teaching.

Good recording sheets will link in data, such as baseline, predicted levels/grades, whether the student has special learning needs or is recognised as 'gifted and talented'. This again helps to build up an 'at a glance' picture of your students that is very helpful when you are planning your lessons. You may want to include a method of identifying the type of special need the student has to make your planning quicker and simpler, e.g. 'dy' for dyslexia.

Your records must be:

- Ongoing, up to date, and cumulative
- Accessible, useful and used as a base for planning
- Based upon reliable evidence supplied through assessment procedures and practices.

An example of a recording sheet is shown in Figure 9.1.

If your school has a Managed Learning Environment (MLE) or Virtual Learning Environment (VLE) there may be a facility for students to submit their work electronically,

Surname	Forename	Gender	SEN	Gifted & Talented	Predicted Grade	Baseline Data													
							Mark												
							Effort												
							Mark												
							Effort												
							Mark												
							Effort												
							Mark												
							Effort												
							Mark												
							Effort												
							Mark												
							Effort												
							Mark												
							Effort												
							Mark												
							Effort												
							Mark												
							Effort												
							Mark												
							Effort												
							Mark												
							Effort												
							Mark												
							Effort												
	Boys																		
	Girls																		
	Class Size																		

Figure 9.1 Example of a recording sheet

for you to mark and provide feedback and targets that are then recorded electronically, and this will then automatically enter their marks/grades into an electronic mark/grade book facility. This can be made available to parents, who can then see how their child is progressing, whether they are completing homework, and so on.

Your assessment practices will help you to get to know your students. By keeping and maintaining your records you will be able to:

1 Relate your teaching practices and processes to your scheme of work and planning for the year/team

2 Provide information about your students and have that information at your fingertips

3 Aid planning and subject delivery

4 Contribute towards setting

5 Compile effort and attitude checks to forward to your Head of Department, Head of Year and parents

6 Be able to compile subject reports for parents

7 Be able to monitor and determine the effectiveness of your:

  - Class teaching and teaching performance
  - Use of resources
  - Student progress.

Student diaries

Some schools will issue students with a diary in which they will log their homework and may be required to evaluate their own learning. These can be very useful but will not be as detailed or focused as the records you will keep. Increasingly, schools are encouraging students to record their progress, where they need remedial help, received support, and so on. The difficulty with relying on these diaries is that they can be lost or damaged, and it can be difficult to collate the data. It is therefore essential that you keep your own records. However, if your school uses them, you must ensure your students make use of them and you follow your school's policy in using them.

Peer assessment

One issue coming from the National Strategy materials is the need to be interactive with students and involve them in their own learning. All teachers should challenge students to develop their ideas further. You need to encourage students to evaluate their own work and discuss with them why they have made decisions and how they can improve their work.

Encourage students to use peer assessment. You need to develop a 'safe' environment where they feel able to discuss each other's work and encourage other members of their class to extend their knowledge and skills. Again, they will need criteria to use in carrying out the peer assessment and you will need to consider how you are going to pair students. This can be a very useful exercise during a plenary, with students reflecting on their own learning, evaluating the work of their partner, providing feedback, discussing targets, then setting their own targets for the next lesson and future development – if you collect these in at the end of the lesson it can be very helpful in planning your next lesson.

Critical synthesis

Look up definitions of feedback and feed forward in text books on assessment and learning. (You could try books by Gardner or Blanchard, for example.) Try to analyse just how different those two things are. If you feed forward – that is, set targets for learners, when you feed back on work they have handed in – does feedback then subsume feeding forward, so that the two are not really that separate at all?

Marking

Marking is an essential part of your professional role. Ideally you need to plan an assessment task for each lesson that you can mark and use to record progress. If students are involved in a large project that is going to last several lessons, break down the project into smaller stages and record each stage so that you have a record of individual progress. It is essential that you develop clear criteria when marking, so you will need to refer to the National Curriculum levels and descriptors for your subject, or the exam board website, whichever is appropriate for your class. Remember that you need to ensure the criteria is written in a language that is accessible by each of your students. Consider a variety of assessment tasks, and make use of technology to reduce your marking load – for example, designing on-line quizzes, using interactive technology such as voting systems, or encouraging students to mark their own work – this can then lead to dialogue and target setting.

When you are setting and marking work for Key Stage 4 or post-16 that will lead to an external qualification it is important that you guide and prepare your students for their final examination or coursework. In doing this you need to go to the exam board website for their qualification and access the guidelines for coursework and examine past examination questions and answers. Some teachers will build a database of past examination questions, then use searches to locate questions related to specific topics. Appropriate questions related to exam boards can also be found in textbooks. To support the answering of the questions and the coursework there are the Examiner's Reports for each year; these are useful in identifying weaknesses and strengths in previous years and giving guidance on the expectations of the exam board for answering the questions or completing the coursework. When planning the learning of your students these websites are an excellent resource for you.

Case study

While on teaching practice, a trainee teacher, on a one-year postgraduate Certificate in Education contacted his university tutor to ask for help with a Y9 class that he was finding difficult to teach. They arranged that the university tutor would visit the following week to observe the lesson. Despite planning the lesson carefully and providing a variety of activities, they experienced some minimal disruption throughout the lesson. After the lesson the university tutor asked what levels the group were working at. The trainee teacher responded that he thought they were all working somewhere around level 5, but was not able to articulate what a level 5 in his subject was. The university tutor asked what information he had gathered in terms of baseline and predicted levels. Unfortunately the trainee teacher had not found out this information. An action plan was agreed, which focused on a list of data that the trainee teacher needed to gather, where he could access the information, and how he would then use it in planning. A further observation of the same group was agreed for the following week.

The second lesson observation was much more positive. The students were on task throughout the lesson and there was no significant disruptive behaviour. In the review following the observation the trainee teacher talked through how he had drawn on the data to plan his lesson. He had accessed the school management information system to gain the group's Key Stage 2 levels and predicted Key Stage 3 levels. He had also used this system to access IEPs for the students in his group, which gave helpful strategies for lessons. He had then talked to the previous teacher for the group and found out what levels the students had been working at. He had then marked the work from the previous lesson and 'levelled' it in line with the Key Stage 3 National Curriculum levels. He had then prepared differentiated resources which linked to topics he knew his students were interested in from informal conversations with them. Within his differentiation strategies he included the IEP lesson-strategy suggestions for the two students with IEPs. At the start of the lesson he shared the lesson objectives with the students in terms of levels. He handed back the marked work from the previous lesson, which included the level the student was currently working at, and targets that would help them to move to the next level. He had included all baseline, IEP information, and predicted level data on his marking sheet so that he knew at a glance what level each student was working at/towards and any specific planning from the IEPs.

Moderation of assessments

Moderation is a process of ensuring all teachers within a subject/key stage have a shared understanding of the different levels/grades. This provides an opportunity to ensure all students are being assessed equally and fairly.

At KS 3 moderation is normally carried out internally and for some subjects there are external tests – these were the end of Key Stage 3 SAT tests which have now been abolished, but some schools still use them internally to measure achievement. As a minimum, internal moderation should always take place between teachers within the same subject, and sometimes across subjects. In addition, Ofsted inspectors are encouraging LAs to provide opportunity for teachers to cross-moderate KS3 work across schools. This will also provide an opportunity for discussion about the interpretation of the levels and increase standardisation nationally.

At KS 4 and post-16 there are a variety of external courses schools can choose, each with its own process of external moderation. Internal moderation will also take place. If you look at the exam board's website for the examination course your school follows, you will find detailed information about their moderation processes. Where coursework is involved, external moderation usually involves the exam board requesting a pre-selected set of coursework. Exams are also externally moderated by the exam board. The main argument in favour of external assessment is that it provides a comparison of standards both locally and nationally.

Feedback

Feedback has been found to be essential for the motivation and progression of students, and has been shown to raise achievement, particularly when linked to target setting (Black and Wiliam, 1998). Feedback should be given regularly as part of the learning experience. It may be given verbally to the whole group or individuals, or it may be given in writing. Which ever method you use, it is good practice to keep a record of the feedback you have given – if you provide it electronically via a VLE/MLE it will be recorded automatically.

Feedback must be accurate and consistently used. Ideally it should be linked to national curriculum levels or exam board criteria to ensure it is accurate and will help with raising achievement. Feedback should include targets which should be achievable and, where appropriate, are linked to dates for completion. Nicol and MacFarlane-Dick (2006) give seven principles of good feedback which can be applied to teaching in the secondary environment:

1 It helps clarify what good performance is (goals, criteria, standards)
2 It facilitates the development of self-assessment and reflection in learning
3 It delivers high-quality information to students about their learning
4 It encourages teacher and peer dialogue about learning
5 It encourages positive motivational beliefs and self-esteem
6 It provides opportunities to close the gap between current and desired performance
7 It provides information to teachers that can be used to help shape teaching.

Following feedback it is important that students are given the opportunity to understand what the feedback tells them about their performance, what they need to do to improve and how to move to the next level of achievement.

Target setting

Target setting is very important to help students to achieve their target levels/grades. There are internal targets set by the school, and external targets set nationally by the government. Target setting focuses students' efforts on areas earmarked for improvement. Your school should have a policy that says how regularly targets should be set. These may be different across subjects to reflect the nature of the topics and the way they are taught. Targets are often shared with parents/carers as well as the students.

The key to effective target setting is to think SMART (Table 9.4).

Table 9.4 Target setting for students in lessons

S	Specific	Specific targets relate to a defined area of competence – perhaps related to NC levels
M	Measurable	Measurable targets are couched in terms which allow the teacher – and students – to point to evidence that they have been achieved
A	Achievable	Achievable targets are ones which students can achieve – that is, they are do-able rather than vague aspirations
R	Realistic	Realistic targets are defined in relation to the context in which students are working and – most important – the standards to be achieved
T	Time-related	Time-related targets have clear dates for review and monitoring in relation to the time scale available

Source: Brooks, 2002

The government is currently moving towards individualised target setting, as part of the Every Child Matters agenda, for all students in consultation and discussion with parents.

Producing school reports

Writing reports for parents can be time-consuming but is an essential part of the teacher's role. If you have kept good records of progress, as discussed above, this will help to reduce the amount of time that can be involved in completing reports. Schools may use different forms of reporting to parents.

Computerised reports

These can be prepared using an Optical Mark Recognition (OMR) system. It is initially time-consuming to write the statements you wish to use, but once the system is set up it can be quick to check the boxes on your OMR sheet for each student. Training may be required for writing the statements or these may be provided by the software company providing the system. Some schools that have invested in electronic registers have a facility for computerised reporting linked to the electronic register, rather than filling in OMR forms by hand. Parents sometimes complain that these reports are not sufficiently individualised.

Individual reports

These can be time-consuming to write. If you teach an entire year group you can find yourself writing 180+ reports in a two-week slot, alongside your marking, preparation, and so on. However, these reports are individual and therefore provide more opportunity for teachers to praise individual achievement and suggest targets for improvement.

What to include

Parents want to know that their child is valued by you, so try to make the reports personal and reflect each individual student's strengths and weaknesses. Your school should provide you with guidelines on the information to be included in the report. Generally the following will be included:

- Attendance at lessons
- Punctuality
- Effort
- Attainment – including grades/marks the teacher wants to highlight to the parent
- Any exam results
- Termly assessment results
- Progress
- Achievement in context, i.e. position within the group
- Identification of strengths and weaknesses
- Targets for future success.

Practical task

In order to produce good quality reports consider the following:

- Ensure they are legible.
- Make sure you spell the student's name correctly.
- Report on their progress over the year/term as well as their more recent performance.
- Include examples of particularly good work/team work/individual work.
- Include targets for future development.
- Be fair.
- Avoid using jargon.
- Include explanations of project work where you feel the parents may not understand exactly what their child has done.

Evaluate any reports you have already had to produce and analyse whether or not they met the above criteria.

Parents' evenings

It is important during your training to become a qualified teacher to attend a parents' evening and sit with your mentor to observe what they do and say. You might be asked to give some of the input because if you have been taking the class for a significant part of their recent lessons. If this is the case you need to prepare carefully – see below. The following advice has been adapted form the leaflet 'Making the Most of Parents' Evenings' available from the Parents Centre website:

Preparation

It is essential you prepare carefully. Make sure you have your assessment recording records. Not all parents/carers will understand what projects/modules their child has been involved in, so it is useful to take some examples along. Some schools encourage teachers to take portfolios of each student's work to show their parents – if you do this make sure it is in alphabetical order so that you can access it quickly.

If you have recently written reports that have gone home, make sure you have read these through, or have them available at the meeting – it is good to be able to comment on improvements.

- Before the meeting reread your most recent reports.
- At the beginning set out what you are going to cover and check this is what the parents want.
- Take your progress records and make sure they are up-to-date.
- Make sure you know who the students are.
- Take examples of their work.
- Know where your Head of Department/mentor is in case you need advice/support.

Here is a checklist of aspects of the student's work and attitude that you may wish to discuss with parents.

- What are the strengths of their child?
- Has he/she shown any special talents/completed a project or module well?
- What is he/she finding difficult? How can the parents/carer help with this? Show examples of these where possible.
- Does he/she try hard enough?
- Does he/she arrive on time and complete homework and class tasks on time?
- Does he/she join in class discussions?
- How can the parent/carer help with his/her work in general?
- Has he/she made sufficient progress since his/her last report?
- Does his/her behaviour give any cause for concern?

Remember to use clear explanations supported by examples where necessary. Some parents will be nervous so it is important to put them at their ease. Parents' evenings are generally enjoyable and give you an opportunity to talk to parents and guardians, and develop your understanding of the students' background and experience away from school as well as sharing targets for development.

Linking assessment and feedback to lesson evaluations

As a new teacher it is essential to reflect on the assessment and feedback element of your teaching. This will in turn help you to improve your practice. It is also good practice to involve your students in reflecting on their progress, the assessments they have been involved in, the feedback they have been given, and ways to develop this aspect further. You may want to do this at the end of a project, coursework, module, and so on. Most departments will have a policy on when to involve students in feedback. You will often get useful feedback, and sometimes students will raise issues you had not even thought of.

Evaluating your lessons is essential. As a teacher you need to become an expert at reflecting on your own practice, accepting feedback from various sources, and developing your lessons (see Chapter 2). If you ask a teacher whether they ever teach the same lesson twice, they will generally answer 'no'. You need to constantly learn from experiences that didn't go as you planned, and refine, and improve. Don't worry if you experiment with a new teaching method and it doesn't work out – critically reflect on why not, what went wrong, what do you need to do to ensure it works well next time.

Aspects you need to include in your evaluations are:

- Reflection related to each objective
- Ensuring your reflections are student-centred
- Including realistic targets for your future development.

When you have finished your lesson evaluation, you then need to use it to plan your next lesson. For example, if when you evaluate your lesson you feel you have not covered an objective in a way that all students have understood, you will need to include this in the next lesson. You may alter the objective, or use a different method of teaching/assessment of the objective, but you are still using it to inform planning. Also, when you are planning your lesson introduction and are linking back to the previous lesson, you need to include questions that will link that knowledge to the current lesson in the minds of the students.

Suggested areas for evaluations are listed below. You won't be able to respond to all of these areas for every lesson, so pick out the ones that are most appropriate to your teaching and the lesson:

- Learning objectives – context, purpose and criteria for judging
- Interventions, interactions and classroom management
- Use, deployment, and quality of the resources you developed for the lesson
- Pace and use of time
- Expectations and challenge for your students
- Grouping – how did you group them, did this go as planned, did all your students have opportunity to contribute?
- Student responsibility, autonomy, response and skills
- Questioning strategies and class discussion
- High- and low-order tasks
- Match in the level of your teaching and the learning of your students
- Differentiation and meeting the individual learning needs of your students
- Specific planning/requirements for EAL students
- Problem solving and enquiry
- Assessment and target-setting
- Homework – for example, was it used constructively to raise achievement?
- Supporting planning and preparation
- Preparation of any adults other than yourself in the classroom
- Teaching and learning styles used
- An orderly and purposeful atmosphere
- High expectations for each student
- Noting which students asked for help and what response they got
- Noting what kinds of help they asked for
- Room layout
- Clear instructions/guidelines
- Acknowledgement of achievement by appropriate assessment methods.

As you develop your lesson evaluations you will probably develop other areas to include that reflect your professional development targets and the subject matter you are teaching.

Challenge your thinking

The following quote is from *Inside the Black Box (*Black and Wiliam,1998)

> 'All teachers have to undertake some summative assessment, for example to report to parents, and to produce end-of-year reports as classes are due to move on to new teachers. However, the task of assessing students summatively for external purposes is clearly different from the task of assessing on-going work to monitor and improve progress. Some argue that these two roles are so different that they should be kept apart. We do not see how this can be done, given that teachers must have some share in responsibility for the former and must take the leading responsibility for the latter. Indeed, from the information that teachers gather for formative purposes, they should, with selection and re-interpretation, be in a strong position to contribute to a fair summative report on each student. However, there are clearly difficult problems for teachers in reconciling their formative with their summative roles, and it is also evident from several evaluation studies of teachers' assessment practices in the UK in recent years that confusion in teachers' minds between the roles has impeded progress.'

- Why do you think that Paul Black and Dylan Wiliam point out the possible conflicts between summative and formative assessment roles?

- If high-quality feedback to learners can enhance their learning, why is so much emphasis placed on summative assessment and league tables when measuring the effectiveness of schools?

- How much pressure do you feel under to report student progress in terms of grades and levels rather than concentrating on supporting learners through effective formative assessment?

- How much of your assessment activity is carried out for the learners and how much for other 'stakeholders'?

Summary

This chapter has introduced you to the purposes of assessment and different types of assessment. You have been given advice on how to set out your monitoring of profession record sheets and where to obtain baseline and predicted grade information and how to use this in your planning. The chapter has discussed the importance of feedback and target setting, how and when to give it, and discussed various methods that you can use. Advice on reporting to parents and how to write reports has been provided. Assessment and feedback are essential elements to the professional role of a teacher, and it is not possible to include everything in this chapter. The Further reading section therefore guides you to useful additional reading for this aspect of your role.

References

Assessment Reform Group (1999) *Assessment for learning: beyond the black box*, University of Cambridge, Faculty of Education.

Black, P. and Wiliam, D. (1998), *Inside the Black Box: Raising Standards Through Classroom Assessment*, London: King's College.

Black, P. and Wiliam, D. (1998) 'Assessment and Classroom Learning', *Assessment in Education,* 5(1): 7–71.

Brooks, V. (2002) *Assessment in Secondary Schools,* Buckingham: Open University Press.

Fuchs, L.S., Fuchs, D., Karns, K., Hamlett, C.L., Katzaroff, M. and Dutka, S. (1997) 'Effects of Task Focused Goals on Low Achieving Students With and Without Learning Disabilities', *American Educational Research Journal,* 34(3): 513–43.

MacIntosh M.G. and Hale D.E. (1976) *Assessment and the Secondary School Teacher,* London: Routledge.

Marton, F. and Saljo, R. (1984) 'Approaches to Learning', in Marton, F., Hounsell, D. and Entwistle, N. (eds) *The Experience of Learning,* Edinburgh: Scottish Academic Press.

Nicol, D. and Macfarlane-Dick, D. (2006) 'Formative Assessment and Self-regulated Learning: A Model and Seven Principles of Good Feedback Practice', *Studies in Higher Education,* 31(2): 199–216.

Somers, J. (2000) 'Knowing the Shadow or Knowing the Bird', in Sefton-Green, J. and Sinker, R. (eds) *Evaluating Creativity,* London: Routledge.

Stobart, G. and Gipps, C. (1997) *Assessment: A Teacher's Guide to the Issues,* Trowbridge: Hodder and Stoughton.

Further reading

Black, P. and Harrison, C. (2001) 'Feedback in questioning and marking: the science teacher's role in formative assessment', *School Science Review* (June).

Black, P. and Harrison, C. (2001) 'Self-assessment, peer-assessment and taking responsibility: the science student's role in formative assessment', *School Science Review.*

Black, P., Harrison, C., Lee, C. and Wiliam, D. (2001) 'Theory and practice in the development of formative assessment', Paper to the AERA Conference, Seattle.

Black, P., Harrison, C., Lee, C., Marshall, B. and Dylan, W. (2002) *Working inside the black box: assessment for learning in the classroom,* London: King's College.

Dymoke, S. and Harrison, J. (ed.) (2008) *Reflective Teaching and Learning,* London: Sage.

Ofsted (2003) 'Good Assessment in Secondary Schools', available electronically from *www.ofsted.gov.uk.*

Sadler, R. (1989) 'Formative assessment and the design of instructional systems', *Instructional Science,* 18: 119–44.

Web resources

http://www.qca.org.uk

http://www.teachernet.gov.uk

http://www.ofsted.gov.uk

http://dcsf.gov.uk

http://www.lincolnshire.gov.uk

http://www.standards.dfes.gov.uk

http://www.assessment-reform-group.org – Assessment Reform Group website.

http://hotpot.uvic.ca/ – free software that you can use to structure quizzes for students that will be marked by the software.

http://www.aaia.org.uk

http://www.parentscentre.gov.uk/schoollife/getinvolved/studentreportsandparentevenings/

http://www.parentscentre.gov.uk/schoollife/getinvolved/studentreportsandparentevenings/

http://www.qca.org.uk/ca/5-14/afl/ – Assessment for Learning website.

Chapter 10

Behaviour management in the classroom

Learning outcomes

By the end of this chapter you should be able to understand:

→ Some of the causes of classroom behaviour problems

→ The causes which are in your control and what to do about them

→ The role of classroom layout and seating plans

→ The importance of relationships and routine

→ The importance of planning for the behaviour of your class

Introduction

Classroom behaviour is probably the key area for concern for teacher trainees and qualified teachers alike. Poor behaviour by the students and the stress that than can bring is one of the most common reasons given by teachers for leaving the profession; 'if only they would listen', 'if only they would behave' are the complaint's which we hear the most. The government has placed the issue of classroom management at the heart of its educational policy, understanding that poor and/or disruptive behaviour impacts on both teachers and students. To this end, the government turned directly to headteachers and other educationalists in the form of The Practitioners' Group on School Behaviour and Discipline, chaired by Alan Steer to look into the wide issues impacting on behaviour in schools. The final report, Learning Behaviour; Lessons Learned, was published in 2009 and forms the basis for they way in which schools approach behaviour management. A section of the introduction includes the following:

> 'The behaviour in school of the large majority of children is good, as it always has been. Where instances of bad behaviour occur intervention must be swift, intelligent and effective. This intervention must protect the interests of the majority while aiming to change the behaviour of those causing the difficulties. Children need to be taught how to behave in an acceptable social manner, and there are few children who are incapable of learning these lessons. A clear and consistent approach is essential for teachers and parents, but this needs to be balanced with a recognition that it is the nature of childhood that it is a period when mistakes are made and lessons learned.'
>
> (Steer Report, 2005, 2009: 16)

This succinctly summarises some key issues you will need to reflect on as you develop your understanding of, and skills in, behaviour management. First, only a minority of students show poor behaviour. Second, swift and effective intervention when poor behaviour is exhibited is crucial. Finally, appropriate behaviour is learned and it is the behaviour that is poor, not the student.

This report looks across a broad spectrum and covers many areas of whole school policy and it makes highly informative reading. However, it is the intention that this chapter will look directly at your practice within the classroom rather than whole-school policies.

Everybody wants to be able to go into the classroom to be faced with a sea of smiling faces, keen to answer questions when asked, always on target and always allowing us to complete the model lesson which fits the prescriptive structure. Well, let's be honest, it's not like that, nor would we really want it to be. The classes which you teach will be full of individuals, all with their own experiences and lives, all of which will impact on their moods, their behaviour and their approach to that lesson on that day. If you do have a classroom with a sea of smiling faces, it will have taken a lot of work to get it to this state, and you will probably be up for an award as teacher of the year and there is little or nothing I can tell you.

However daunting classrooms may be, you should always remember that, as the Steer report states:

> 'the great majority of pupils work hard and behave well'.
>
> (Steer 2005, 2009)

You should not go into a classroom expecting poor behaviour and confrontation. There may be times when this occurs, but there will be reasons for this, and the way you deal with it will impact on how your students see you and how you see yourself as a teacher.

Silence in the class – the perfect teaching world?

Before we investigate this section of the chapter, take a little time for a reflective activity to help you to understand your preconceptions about teaching environments.

Stop and reflect

- Reflect on your teaching experiences so far.
- Describe your perfect teaching environment.
- Describe what you would see if you went into a classroom which was out of control.

As a school student, many years ago, I remember being taught for a year in an atmosphere of silent terror by a teacher who intimidated his class so much that we dared not speak for fear of being shouted at, not even to ask a question if we did not understand something. The total fear is the only thing which I remember about those lessons, I remember no content. To an outsider, it would look like a situation of perfect control, but the real question must be, what learning was going on? I would argue that no learning occurred at all. Is that what teaching is about? I think not. Obviously, things have moved on considerably from this time. Classroom and behaviour management has moved away from fear and intimidation and is now more concerned with the positive behaviour management advocated by Canter and Canter (1992), Roffey (2004) and Cowley (2003), and it is this more humanist approach where students are treated with respect and understanding that is the expected norm.

Some of the questions which we must all ask ourselves as teachers are: 'What sort of an atmosphere do we want in the classroom?' and 'What atmosphere do we work best with?'

Is the classroom one where the students are happy to be there, keen to learn, confident enough to ask questions and give their opinions when asked, and where is a 'buzz' to the lesson? If this is what we want, then one of the consequences of this lesson is that it may be a little noisy at times and the question must be 'Does it matter?' A silent lesson where every student has their head down does not mean that they are happy to be there, nor is it proof that they are learning.

To some people, a noisy classroom may give the appearance of being out of control, but this may simply not be the case. This may be an active classroom where productive learning is going on, especially if it is a practical lesson. What a teacher really needs is to be in control of the situation. If it is noisy but on task, then there may be no problem to address. If it is silent, but without learning, then there are huge problems.

This chapter is not intended to solve all of the classroom behaviour problems, but it is intended at least to make you think about possible causes of poor behaviour and what you can do to help improve behaviour in the classroom and to make that classroom somewhere where all students want to learn and in which you enjoy teaching. The first things to consider are the possible causes of poor behaviour.

It is important to stress that, although a few cases of extreme behaviour by school students make headlines, the vast majority of cases of behaviour problems faced by teachers can be defined as low-level disruption (Elton, 1989; Steer, 2005, 2009)

Causes of behaviour problems

There are a range of possible causes of behaviour problems. Some may be within your direct control, and some may not be.

Stop and reflect

Remember, every time you go into your classroom, you will be dealing with a number of individuals, not one single body, and they are not all going to act and behave in the same way.

Try some critical self-analysis:

- Are you in the same mood every day?
- Are there some times when you are more receptive than others?
- Do you feel at your best when you are cold, hungry, upset?
- How responsive are you immediately after lunch?
- Would you rather have a nap or do some maths?
- Do you feel ill?
- Does the medication you take make you drowsy or affect your ability to concentrate?

It is obvious that being self-aware will enable you to be more empathetic with your students, and the quicker you can get to know your students on an individual basis the better.

The causes of behaviour problems can be split into two groups: those within your direct control which you can do something about; and those out of your control – i.e. those factors which have nothing to do with you but that you have to handle.

Practical task

1. Reflect on your classroom experience to date.
2. List those factors which may not be under your control but which may have an impact on behaviour in the class: for example, lateness.
3. List those factors which are under your control and which may have an impact on behaviour in the class: for example, the content of the lesson.

You will no doubt have come up with a range of factors in task 1 above. It is very easy to identify factors in others which you may or may not be able to identify with yourself, but you may well have come up with more factors in task 2 than you thought. Let's unpack some of these issues now and think what could be done about some of them.

External factors influencing classroom behaviour

Obviously, some of these factors will vary from school to school and individual to individual and I will no doubt miss a number of them. Although I may make some suggestions as to how to deal with some of the external factors, some may be whole-school solutions and some may simply be down to being caring, human and responsive to the problem. Here are a few of the problems which are frequently encountered in the school environment:

- An argument/fight at break/lunchtime
- A fallout with a friend
- Late to lesson
- Feeling ill/medical
- Side effects of medicine
- Home life
- Being bullied
- Poor diet
- Hormones
- The weather
- Lack of food
- SEN issues
- Lack of confidence
- End of the day
- End of the week
- General excitement.

There are many different problems here and they may manifest themselves in your classroom in many ways and at any time. The person being bullied may thrash out, the person with medical side effects may be short-tempered, the person with a falling out may be confrontational, the teenager with hormone issues may simply be unpredictable. This does not mean that, because they are not in your direct control, you cannot do something about the situation.

Stop and reflect

Critically evaluate the following scenarios and think about what could have caused them and what action could be taken.

- *Scenario 1.* Students X and Y turn up five minutes after your lesson has started, clearly a little flustered and in the middle of your introduction to the task for today's lesson. What would you do?

- *Scenario 2.* Student Z, someone with whom you have always had a reasonable relationship, is failing to follow instructions, is uncooperative when asked to work and abusive when pressed.

- *Scenario 3.* A student who is new to your class is refusing to do the work set and becomes argumentative when asked to get on with his work.

I have seen each of these situations on a number of occasions and have observed them handled with different levels of success by different teachers. I have found that the worst way to deal with any one of these situations is to confront it in a domineering manner. It does not work, it creates resentment, it stores up future problems for yourself and solves nothing. Recent publications by Dunn (2005), Swainson (2007) and Cowley (2003) all stress the importance of dealing with behaviour issues in a calm, controlled and non-confrontational way. Shouting simply does not work, nor does aggression and it simply stores up problems for the future. Rogers (2002) is keen to advocate that the language which we use when we wish to address behavioural issues is vital, and that we should communicate our expectations in an assertive tone which is supported by non-confrontational but confident body language. Remaining calm and in control shows the students that you are dealing directly with this in a professional manner with the intention of resolving the situation to everyone's satisfaction. It will also show the rest of the class that you are someone who can be trusted to react to situations in a fair and positive manner.

Let us consider scenario 1. This situation can be dealt in a range of ways, depending on the teacher. It is wise not to shout at the students for being late. It interrupts the flow of the lesson more and shows the class that you are not truly in control. There could be 100 reasons why that person is late to the lesson and 99 of them may be valid. You must find out why they are late first. Another poor way to handle the situation is to do nothing at all, since this puts out the message that you can turn up to the lesson whenever you want and that this does not matter, which is obviously not the case. An appropriate response is to acknowledge the presence of the latecomer, getting them to sit down at a desk as close to the door as possible and to speak to them quietly, asking them to explain why they are late, as soon as possible. By doing this, the lesson can continue, a possible flashpoint is avoided and you are seen by the class to be doing something. Always stress to the latecomer that being late to the lesson is not acceptable and that they need to be on time next session or face a sanction. Log this incident and follow it up if there is a repeat of the lateness. Depending on the situation, you may decide to follow this situation up with a Form Tutor or Head of Year or simply check that things are OK with the student the next time you see them in the corridor.

Again, for scenario 2, a possible way of escalating problems is to shout at the student, but this is unlikely to achieve anything in the long term and may simply cause resentment. There could be any number of reasons for this behaviour. He/she is being bullied, is a confused teenager, has been abused at home and is feeling resentful. Again, the best thing to do is to remain calm at all times. Obviously, as there is a class as an audience, all of whose members want to see how you handle this (they may be the next one in this situation), you must act professionally. Explain to the student that being abusive is not the sort of behaviour that you would expect from him/her and this is not acceptable, but that the work is set and that you would like them to get on with it now and do the good work that you are used to from this student. By doing this, you are emphasising that you have high expectations of this student in terms of behaviour and output. Most important, you have avoided confrontation; you have been seen by the class to have done something and, also most important, the student has not lost face in front of his/her classmates. As with scenario 1, follow this up with the student the next time you see them in the corridor, another classroom or wherever. Being seen as someone who genuinely cares for their students and takes the time to show it will help to develop positive relationships, and this is crucial for effective behaviour management.

By now you will have worked out that scenario 3 is very similar to 2. Shouting at students solves nothing. There may be times when you raise your voice, but it should be back to normal as soon as possible to make sure that the students know you are in control of yourself and that shouting is not an appropriate way to behave. It has been known for students and teachers to shout at each other with both parties out of control, and one of them is supposed to be an adult!

Always be calm, always be in control. In scenario 3 you have a new student who is refusing to do the work set. The first thing to do is to find out from the student what the problem is; you would do that for a colleague, why not a student? He/she may not be able to read and may be embarrassed by this. They may not understand the task you have set, which you may have pitched at the wrong level. Recently a teacher complained about student X who had entered his room, sat at his desk with his head in his hands and had done very little work that day. When asked if the teacher had found out from the student what the problem was, he said no and that he assumed that the student was not interested in the lesson. What the teacher had not found out was that the student was on medication. This made him drowsy, but was a treatment for a condition which made him uncomfortable and irritable. The reality of the situation was that the student was trying his best to keep calm. By doing nothing, the teacher sent a clear message that he was not interested in the child and that he was unwilling to find out. How different the situation could have been with a little effort from the teacher!

With all three scenarios, and many others besides, you are being asked to act on behaviour which may have had nothing to do with you, so that you are just getting the brunt of it, and this may seem unfair. However, with a careful and thoughtful attitude, you can make sure that the students understand that you are in control, that you are interested in them and that you care. Teachers who have this reputation get a more responsive class and a better quality of teaching life than those who have a reputation for shouting and nothing else.

The golden rules for handling behaviour are:

1 **Stay calm.** If you do not, you will lose face with the students and are more likely to make mistakes which you will regret later.

2 **Find out what the problem is before you react.**

3 **Always do something positive.** Make sure that the student understands what is expected of them.

4 **Make sure that the student does not lose face or is humiliated.** They will resent you for a long time and the relationship may never recover.

5 **Follow situations up.** Make sure that you speak to your students to check on them after the event. Your behaviour will determine whether the relationship continues.

6 **Be flexible.** By giving your student a little space, but insisting that you need the work to be completed, you will make a positive impression with the student. They are more likely to go the extra mile for the teacher who was supportive of them when they needed it.

What if they don't respond?

You may well now be saying, 'Well, what if they have not responded?' 'What if they have not done what I ask?' 'Where do I go from here?' Well, basically, the first thing to do is to not give up at the first hurdle. A number of educationalists advocate the importance of a consistent and assertive approach where the student is given the option of altering their behaviour or accept the consequences (Roffey, 2004; Cowley, 2003; Swainson, 2007). All point out that it may take some time before the students accept that you mean what you say and that you will always follow up what you say. In short, the message is be clear about what you want, be consistent and put the choice of whether the student who is giving you the problem does as he/she is told or accepts the consequences of their actions, which must be a sanction.

Most schools now have a behaviour policy which is clearly stated and may have a number of stages ranging from simply talking to the child to removing then from the lesson and contacting their home. If this is the case, follow the school's policy as this should be something which the school has enforced and the students should be used to. Involve more senior members of staff where appropriate, but avoid using this as a first port of call, since the impression that it gives the students will be that you are not in control and that you are depending on someone else to enforce discipline. Consequently, you may be seen as someone who does not have the backbone, and you may well lose respect.

If you do involve more senior members of staff, try to use them in an advisory role at first. They will have more experience than you, may well know the student concerned and be able to advise you on what works for that particular student.

If you have had cause for concern with a student over their behaviour and have had to act on it, make sure that you make every effort to see the student before the next lesson. Also, make sure that the student knows that, as far as you are concerned, that lesson is in the past and the next lesson is a fresh start. You, as the adult, are modelling the attitude and behaviour that you expect from the student. Explain to the student that that is not the behaviour that you expect from them, and it was the behaviour that was the problem, not them personally. By doing this, you should be able to rebuild your relationship with the student quickly and positively.

Case study

A trainee was placed in a large newly built academy in the north of England, in a rough area on the outskirts of a large city. One particular day in class, the trainee was taking a Y10 lesson in which there were also three other adults present: their mentor (who was the usual class teacher), a classroom assistant and the university tutor who was there to observe the lesson.

Despite the adult presence in the class, the students were out of control for the whole lesson, among other things, threatening to throw each other out of the windows and messing with the chairs; there were overt, loud, sexual conversations between boys about girls in the class; a student from the corridor entered the class and went unnoticed while they talked to a member of the class for over five minutes; some threatened each other with violence, and on it went for the whole lesson.

This carried on despite a succession of warnings, leading eventually to detention sanctions from the class teacher, and admonishments from the other adults in the class. No one learned anything that day.

So, if four adults cannot maintain discipline and control in that situation, where would you go from here if it was a class in your school?

Factors within your control

As indicated earlier, there are as many factors within your control as there are outside it. These may be approached in a proactive rather than a reactive way. All of these you can either plan for or can take control of as a professional, reflective practitioner. As these are within your control, they can be linked directly and easily with the QTS standards. For example, dealing with things in a professional manner, using appropriate language, appropriate dress and all of those indirect signals you give to the students reflect QTS standard 2 in which you are expected to demonstrate those values and behaviour you expect from your students. You are modelling what you want your students to do. Ensuring that you have planned your lesson well, with appropriate resources and a good understanding of your class in terms of their learning styles, reflects that you understand the requirements of QTS standard 25. Creating a positive atmosphere in the class where your students feel confident enough to ask you questions and are willing to share their ideas can be used as evidence for QTS standards 30 and 31.

Stop and reflect

Reflect on the types of teachers you have seen in school so far.

● Write down a description of what a professional, respected teacher may look and act like.

● Critically analyse whether or not this could be you.

Here are just a few of the things of which you are in control and your students are not:

● Your dress and appearance
● Your professionalism
● Your relationships
● Your language
● Your presentation
● Your resources
● Your room
● Your displays

- Your assessment and feedback
- The seating plan
- The ambiance of the room
- The task set
- The routine.

Again, as for the factors outside your control, there will be a number of these which I have not included which you feel are important. That is fine, it shows that you are thinking about yourself as a teacher.

Many people seem to think that the behaviour in the classroom is the responsibility of the students and that the teacher is somehow secondary to this. Wrong! You, as an individual teacher, have the most important role to play in classroom management. You are the adult in the classroom, you are the role model and how you project your behaviour and attitude will have a direct impact on the students' behaviour.

The first item on the list within your control has to be the way you present yourself to your students and colleagues in terms of dress and appearance. Now it may seem odd to advise teachers about their dress and some may say that it is out of place, but if you want to be treated as a professional, then dress like one. Male teachers may well be expected to wear a collar and tie, female teachers may be well advised to think about the neckline of their dresses and the length and style of their skirts. Like it or not, hormones can exercise a powerful influence on our students and can cause problems and, in some instances, conflict. If you are a young trainee teacher, there may only be a few years between you and the people you want to teach. You may have a similar style of dress, and similar musical interests and hobbies to some of your students. Sometimes the age similarity can make it difficult to win the respect that you feel that you deserve and you may be tempted to go for the 'I'm one of you' approach in a hope of getting through to the students. For most students, this will not work and will only backfire on you later. It will also impact on the way that your colleagues see you. You are a role model for your students and a professional responsible for the education of your charges, so remember that at all times. You do not want to be discussing what you wear with your students.

Connected to dress and appearance must be the way in which you conduct yourself outside school. This is always a difficult area as many will justifiably say: what has my social life got to do with my teaching? Well, when it comes to the impact on the students you are trying to teach, the answer is, a great deal. If you are a young teacher, should you, for example, go to the same clubs where, rightly or wrongly, you may meet some of your students or their siblings and where what you have done in your free time gets round the school in minutes? If you are part of a social networking site such as Facebook, do you want your personal details and that humorous picture taken at a stag do or hen party published round the school? Students will find enough reasons to avoid taking you seriously without giving them more ammunition yourself.

The next thing to consider is your professional relationships with your students. It is vitally important that you create an atmosphere in which the students can work. They should recognise you as a friendly person who will support them and that you are, above all, human. What you are not is their friend. (See also Chapter 4.) It is vital that you take a personal interest in each and every student in your charge. Find out what you can about them, show interest in their interests. Make each student feel that they are a valued individual, so that you will get the most out of them, but be clear about where the line is drawn. Some teachers are willing to take what appears to be, at first, the easy route of being overly friendly in the classroom, letting the students get away with things and giving free time to get the students on their side. At first this may work. But very quickly some students will take advantage of this, classroom discipline will fall apart and then it is an uphill battle to get the students back into a situation where they are actively learning.

So, having considered how you will approach your class in terms of dress, having understood the possible impact of your social life on your teaching life and looked at how your relationship with the students can impact on your ability to effectively manage the classroom, the next thing to consider is the room in which you teach.

The environment in which you teach is key to effective behaviour management and more attention needs to be paid to this. Your room needs to be tidy. It should have up-to-date displays of the students' work. Your desk needs to look well-ordered and your resources should be ready for when the students come in. Make sure that there is no litter around and that all chairs are under the desks. Ensuring that the room is returned to this state for the next class should be part of the routine for the next class. In doing this you are showing the students that you care about the environment that they work in and that their work is important. If you do not show this, then how can you expect them to? You are modelling the standards that you expect from your students. Both you and your room are ready for your students.

The next thing which is in your control and that can impact on behaviour is the seating plan. This gives you the opportunity to decide who sits where and why. This is a powerful method of defusing possible hotspots of trouble. It is up to you to decide where people sit, but it is always a good idea to run your seating plan past a more established member of staff or head of department who may have more insight into, or experience of, the students in the class.

Resources and tasks should be achievable by all in the class. This may mean considerable planning and differentiation on your part, but the time invested in this activity will more than make up for the time it will take to explain a task if you have done this poorly. Two of the most common reasons for students being disruptive is either that they are bored by a task which is too easy, or they are reacting to a task that they cannot do by a displacement activity such as causing disruption. Everyone likes to be able to feel that they can achieve a task and no one likes to feel a fool, so develop your resources accordingly.

The final areas which you will wish to reflect on are routine, and your delivery. Routine is vital for students. They like to know where they stand and what they are going to do and, while variety in a lesson is effective in stimulating the mind (ensuring progression and student involvement), it is a good thing to have an overall structure to clarify what will happen. This is obviously part of the planning for the lesson. If a student detects that you have not planned and you do not know what you are doing, then they will lose confidence in you and your credibility will be lost.

The routine should include a starter activity with which the student can get involved as soon as they get into the room (rather than five minutes into the lesson). The register should be called early in the lesson. Following the starter should be the main activity/activities followed by a winding-up/plenary session. This standard routine should become the norm for the students and, because they know what will happen and when, it will help with overall behaviour management.

Last of all would be your own delivery. No one likes a monotonous, dull delivery which does not engage anyone. Consequently, you need to be confident and clear in your delivery, animated and proactive with your students and quick with your use of positive praise. You are key to creating the positive atmosphere in your class and although it may take a couple of lessons before these norms are established, once they are, they make teaching one of the best occupations there is.

Relationships matter

One of the most important skills for a teacher to develop is that of the relationship with students.

Stop and reflect

Reflect back on your school days.

- Who can you remember as a good teacher?
- Who was the bad teacher?
- What was it about them that made you feel this way?

If you ask most students, the poor teachers are those who do not have the time for them, who do not go that little bit further. Good ones go beyond the normal classroom requirements, show an interest in them, use their names, and they ask them questions other than 'What is the square root of 125?' If this is the case, then surely establishing this relationship and in so doing, creating a positive working environment, is the most important task for the teacher.

A student's relationship with their teacher is crucial to their success in class, their attitude to their work and for their own self-esteem. The student must believe that the teacher has a real interest in them.

'Students' perceptions of their teachers' caring were found to be positively related to their perceptions of their teachers' immediacy, responsiveness and assertiveness while negatively related to teacher verbal aggressiveness.'

(Teven, 2001: 159)

This quote neatly encapsulates what the teacher needs to achieve for effective classroom management to take place. It is also true to say that those teachers who exercise a positive, assertive and non-aggressive style of behaviour management when dealing with students create the best leaning environment for students (Watkins and Wagner, 2000; Rogers, 2002).

There are times when you are the most stable thing in a student's life and they may well share with you things which they may not share with their parents. From this point of view being a teacher is the most privileged job which you can do; but this does not come quickly or easily and you need to work on it.

Think back again to when you were at school. There will have been teachers who gave you the time and teachers who you know were there for the job alone. Which one do you remember most fondly? Which one did you want to work for and to please? There is no magic formula to this, but there are some handy hints and tips along the way.

- **Get to know names.** This is crucial. How would you feel if someone you were working with did not take the time to find out your name? It helps to show the respect that you give to them and which you hope that they will mirror to you.
- **Get to know something about each child** – find out about their interests, what they do and ask them about it. It makes your students feel special.
- **Greet your students** as they come into your classroom by name and with a smile.
- **Be positive about their achievements** and celebrate them, no matter how small. Praise your students, write home to tell parents how well they have done, but do not tell your student that you will be doing it. A great surprise for all.
- **Use their work as an example of good practice** wherever possible.
- **Take an interest in their own individual efforts and mark their work frequently.** In this way you will demonstrate that their work is important and if you do not demonstrate this, then why should they take care over it.
- **Be consistent in your moods and behaviour.** Children want to know what to expect. They may be going through a traumatic time themselves at the moment. Your stability may be very welcome.
- **Get out of the classroom.** Take time to speak to students in different environments. Get involved in some extra-curricular activity that you can share with the students.
- **Be flexible at times.** There may be times when a student has an off-day and not behave in the way you expect. Be sensitive to this, give them space, check if they are OK later on in a discreet way.
- **If you are wrong,** have the guts to say sorry.
- **Be humble.** Remember, you have chosen to be in that classroom, your students have not, and the things you do have a direct impact on the students.

These are a few pointers, but word gets round soon that you are there for them, that you are fair but firm and that you can be relied upon. There may be a number in the classes you teach who do not have that type of positive adult role model at home, and you have a responsibility to provide that structure.

Establish your boundaries clearly with your classes. Be friendly and warm, but be clear that there are boundaries which they must not cross and, if they do, then there will be consequences. If you have established your relationships with your students, then you should express disappointment that they have chosen to cross these boundaries, and that by doing this they have let both themselves and you down. In this way you are making it clear that they have ownership of their behaviour.

Critical synthesis

You need to be able to make links between theory and practice for behavioural management. To this end, look up learning theories in general theory texts, or in notes from your sessions in university. Reflect on whether you have seen evidence of particular learning theories in action in your classes, or in classes you have observed.

> *Try to analyse whether the use of a particular learning theory applied in class had an effect on behaviour in that class. For example, are there clear links between students being on task when experiential learning is used for activities in the class, or when students are asked to work together, as purported by Vygotsky? Do specific learning theories lend themselves to better-behaved classes?*

Meeting the class for the first time – first impressions matter

When they first meet their new class all teachers are nervous, whether new, trainees or experienced, it's all the same. You are an individual meeting a group of individuals who may already know each other. Their group dynamics may have already been established so that they carry with them a shared history which you will not know about. You may only know some of them by reputation: good students, poor students, argumentative, and clown. You will be meeting them for the first time and first impressions do count.

Practical task

- Write down how you will be feeling when meeting your class for the first time, what your expectations of them are and what information you would like to have?
- Put yourself in the place of the student. What would you like to get from this first meeting? What sort of activities would you like to take place in this lesson?

If you are an established teacher at a school, you will have established your own reputation, which the students will be aware of. You may have taught their siblings, or there may be something about you that they are aware of. On the other hand, you may be a new teacher at the school meeting the class for the first time. The most important piece of advice is to be well prepared for this meeting. You may well be nervous, but it is important not to let that show. You must appear confident, in control and clear about your objectives, even if inside your guts are doing cartwheels.

Students tend to make their mind up about a teacher very quickly, usually within the first ten minutes of meeting them, and from then on it is difficult to change that opinion. The first time you meet, most of the class will be as apprehensive as you will be; consequently, this is the best time to establish the way in which your classes will be run and what you expect.

It is always a good idea to be as well prepared as you can be. You need to have as much information as possible about your class. Most schools now operate centralised registration system such as SIMs, and many of these systems will provide photos of the students within the class. Consequently, as well as a class list, you will have an image of a student. One of the traditional excuses which students have used – claiming to be someone else – is instantly removed, and this puts you at an advantage if you can put names to faces straightaway.

There are things which you must prepare before the lesson. Obviously the lesson plan will need to be as detailed and varied as possible. You must make sure that you have all of your resources prepared and that there are enough of them. You need to make sure that the activities you have prepared are interesting and varied with extension activities. It is a good idea to have a reserve activity just in case. Make sure that the class is laid out in the way that you want it and that any resources which need to be on the desks are on the desks.

Once you have made sure that you have your resources ready, your class list and the seating plan, it's time to meet the students.

Where possible, meet the students at the door and allow them into the classroom only when you are ready to let them in. It is a clear statement that this is your territory and they are being invited into it, but on the understanding that you are in charge.

Students should enter a class one at a time, not in a crush. This is not only for health and safety reasons, but also to establish an atmosphere of calm. They should also enter the class for the first time in the way set out in your seating plan. This may take a little time to do, so I would recommend having a written starter activity on the desks for the earlier students to complete while the remaining students enter the room.

Thank the class for entering the room, for sitting according to the seating plan and undertaking the starter activity. Introduce yourself and take the register, explaining to them that you need quiet while you do it and that they should respond in a polite manner.

Again, thank the class for following the instructions and explain what would be the normal start to a lesson – that they enter to a starter activity which will usually be linked to the lesson, that you will then call a register and then explain what form the day's task will be – in fact, describing the way that the normal lesson will progress.

In your first lesson, it is important that you establish the ground rules with your class. Most schools have a behaviour policy which the students will know about and be expected to follow, but these ground rules are going to be yours and worked out with the students in this first lesson. Explain that they will be part of this decision-making process and that, because of this, they will be expected to follow it. Making such an agreement is empowering to the students, shows to them that you are a reasonable person and gives you a good base from which to build your relationships and your classroom management, since you can refer back to it throughout your time with them.

Seating plans and room layout

Seating plans are very important for classroom control. Cowley (2003) points out that using seating plans not only sends out a signal to the students that you are in control, but also that using the plan to allow students to sit where they want in return for good behaviour can be used as a reward. There are many models for this – alphabetical order, boy/girl, ability grouping – but the message is clear: it is you who are in control and it is you who decides who sits where. There will obviously be cries of 'Mr/Ms — lets us sit where we like.' Well, that may be the case, but has Mr/Ms — already established his or her own classroom rules and arrangements? Letting students sit where they wish to sit should be used as a reward for good behaviour, following the rules, being productive. It can always be sold to the students as a way of you, the teacher, wanting them, the student, to make the best possible progress and of their proving to you that, if they can be trusted to behave in a mature and responsible manner, they can benefit from this.

If possible, ask a more experienced member of staff about a seating plan you are proposing. Without advice, you may be setting yourself up for a fall. For example, you may want to keep Margaret and Lorraine apart because they will talk and not make progress, you may need to keep David and Ali apart because they will always fight, and so on.

The layout of the room is also important and will impact on your seating plan. Are your desks in rows facing the front? Do you have islands where students face each other, but not necessarily you? Are you in a computer room where there are potential distractions and students looking at things other than you?

You may wish to arrange the room for the first meeting with a class so that your students are sitting in rows facing you. This could be a square with you on one side of it, or it could be three rows of tables facing you. Whichever it is, the objective is to make sure that they are facing you and not their friends (thus reducing the temptation to chat), and that you are able to have eye contact with each and every child in that class when you want to. This may of course change when you have established your boundaries and relationships; however, the set-up you start with is the default one which you can return to. If you are going to be doing group work in a lesson, then set the tables and chairs out accordingly for that lesson, but then return to the default.

Make sure that you keep a seating plan available at all times. At the start when you are getting to know your class, it will be a valuable aid in helping you to establish good classroom-management techniques. For the cover teacher who may have to take your class at some stage it is invaluable.

Challenge your thinking

The Elton Report (1989) noted that a school with an effective rewards and a sanctions system would have a ratio of 5:1 in favour of rewards. This is echoed in the Steer Report (2005), with the Elton Report actually quoted there.

Interestingly, the Steer report then goes on to devote two pages to recommendations about use of rewards, but takes five pages to list the sanctions!

Are your experiences of schools and classrooms in a 5:1 ratio in favour of rewards over sanctions? Reflect on your own lessons and gauge the number of instances of rewarding good behaviour, and then contrast this with the use of sanctions, warnings or punishments for interruptions, disruptions and lack of attention.

Is it time to re-think the balance between rewarding learners for their efforts and the punishment of their example of what we regard as poor behaviour?

How can you increase your efforts to influence behaviour by rewarding the good?

Summary

In this chapter we have considered:

- Some of the causes of behaviour problems
- The factors that are outside our control and the factors we are in control of
- Some scenarios of possible situations and how to deal with them
- Some possible actions which may be taken if situations escalate
- The importance of the first few lessons in your relationship with the class
- The crucial role of your relationship with the students
- The importance of seating plans and layout.

References

Canter, L. and Canter, M. (1992) *Assertive discipline: Positive behaviour management for today's classroom*, Los Angeles: Canter Associates.

Charles, C.M. (1981) *Building Classroom Discipline*, New York: Longman.

Cowley, Sue (2003) *Getting the Buggers to Behave*, London: Continuum.

Dunn, R. (2005) *Dos and Don't's of Behaviour Management*, London: Continuum.

Elton (1989) *The Elton Report: Discipline in Schools*, London: HMSO.

Hallam, Sue and Rodgers, L. (2008) *Improving Behaviour and Attendance at School*, Maidenhead: McGraw-Hill.

Leaman, Louisa (2005) *Managing very challenging behaviour*, London: Continuum.

Leaman, Louisa (2007) *The dictionary of disruption: a practical guide to behaviour management*, London: Continuum.

McManus, M. (1989) *Troublesome behaviour in the classroom*, New York: Routledge.

Newell, Sandra and Jeffery, David (2002) *Behaviour management in the classroom: a transactional analysis approach*, London: Continuum.

Roffey, Sue (2004) *The New Teacher's Survival Guide to Behaviour*, London: Paul Chapman Publishing.

Rogers, B. (2002) *Classroom Behaviour*, London: Paul Chapman Publishing.

The Steer Report (2005) *Learning Behaviour: The Report of the Practitioners Group on School Behaviour and Discipline*, London: DCSF Publications.

Steer Report (2009) *Learning Behaviour: Lessons Learned. A review of behaviour standards and practices in our schools*, DCSF Publications. Also downloadable from: *www.teachernet.gov.uk/publications*

Swainson, Tony (2007) *Behaviour Management*, London: Continuum.

Teven, J. (2001) 'The relationships among Teacher characteristics and perceived caring', *Communication Education*, 50(2): 159–69.

Thody, A., Gray, B. and Bowden, D. (2000) *Teacher's Survival Guide*, London: Continuum.

Watkins, C. and Wagner, P. (2000) *Improving School Behaviour*, London: Paul Chapman Publishing.

Wragg, E.C. (1993) *Class Management in the Secondary School*, London: Routledge/Falmer.

Web resources

http://www.angus.gov.uk/atoz/pdfs/BB-BLAPracticalApproach.pdf – Angus Council website.

www.behaviour4learning.ac.uk – Behaviour 4 Learning website.

http://nationalstrategies.standards.dcsf.gov.uk/node/86931 – National strategies website.

http://www.teachingexpertise.com/articles/behaviour-management – Teaching expertise website.

Part 3

HOW SCHOOLS ARE ORGANISED

Chapter 11

The mentoring process

Learning outcomes

By the end of this chapter, you will have:

→ Explored how to get the most out of your relationship with your mentor

→ Considered how to deal with difficult situations with your mentor

→ Developed an understanding of different approaches to mentoring

→ Reflected on the stages of development that teachers may experience

Introduction

'Mentoring is a brain to pick, an ear to listen, and a push in the right direction.'

(John Crosby)

Definitions of mentoring are numerous, perhaps because the mentoring model for supporting a novice is seen in many fields and spheres. In education the notion of mentoring and coaching has become deeply embedded in recent years and now merits a mention in teaching standards, not only for trainee teachers, but also for those who are qualified and experienced (TDA 2007 – c.f. Q9, C9 and P10). Trainee teachers have mentors, NQTs have mentors, middle managers have mentors, staff who are newly appointed to the senior management team have mentors; the mentorship model is recognised as being a valuable and important way of helping an individual settle into a new role. For the purposes of this chapter we will take our definition of mentoring from an article by Hobson *et al.* (2008). They state:

> *. . . mentoring is defined as the one-to-one support of a novice or less experienced practitioner (mentee) by a more experienced practitioner (mentor), designed primarily to assist the development of the mentee's expertise and to facilitate their induction into the culture of the profession (in this case, teaching) and into the specific local context (here, the school or college).*

(Hobson *et al.*, 2008: 207)

Here we are concerned with the nature of that 'one-to-one support'. How can a mentor 'assist development' and facilitate induction into the culture of the profession? Crosby (see quote above) suggests that this is done through the sharing of expertise, listening and discussion, and gentle guidance. This chapter will explore these in more detail.

The mentor–mentee relationship

Why is it important?

School-based mentoring has been a significant element of teacher education since the early 1990s when it was decided that the majority of time for students on PGCE courses would be spent in school. Currently the requirements dictate that students on a graduate QTS programme should spent 120 days (24 weeks) in school (TDA 2009: 97). The major part of a year-long teacher training course is, therefore, spent under the day-to-day guidance of a school–based mentor rather than an academic tutor. The relationships that you form with your mentors in school are likely to be some of the most important ones you develop while undertaking your training. Those training via GTP or other school-based routes will look to their mentor for help and advice on every aspect of their training. So, forming a good working relationship with your mentor is essential.

Why is it complicated?

> **Practical task**
>
> Make two lists; one should list of characteristics you expect in a mentor (e.g. friendly, helpful) and the other should be list of things you expect them to do (e.g. look at lesson plans, observe lessons).
>
> When you have completed this, analyse both lists. Are they realistic, especially given the other responsibilities that your mentor is likely to have (for example, they might also be a head of department, a form tutor, and have other additional responsibilities in their department or extra-curricular commitments)? Evaluate the lists to consider whether there are there any conflicts between them? Can you suggest any solutions to ensure that potential conflict is avoided?

This important relationship is also quite a complicated one. It is complicated because what you want and what you need from your mentor are sometimes in conflict. For example, you want a mentor who will be friendly and supportive and encouraging. However, you also need a mentor who will assess your progress carefully, making sound judgements, pointing out when mistakes have been made and encouraging you to rectify them. It can be hard for a mentor whom you are beginning to think of as a 'friend' to tell you that your work is not up to scratch. Your 'friend' has a responsibility for making judgements about your progress. One approach is to view your mentor as a 'critical friend'. Remember that they have your best interests at heart, but sometimes that means offering constructive criticism.

One of the major causes of conflict between mentors and their mentees is the issue of time. As a trainee teacher you spend all of your time thinking about your planning and your teaching and you are keen to discuss and share at every available opportunity. However, your mentor will have other roles within the school and cannot spend every minute they have when they are not teaching talking to you. Mentors agree to take on this role knowing that it will require a time commitment from them and, in most schools, mentors are given time each week to meet with their mentee. However, when students abuse this and constantly demand significant amounts of time, resentment can quickly build.

A professional approach

The good news is that many of these potential areas of conflict can be avoided if both parties adopt a professional approach. For the mentee, there are some points that are worth bearing in mind:

● *Your mentor has other calls on their time* – mentoring you is one thing in a long list of responsibilities for them. If you are concerned that your mentor does not have much time for you, make the most of the time that you have. For example, turn up at your mentor meeting with a focused and prioritised list of questions so that you can ensure that pressing matters are dealt with.

A newly qualified art teacher having an appraisal with a more experienced teacher
Source: Education Photos

- *You and your mentor might disagree* – that's life! There may be situations that you would handle one way and your mentor would resolve differently. However, remember that they are the one with the experience, not only of teaching but also of operating within that particular school. If they want something done a particular way, follow their advice. You will have plenty of time to make your own rules when you have a school and classes of your own.

- *You and your mentor don't have a lot of time to discuss observation feedback* – talk to your mentor about this. Perhaps they think that you are doing well and feel that they have little to contribute. Nevertheless, you do need feedback and, if you are not getting any, this should be discussed. However, think carefully about what it is that you need. Do you need detailed, written feedback from every lesson? A lot can be covered in a short conversation while you are packing away, and you can initiate that conversation.

- *You and your mentor might not get on well; it's a personality thing* – this one is tricky but, again, that's life! In your career you will encounter people in your schools that you do not get on well with: sometimes they will be individuals within your own department. This is true in any profession. If you and your mentor don't get on, you are in the lucky position of knowing that you only have to work together for a limited time, but it is up to you to make it work for that limited time. You should be able to develop a professional working relationship and a respect for their skills without needing to be their best friend.

- *Resources can be an issue* – space and materials can be in short supply. Established members of staff in your school are likely to have their own workspace, but they may not be able to provide this for you. Be prepared to 'hot desk' and ensure that you don't miss messages and memos because of the lack of a pigeon hole. If you do encounter issues like this, consider whether they are really your mentor's problem. They can't create space or make you a pigeon hole; perhaps you really need to speak to the person who looks after all the students within your school or someone on the admin team.

Stop and reflect

How good are you at dealing with conflict? Have you ever had to work alongside someone with whom you did not relate to easily? If so, what did you learn from that experience?

In a very small number of cases there may be more serious situations that cannot easily be resolved by you. Luckily these are few and far between, but when they do occur they can be the cause of much upset and worry. In these situations the main thing for you to do is to seek help and advice. There are several people who may be able to offer you support.

In your placement, in addition to your mentor, you are likely to have a professional mentor (although what this person is called can vary from school to school). It is usually their job to oversee the experience of all of the trainee teachers within the school and

Good mentoring requires great skill. How would you give feedback on a poor lesson in a way that was honest, constructive, did not damage the trainee's confidence, yet still set high standards?

Source: Pearson Education Ltd/Ian wedgewood

their role normally involves monitoring the quality of your school-based training. In some settings the professional mentor will meet with all the trainee teachers every week and spend time exploring whole-school issues with them. They may also observe your teaching, either to check on your progress or to monitor and moderate the support that you are being given by your subject mentor. The relationship between you and your professional tutor will be different from the relationship that you have with your subject mentor. He or she will see you less frequently, yet they will be actively involved in your training and have a particular interest in the quality of the experience that you are having. Therefore, if you and your mentor are struggling to build a working relationship, in the first instance you should probably speak to your professional tutor in school. They will know your mentor and the school and they are the person who is best placed to support you and attempt to resolve the issue.

You may also wish or need to speak to your academic tutor to keep them informed about the situation and perhaps seek their advice. It is also worth remembering that you would not have been knowingly placed in a difficult situation. In these rare circumstances, one of the major complicating factors is often a clash of personality and this is something that no one could have foreseen. Everyone involved will be working hard to help you; and the right support and a professional approach will go a long way to improving the situation.

Models of mentoring

'Successful people turn everyone who can help them into sometime mentors!'

(John Crosby)

Whatever your background it is likely that you are already familiar with the concept of mentoring and being mentored. Even if we were not being formally mentored, most of us can point to a time and an individual who has helped us through a new stage or challenge in our lives.

Practical task

Think back over the course of your life. Make a list of people who have influenced you, also noting down why you think that they are particularly memorable and have come to mind. Then consider *how* they helped you. Recall the form that their support took. Did they model a behaviour or practice? Did they let you get on with it and make your own mistakes? Did they encourage you to ask questions?

Synthesise your reflections to consolidate what you already know about providing effective support.

There are various approaches to mentoring. You may recognise one of the following as the model to which your own mentor seems to subscribe. Alternatively, you may recognise several of them if your mentor adopts different approaches depending on the situation.

Maynard and Furlong identify three distinct models of mentoring: the apprenticeship model, the competency model and the reflective practitioner model (1995: 17). They argue that, taken individually, each of these models may be appropriate in particular situations. However, considered together they provide an approach to mentoring that is capable of responding to the changing needs of student teachers as they develop throughout their placement. As you read about each model, consider how and when it might be useful to you.

The apprenticeship model

This model advocates that new skills are best learned 'by the emulation of experience practitioners and by supervised practice under guidance' (Hillgate Group 1989: 9). The expression 'sitting with Nellie' is often used to characterise this model as the mentee observes their more experienced mentor and learns the required skills through this observation. Maynard and Furlong point out both the strengths and weaknesses of this model; it has the advantage of giving student teachers first-hand experience of real students, situations, classrooms and subject matter (1995: 18). However, they also point out that the mentee may need help in understanding what they are observing. To sit and watch is not enough – they need an interpreter to help them understand what they are seeing.

The competency model

Supporters of this model argue that learning to teach involves practical training against a list of pre-defined competencies (e.g. the standards for QTS). In this model therefore, the mentor takes on the role of systematic trainer. For example, they would observe their mentee teaching, perhaps focusing on a predetermined area, and provide feedback in relation to the list of competencies (Maynard and Furlong 1995: 20). This model currently underpins the British system for training and assessing the development of teachers and has the advantage of giving structure and focus to the complex tasks involved in teaching and learning.

However, Maynard and Furlong caution against complacency as a result of this model. The danger is that, once the mentee has set up routines and systems that work for them, they can stop learning. They stress that the mentor, in this situation, must continue to encourage the mentee to experiment with different teaching styles and strategies (1995: 19).

Critical synthesis

In the context of thinking about how you learn to teach you should evaluate the competency model. Once again, read through all 33 of the standards for QTS.

- *Analyse each one in turn and consider how you are going to be able to meet this standard.*

- *Reflect on the role of your mentor in this process – do you want them to help you 'tick off' each one, or do you want them to do more than that? If so, what else do you want from them?*

- *Consider Maynard and Furlong's criticism of this model. Can you identify some standards where to be a good teacher you will need to go beyond this 'tick off' approach and suggest what extra help you might require?*

The reflective model

Most, if not all, Initial Teacher Education (ITE) courses promote the idea of students becoming reflective practitioners. In fact, as Maynard and Furlong point out, courses are often structured to encourage the process of reflection (e.g. through the use of blogs or coursework tasks) even without reference to the school-based mentor (1995: 21). However, they suggest that as students progress through their ITE course they need to move on from reflecting on their own teaching to focus on the learning process and how they can make it more effective. They argue that, to support this process, mentors need to move away from being a model and an instructor to being a 'co-enquirer', since a more equal and open relationship is essential if the promotion of this critical reflection is to happen (1995: 21). This is a very different relationship from those hinted at by the earlier models where the mentor offers expert example (as in the apprenticeship model) or offers support and makes judgements within the framework of a set of competencies (the competency model). This reflective model requires a spirit of openness and offers a shared journey.

Stop and reflect

If you have already started a school placement, think about the models outlined above and analyse the support that you have been receiving in the light of them. Does your mentor tend to follow just one of these or have they utilised different approaches at different points during your placement. Are they encouraging and helping you to be reflective?

The practicalities of mentoring

The responsibilities of mentors will vary from one ITE course to another. They will have responsibility for reviewing your planning, observing your teaching and giving you feedback, meeting with you regularly to discuss your progress, set targets and complete assessments. However, the frequency of meetings, the nature of the assessment, the type of support given to help with planning and the number of formal observations can vary from course to course. It is important that you know what is expected of your mentor and what they are tasked to do in relation to your training.

Supporting planning

Your mentor will be the person who helps you put the theory your have learnt about lesson planning in university-based sessions into practice. At first, they might plan lessons with you, sharing ideas and resources. However, as your progress through your placements you will quickly take responsibility for this yourself. You might still ask for advice and ideas, but you will gradually be trusted to plan your own lessons.

Some mentors (often in line with school policy) will ask you to hand in your lesson plans in advance to be checked. Don't be worried or offended by this. They are simply doing their job in supporting you. This gives them an opportunity to check your plans and make suggestions or comments for improvements where appropriate. This system has the added advantage of helping to keep you more organised! You will always be prepared a few days in advance.

The potential downside of working so closely with someone else in the planning of your lessons is that you are advised or asked to do things in a way that you wouldn't choose. Try to keep in mind that you have to conform to the school's conventions and systems and that the advice of your mentor is based on years of experience. A good mentor will let you experiment (or, more likely, encourage you to experiment) when the time is right.

Observation

Trainee teachers sometimes get very nervous about the idea of being observed while teaching, but there really is no need. It is something that you will quickly get used to and is one of the best things for helping you to make progress. You may be in a position where every lesson you teach is observed; in some placements they may leave you alone in the classroom for short periods (although if this is the case it must be easy for you to summon help if you need it). You should ensure that you know what the requirements are for your course in relation to the observation of lessons.

It is important that you make the most of your observation feedback. Consider the following:

- *Select a focus*. You are likely to learn more as a result of being observed if the observation has an agreed focus. For example, rather than having your mentor try to observe and comment on *everything* that happens in the room, decide what your priorities are. You could just focus on the student response to learning activities, or behaviour management, or teacher–student interactions, or transitions between activities; the possibilities are limitless. Consider what your current targets are and ask for feedback on those.

- *Evaluate your own lessons*. The fact that you are being observed by someone does not remove the need for you to reflect on and evaluate your own lessons. Sometimes this will be done in the light of feedback you have received from others, but try to evaluate some lessons *before* you are given feedback. This way you can see if your own conclusions match those of your observer to see how accurate your own assessments are.

- *Set targets*. Ensure that after an observed lesson targets are set. They might be in relation to that particular class, or they might focus on your planning or teaching skills. Use comments from your mentor to help you set appropriate targets to continue your development.

Mentor meetings

Again, whilst different courses have different requirements, it is likely that you will meet with your mentor on a weekly basis to check on your progress, discuss current concerns and set targets. When you are placed in a large department where you perhaps only see your busy mentor in passing each day and you may only teach one of their classes, it is very important that you have time each week to sit with them and discuss your progress.

Occasionally both the mentor and the mentee feels that a regular meeting is unnecessary, especially when the student is placed in a department that only has one or two members of staff. In these situations it is likely that the mentee will teach several lessons from their mentor's timetable and see them many times each day. In this situation, even though you have regular access to your mentor, it is still very important that you have regular, formal meetings. If everything is done informally, there is a danger that important things get overlooked, or you never have the opportunity, in an appropriate and confidential setting, to discuss your concerns.

The content and nature of these meetings will vary from situation to situation. This is a time when you are likely to review the achievements of the previous week and discuss the planning you have done for the coming week. You may also discuss your progress against the standards and consider other, whole-school activities with which you are involved. This should also be the time that you can bring up any specific concerns or questions that you have. This meeting is an important opportunity to focus on your progress; it should also be a time to set targets for the coming weeks. It is a good idea to keep notes as a record of these meetings (even if you are not required to do so). These could potentially act as a 'things to do' list, a record of current targets and a summary of your achievements (with the latter perhaps providing evidence for the QTS standards).

Case study

Alice is completing a teaching practice placement at a large comprehensive school. The school gets above average results and is judged by Ofsted to be a good school. The department in which she is working has four members of staff, and Alice is getting on well with all of them. Three members of the department have handed classes over to her for the duration of the placement, but most of her timetable is filled with her mentor's own groups. She is getting on well with her mentor. He is being very supportive, has given her access to all of the department's resources and has made her feel very welcome. She finds that the verbal feedback that he gives her after every lesson she teaches is very constructive and helpful.

However, even though Alice is now over half way through a 12-week placement, she has only had one formal mentor meeting (her university expects a meeting to take place every week). Her mentor has commented that as they are both in the same office all of the time and that she can ask him questions whenever she needs to, a weekly meeting is unnecessary. However, Alice feels that she is missing out. The conversations they have on a daily basis are often hasty and conducted in the midst of a lot of background chatter. They also tend to discuss practical issues, but they never have conversations about pedagogy, her general progress or ongoing targets (or even what those targets should be). As these meetings rarely take place, she does not have any notes from mentor meetings. She is also finding that, although his verbal feedback is very helpful, he never gives her written feedback following her lessons.

Alice does feel well supported, but she does not have a sense of her own progression. She likes both her mentor and the school very much. Therefore, although she feels that she needs to do something about this situation, she is not willing to do anything that will damage their working relationship or make her appear ungrateful.

Consider the following questions:

- *Can you identify the key issues here?*
- *Are there any other questions that you would like to ask Alice?*
- *Can you see similarities between this situation and a situation that you (or a friend) have found yourself in?*
- *Can you see a possible solution to this situation?*
- *What advice would you give to Alice?*

Assessment and target setting

A major part of your mentor's formal role is to assess your progress. This is likely to be done both informally (for example, in a quick chat about a lesson over lunch) as well as formally (such as in a formal lesson observation). The feedback you receive will also be both formative and summative.

Most of the conversations and activities you engage in with your mentor will provide you with feedback about your progress and some formative assessment of your abilities and progress. Comments following a lesson observation, a consideration of your planning in a mentor meeting or a discussion to moderate your marking are all examples of ordinary day-to-day activities which will provide you with formative feedback to help you develop and improve your skills. This formative feedback will be very valuable to you. You can both reflect on and learn from your successes and failures, and guidance from your mentor in this reflective process should enable you to get the most out of these experiences.

At certain points, this formative feedback should be formalised through appropriate target setting. Teaching is a complex activity and you cannot tackle everything at once. Following formative feedback and in discussion with your mentor you should regularly set yourself targets to help focus your development. These targets should be specific and achievable and, as you make progress, they should be regularly reviewed and revised to help you focus on the next stage of your development.

There is, necessarily, a place on teacher training courses for summative assessment. The summative assessment of your teaching is likely to be carried out by your mentor, although this may well be informed by discussions with you. It is very easy to focus too much on this and find the process very stressful. However, you should try and see it as a helpful and supportive process; comments made at the end of one placement should help you set targets for the next, or comments made at the end of the course should help approach your NQT year. As previously discussed, one of the issues here can be the fact that you are being assessed by someone with whom you have develop a close working relationship. Again, in most cases this becomes a positive thing. You have someone who knows you well and who has your best interests in mind offering an honest assessment of your progress and helping to set targets to progress you further in the future.

Practical task

What are your current targets in relation to your school placement? Where are these recorded? If you can't answer these two questions, why is that the case? Do you have targets but they are not recorded anywhere, or do you not have clear targets?

If the latter is true you need to discuss this with your mentor. You could use the 'SMART' approach to target setting. This says that targets should be:

S	Specific	The target must be clearly defined
M	Measurable	You should be able to assess in some way whether or not you have achieved your goal
A	Achievable	It must be something realistic that you can be reasonably expected to achieve given the constraints of your context
R	Relevant	It must be relevant to the context in which you are working – don't worry about the bigger picture
T	Timed	There must be an end date – there is no point setting a target that you have no chance of seeing yourself achieve.

Before you and your mentor work on your new targets, consider those listed below. Decide for yourself whether or not you think that they are SMART targets:

1. Work on behaviour management
2. Out-of-school learning opportunities – write one section of the materials for the Y7 field trip after half term (must be done by 23rd)
3. Get better at working with parents and guardians
4. Plan a lesson using the wireless laptops for my Y8 class in two weeks' time
5. Plan a sequence of lessons
6. Do some group work
7. Work on improving the behaviour of the girls in 9C over the next three weeks
8. Make use of ICT
9. Attend next week's Y10 parents' evening with the class teacher and aim to get involved in some discussions
10. Mark some Y10 mock exam papers ready to contribute to the departmental moderation meeting on 25 June.

The learning curve: stages of development

However mentoring is approached, the aim is always the same; to help you progress and develop your skills in the classroom. It is important that you see yourself making progress – both you and your mentor need to know that your hard work has not been wasted. Let us consider some common models for categorising the stages of development in teacher skills, both for those in training and for teachers further along in their career.

Maynard and Furlong's stages of development

Maynard and Furlong suggest a series of stages that they believe are experienced by many trainee teachers. Each stage has its own distinct characteristics and concerns (1995: 12).

1 **Early idealism.** This stage is one you have probably gone through before you embark on your ITE course. It is the stage when you are idealistic in your feelings towards your students and about what you hope to achieve. At this stage you have a clear image of the kind of teacher you want to be (Maynard and Furlong 1995: 12). Perhaps it was when you were at this stage that an advert attracted you to teaching (see examples below). Many of the campaigns we see encouraging people to consider the profession focus on this idealism, persuading us that we can make a difference.

2 **Survival.** This is likely to be the stage that you go through early in your teaching placements when the realities of life in the classroom quash your idealism and your main focus is on your own survival. Main concerns at this stage are likely to be on settling into life in the classroom and school, and on behaviour management (1995: 12).

3 **Recognising difficulties.** At this stage Maynard and Furlong suggested that trainee teachers are very aware of the varied demands placed on them and are keen to do well. This is the stage when they start to worry about their performance and progress and are concerned with the possibility of failing their course. At this stage you are also aware of other constraints (such as a lack of resources) that can impact upon your teaching (1995: 13).

4 **Hitting the plateau.** This is the stage when you have established what works for you. You have set in place some basic rules and techniques for managing the classroom and your teaching and you are keen to stick with it. Maynard and Furlong suggest that, at this point, trainees are likely to 'hit the plateau' (1995: 13). They refer to Feiman-Nemser and Buchmann (1987) who argued that, at this stage, trainees have difficulty in moving their focus away from themselves and their subject and onto their students and what their students need to learn. Instead they are focused on sticking to what works for them and helps them achieve their own ends.

5 **Moving on.** The final stage is the one in which trainees eventually go on to experiment within their own teaching and show concern for their students' learning. However, they point out that the level of reflection at this stage may still be shallow.

Consider where you see yourself in Maynard and Furlong's stages. This is likely to change as you develop throughout the course and be prepared to feel as though you are moving backwards as well as forwards at times. For example, you may feel as though you are at the 'recognising difficulties' or even the 'hitting the plateau' stage, but then you move to a new placement and suddenly find yourself back at the 'survival' stage. This is not a problem and you are not alone!

Conscious competence

One commonly used model for reflecting on the progress of learners is the Conscious Competence model, often attributed to Howell (1982). He highlights four stages of development through which you may pass (Table 11.1).

The above model is often illustrated with reference to learning to drive. When we are babies we don't understand the concept of driving or what it involves (stage 1). As children

Table 11.1 The Conscious Competence model

Stage 1	Unconscious incompetence	At this stage learners don't know what they don't know
Stage 2	Conscious incompetence	Learners become aware of what they don't know and how much they have to learn
Stage 3	Conscious competence	At this stage learners know the theory or have learnt the relevant skills, but perhaps can only apply this with difficulty
Stage 4	Unconscious competence	Learners have the necessary knowledge and skills and apply and practise them with ease – perhaps without really having to think about what they are doing

we may sit in the driving seat and try to move the steering wheel, but the car doesn't move and we don't understand why (stage 2). Later on we then learn to drive. As we pass our test we have all the necessary knowledge and skills, but it still requires a lot of thought and concentration (stage 3). Gradually our skill develops until we can drive easily and instinctively, without thinking through every action and manoeuvre (stage 4).

Prior to embarking on your course you were likely to have already passed through stage 1 and into stage 2. However, consider how you might work on moving from conscious incompetence into conscious competence, and then on towards unconscious competence. How could your mentor help you, in practical terms, with this challenge?

From novice to expert teacher

Another model which you might like to use to consider your progress is that outlined by Berliner (1995: 108–11). He identifies five stages of development, each characterised by some distinctive features. You may be able to relate to some of these early stages while you are completing your ITE course. However, some of these stages will only be reached by experienced practitioners.

Stop and reflect

As with the previous model it is worth evaluating your own progress and considering where you see yourself within Berliner's model – trainee teachers are likely to be at the novice, advanced beginner or maybe the competent stage, depending on where they are within their course. However, you should also assess where your mentor would be within this model; are they proficient or are they an expert? Don't be deceived by what you see. When you are watching them in the classroom their teaching may appear effortless, but they have moved through all of the previous stages to reach that level of skill.

Berliner also points out that there are differences in the way that teachers at different stages may interpret the same events (1995: 111). This is an important point for you to

Table 11.2 Berliner's Five Stages of Development model

Novice	This is the period when the beginning teacher is learning to make sense of the classroom. They are coping with the 'mechanics' of teaching and learning the new terminology associated with it. At this stage much use is often made of what Berliner describes as 'context-free rules' such as 'Give praise for right answers' (1995: 108)
Advanced beginner	At this stage knowledge and experience come together and the teacher starts to develop 'strategic knowledge' – they make decisions about when to ignore rules and when to follow them. Context is taken into account. For example, you may begin to realise that praise doesn't always work! (1995: 108–109)
Competent	Berliner identifies two distinguishing characteristics of this stage: 1. The teacher makes conscious choices about what they are going to do 2. The teacher can determine what is and what is not important. For example, individuals at this stage learn not to make mistakes with timing and pitch in lessons and make conscious decisions about lesson content (such as when to stay on a topic and when to move on). At this stage teachers are more in control and take more responsibility for what is happening in their classroom (1995: 109–110)
Proficient	Berliner says 'this is the stage at which intuition and know-how become prominent'. This is the point at which the teacher has developed a wealth of experience and can act intuitively in classroom situations. However, decisions may still be very carefully considered (1995: 110)
Expert	This is the stage at which the teacher not only acts intuitively, but also without analysis. They no longer have to think carefully about choosing their words and actions – they appear to do the job effortlessly (1995: 110–111)

consider when reflecting on your relationship with your mentor, especially when your opinions differ. Your mentor's observations on your work, particularly in the classroom, will be different from your own because they have more expertise. This is not a problem – it is an advantage. Your mentor is there to help you interpret the events that take place in your classroom. Their experience can offer you another perspective.

Challenge your thinking

In their interesting survey of 102 mentors Marion Jones and colleagues concluded:

'Regardless of the sector, in their work with trainees and newly qualified teachers, mentors drew primarily on their professional practice and personal experience acquired as teachers, which was accompanied by an assumption that practice knowledge is superior to theoretical knowledge.

The findings suggest that in addition to their teacher knowledge, mentors need to develop a critical understanding of the generic principles involved in mentoring to enable them to analyse and examine their own practice in relation to mentees' learning and alternative frameworks and models.

However, to promote critical analysis and reflection, time is a prerequisite, a precious resource which according to the vast majority of mentors is in short supply. Consequently, they tend to rely on knowledge acquired in the course of their professional practice and personal experience rather than attempt new approaches in search of solutions to problematic situations. In the light of these findings the following recommendations are made.

This study shows that understandings developed from teaching alone are insufficient to fulfil the role of mentor. The findings are of importance in developing teacher training.'

(Jones, M. *et al.*, 2005)

This study indicates that it is difficult for mentors to find the time to consider any theoretical underpinning in their work with trainee teachers. There appears to be an assumption that their practical experiences of teaching are more important than any theoretical knowledge linked to supporting adult learners.

- What is your view of this issue?
- Do you ever engage with your mentor in discussions related to your learning and development?
- Have you ever discussed the mentoring role and any underpinning models or principles?
- As a potential future mentor do the findings of Jones and her colleagues have any implications for you? Should they?

Summary

The relationship that you have with your mentor is likely to be one of the most important you form while you are completing your training. Studies suggest that it is an important and effective form of supporting new entrants to the profession (Hobson *et al*. 2008: 209). Your mentor is your way into the school; they will help you to settle and they will offer you every kind of support (emotional and practical). Hobson *et al*. draw attention to research highlighting the potential of mentors help to develop their mentees' skills, particularly in the areas of behaviour/classroom management and time management. They also point out the important role played by mentors in helping their mentees adapt to the norms, standards and expectations of both the profession in general and the school in particular (2008: 209).

We have considered the tensions and conflicts that can occur within this relationship, but it is also worth remembering that the vast majority of students have a good working relationship with their mentor. In some cases the friendship that has formed lasts far longer than the duration of the placement. The 'critical friend' simply becomes a friend; although they are a friend who does the same job as you and with whom you can share ideas, resources and tales from the classroom!

The most important thing to remember is that mentoring is a process. It requires active involvement and engagement on the part of both mentor and mentee. Your mentor is there to help, to explain, to advise, to recommend and, in the end, to assess. However, you have to take responsibility for your own development. You have to ask for help when it is needed, listen to the explanations, take the advice, heed the recommendations and, when the assessment process is over, actively engage in target setting.

References

Berliner, D. (1995) 'Teacher Expertise', 107–113 in Moon, B. And Shelton Mayes, A. (eds) (1995) *Teaching and Learning in the Secondary School,* London: RoutledgeFalmer.

Feiman-Nemser, D. and Buchmann, M. (1987) 'When is student teaching teacher education?', *Teaching and Teacher Education,* 3(4): 255–73.

Hillgate Group (1989) *Learning to Teach,* London: The Claridge Press.

Hobson, A., Ashby, P., Malderez, A. and Tomlinson, P. (2008) 'Mentoring beginning teachers: What we know and what we don't', *Teaching and Teacher Education,* 25(2009): 207–16.

Howell, W.S. (1982) *The empathic communicator,* University of Minnesota: Wadsworth Publishing Company.

Jones, M., Foster, R., Groves, N., Parker, G., Rutter, T. and Straker, K. (2005) 'How do mentors know what they know? An investigation into mentors' professional knowledge base', TDA 2005. Available at: *http://www.ttrb.ac.uk/viewArticle.aspx?contentId=11286.*

Kerry, T. and Shelton Mayes, A. (1995) *Issues in Mentoring.* London: Routledge.

Maynard, T. and Furlong, J. (1995) 'Learning to teach and models of mentoring', 10–24 in Kerry, T. and Shelton Mayes, A. (1995) *Issues in Mentoring,* London: Routledge.

Moon, B. and Shelton Mayes, A. (eds) (1995) *Teaching and Learning in the Secondary School,* London: RoutledgeFalmer.

TDA (2007) *Professional Standards for Teachers: Why sit still in your career?* London: Training and Development Agency for Schools.

TDA (2009) *Guidance to accompany the Professional Standards for Qualified Teacher Status and Requirements for Initial Teacher Training,* London: Training and Development Agency for Schools.

TDA Advertising (2009) TDA [on-line]. Last accessed 19 February 2010 at: *www.tdanewadvertising. com/uyh_pressads.htm.*

Chapter 12

School structures, leadership and management

Learning outcomes

By the end of this chapter, you will have an understanding of:

→ How you can expect headteachers and leadership teams to approach the management of secondary schools

→ How leadership of schools has changed or 're-engineered' schools

→ How the staffing of schools has changed and is likely to change in the future

→ The different 'types' of school now operating in England and Wales

→ How the expectation of you as a 'leader in learning' is likely to affect your approach to teaching practice, your NQT year and your future career

→ How your department in school is affected by leadership strategies

Introduction

'Leadership is essentially the process of building and maintaining a sense of vision, culture and interpersonal relationships, whereas management is the co-ordination, support and monitoring of organisational activities. To enact both roles successfully requires a careful balancing act.'

(Day and Harris, National College for School Leadership – NCSL)

Effective head teachers will have a clear vision for the school they lead shared with all stake-holders. Where this is likely to be successful for the school, the vision will be articulated often in different ways by staff across the organisation from deputy headteacher to caretaker and from head of year to teaching assistants and lunchtime supervisors. Most headteachers will be delighted to engage you in conversation about the school's 'direction of travel'. If this has been established through open discussion and consensus, then trainees and NQTs can begin their work with clarity of expectation. If you are able to interpret the 'leadership vision' and see how you can contribute to its achievement by participating in activity in school, you will quickly sense a drive and common purpose. If it is in line with your own philosophy and approaches to children's learning, you might sense this is the school for you!

In this chapter I will share with you the leadership views of headteachers and how a new approach to school leadership is shaping schools and changing the role of the teacher and their relationships with their learners and other professionals on the school staff. As a *leader in learning,* you will be included in the leadership challenge. Leadership teams in the modern school will welcome trainees and NQTs to bring them solutions not problems towards accomplishing the vision for the school and optimum outcomes for the students of the school. Inclusion for staff as well as students has become a central issue. 'Every Child Matters' (DfES, 2004) and all teachers will lead the learners to be the best they can be.

Schools are complex organisations and have to be seen in their historical, social and political context. Their management is about 'getting stuff done' which will help move the school in the right direction determined by the leader(s). Good headteachers will always be looking to delegate the power to lead within clear parameters. One head teacher I met recently spoke of the 'distribution of leadership' in his school. His goal was to empower chosen staff (not necessarily senior) to lead initiatives which would contribute to the school's mission.

This concept of 'distributed leadership' is, according to Harris (2004) very much in vogue. It can be defined as: 'Engaging expertise wherever it exists within the organization rather than seeking this only through formal position or role' (Harris, 2004). This may be in sharp contrast to your notion of hierarchical systems of management. The approach is more collective and participative and helps to ensure that school leaders are more in touch with the people and networks within their organisation. Also, to ensure that such informal but effective systems do not confuse, it is essential for the organisation to have very strong shared goals and purposes.

Some authors have gone further in highlighting the importance of distributed management approaches within schools. Indeed Glickman and colleagues (Glickman *et al.,* 2001) have placed this approach to leadership at the top of their list of characteristics marking out improving schools. Such approaches demand confident managers who have trust in their colleagues.

Appointing the 'right' staff to the 'right' job, and continuing professional development are central in this. You might imagine that preparing for an interview for a post a school with this as a leadership culture would be interesting and challenging!

Practical task

- Write a list of experiences you would like to be able to include in or add to your CV to demonstrate you could lead initiatives.
- Can you 'articulate your vision' on becoming a teacher?
- Prepare a statement you might include in your job applications.
- Do you feel comfortable with the term, 'Leader in Learning' as applied to the teacher?
- Does it change your vision of what becoming a teacher means for you?

According to Hammer and Champy (1993), headteachers are engaged in re-engineering not re-structuring: 'We re-engineer how work is done, how outputs are created from inputs'. They argued that changing staffing structure from 'departments' to 'faculties' did little to change the learning experience of most children in school.

The school planning cycle

The cycle of Ofsted inspections expected in a modern school is accepted by many leadership teams with a professional resignation. Some might regret the fact that Ofsted can be the driver for schools' strategic planning. To be positive, inspection will be seen by some as an opportunity to self-evaluate and improve. Effective headteachers are always 'ready' for inspection in the sense that their vision and direction of travel mentioned above is shared and in evidence through every planned activity for the children. Documents are constantly reviewed in the context of the vision and the SEF (Self-Evaluation Form) is a 'work in progress' not just an Ofsted document to be dusted down for a ceremonial presentation to HMI every four years or so. In well-managed schools, the SEF is revisited and updated often with information from every aspect of the school and therefore from every member of staff and other stakeholders. To be effective, the SEF must be 'owned' by all in the school and have relevance to the planned activities for children. If it is not provided as part of your induction, ask to read the SEF in schools where you are placed.

Put simply, the SEF comprises the school's own judgements in various aspects of its performance. These are reported under the following six headings:

- Achievement and standards
- Personal development and wellbeing
- Quality of provision
- Curriculum and other activities
- Care, guidance and support
- Leadership and management.

Ofsted will visit the school and judge performance against this self-evaluation, also reporting on 'value for money' and the school's 'capacity to improve'.

Many of the judgments arrived at are informed by the growing body of data available to school leaders. The ability to measure performance has enabled schools to assess the effectiveness of strategies designed to affect change. This informs strategic decisions for the next round and so on. The consequence has been to radically alter the approach to school management. This has also had a significant influence on the structure of school staffing and its deployment.

For example: data might indicate that the GCSE performance of white boys from an identified social background lags behind other groups in the school. When analysed further, the contextual value added data might also identify this group as 'underachieving' when compared with other distinguishable groups of students.

Practical task

Before reading any further, make a list of possible actions you think could be appropriate in response to this evidence.

A team of teachers might well agree a package of actions designed to improve this performance indicator including:

- Involving the learning mentor in supporting learning
- Involving the year leader and student support officers in personal support
- Withdrawal from certain lessons for extra support
- Targeted support from teacher assistants
- Introducing such boys to a mentor inside and/or outside school to track and encourage progress
- Single sex lessons
- Small-group work
- After-school or lunchtime work
- Sixth form support
- SEN support
- Looking at rewards and sanctions to encourage the group.

Once implemented effectively, the results for the next cohort could then be analysed and compared with prior attainment. You will begin to appreciate how such an approach to affecting change can inform decision making. Data can be compelling evidence and this is a powerful drive for change and encouragement to achieve improvement.

I hope you will also see how this strategic approach to whole-school development could be readily adapted to provide a model for your own work with classes of children. While on school placement, find out the data available to help build a profile of the children you teach. You will then be in a position to treat each individual child as an individual to be valued. Personalised learning comes into sharper focus.

Stop and reflect

Reflect on your experiences of teaching within a school:

● Find out the information available to teachers about the children they teach.

● Evaluate these data sets and begin to synthesise ways in which the information could inform your planning and preparation, your teaching and assessment.

The School Improvement Plan (SIP) is a document presenting the professional response to the SEF and/or Ofsted Report following an inspection. It will detail the steps a school plans to make in certain targeted areas of performance for the next stage in its development. With a school that is in Special Measures or Notice to Improve (both Grade 4, Ofsted), it might take the form of a 'Recovery Plan'.

Like the good teacher, schools know that effective and open self-evaluation is the key to improvement. You are more immediately aware of some of your strengths and areas for development in your teaching practice than any school-based mentor or visiting tutor. Constantly reviewing your teaching and the planned activities you prepare for children against your learning objectives will inform progress. So it is with a school planning its cycle of actions – see Figure 12.1.

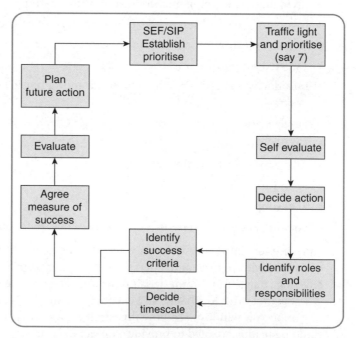

Figure 12.1 Diagram (cycle) with shared vision

Departmental reviews

The SEF requires each subject department within the school to feed in information, data and action plans as will each section of the school from KS1 to Sixth form where appropriate. To improve the quality of teaching and learning, most schools will enact departmental reviews including a full lesson observation cycle. This is almost a 'mini internal Ofsted inspection' of each subject area of the school, one at a time. This ongoing process aims to have a positive and constant impact on standards of teaching and learning in the school.

A member of the leadership team will assume the responsibility of leading a departmental review as part of the cycle. The review will comprise lesson observation of all teachers within the department by the whole leadership team. Prior to the round of observations, children's work samples, staff questionnaires and student questionnaires will have been seen and analysed. Typically, reviews will be completed in a week and a report produced to be agreed with the Head of Department. This period is characterised by a consolidated and energetic focus on teaching and learning across the departmental team. There will be an intensive exchange of professional judgements following lesson observations and a gathering of data to inform judgements not only about the department as a whole but also relating to individuals. As a trainee teacher, you might feel sometimes that you alone have the pressure of lesson observation and judgement. This is not the case and will proceed throughout your professional career. Senior teachers and department heads often remark on how they admire trainee teachers' approach to lesson observation, which is such a routine part of your training, evaluation and improvement. Trainee teachers, newly qualified teachers and established teachers alike are now used to being observed against core professional standards.

Practical task

- In your opinion, in planning and in process, what are the characteristics of effective lesson observation?
- In your opinion, in planning and in process, what are the characteristics of successful lesson feedback?

Select from your teaching files a lesson observation and feedback you judge to be good practice or poor practice.

- Try to identify why this is your view.
- Did you feel the same at the time the observation took place?

During a review, the department can feel 'under the cosh'. Teachers are proud of their work, which is highly personal to them and involves a major personal investment in the planning of lessons and in the relationships they establish with groups of learners. Being an observer requires sensitivity and high levels of professionalism. If undertaken in an atmosphere of rigorous professionalism, reviews can be highly effective in identifying a set of imperatives from which the need for planned action is clear.

There is no doubt that a culture of openness is being established in schools where this is the case. Teachers are increasingly accepting of lesson observation, seeing its importance in school improvement. From a career point of view, too, observations of colleagues' teaching informs the performance-management process. Where teachers wish to move beyond the 'threshold' of main pay scale (six levels) to the upper pay scale they, like trainees, must present evidence of their professional standards. Even teachers with reservations see the benefits of sharing best practice and professional judgements about teaching and learning.

Stop and reflect

- Consider the value of departmental review.
- Draw up a list of actions which might arise from a departmental review as described above.
- Reflect on how each action could improve the quality of teaching and learning in the department.
- Evaluate your own approach to wider-scale planning. How could you contribute to departmental and school improvement planning?

The re-engineering of schools: where you might fit

During the nineteenth and twentieth centuries, schools took on the organisational structures seen in industry and other large institutions which aimed to maximise control: that is, a formal hierarchical structure where power and responsibility as well as work were devolved 'down' a chain of command (see Figure 12.2). Roles were clear and decisions more often than not made 'top-down'. In time, the support work of a school became recognised by the creation of 'pastoral' structures running alongside the 'academic'. Power lay at the top of the pyramid, talent and initiative could be stymied.

'Knowing one's place' was relatively simple for the newly qualified teacher who would take up their position in the pastoral system as a proud first-year (Y7) form tutor and be given their timetable for *real* teaching by their head of department. There was a loud 'splash' as the novice teacher submerged in 'the deep end', hopefully to surface sometime before autumn half-term. Advice from colleagues would run something like '. . . oh and don't smile before Christmas!' as they disappeared into a smoke-filled staff room to take up their established seat by the fire! Forgive my hyperbole.

Managers of these '. . . directive and risk averse bureaucratic structures' (Davies and Ellison 1997) were hardly promoting a climate ripe for the educational 'entrepreneurship' associated with the post-Blair period. The effective modern school leader, according to Davies and Ellison (1997), will understand three key perspectives; global, school and individual.

Now the focus in education is on learning and teaching and 'Every Child Matters' (DfES, 2004) – as if we ever needed reminding. Schools have been engaged in 'stripping away

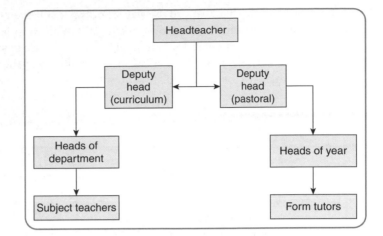

Figure 12.2 **Traditional hierarchical school management structure**

hierarchical structures and reaffirming the skills and talents of students and teachers at all levels' (Dalton *et al.*, 2001). Ofsted praised the work of the headteacher of an 'outstanding school' in a northern city saying,

> *'Together with his very able senior team he is providing very clear educational direction and has created a common sense of purpose among staff. He has very astutely identified influential staff and empowered them to lead key developments. By devolving some responsibilities, he is not only building capacity within the organisation, but has also secured exceptional levels of commitment from staff right across the school. The introduction of the 'change team' ensures that staff at all levels feel consulted and part of the decision-making process.'*

Much of the drive for change in *self-managed schools* at this time is encapsulated here, I believe. Freedom from local government bureaucracy would enable schools to respond to change with agility. Hentschke and Davies (in Davies and Ellison, 1997) use the analogy of the behaviour of minnows (small schools responding sharply and independently but in similar directions to major influences) and that of whales (local authorities, ponderous and slow to adapt). Market forces and the emphasis on competition and consumer empowerment (Davies and Ellison 1997) continue to have huge influence upon schools' missions and how schools achieve their goals.

For the newly qualified teacher or trainee in school, times are challenging and exciting. You will be 'empowered' if you know what you wish to achieve within the improvement plan of the school. Success is not to be identified through the quality of teaching but rather through the quality of learning. Each individual child in your care is an exception to be valued against her or his own ability and potential. Schools are no longer rigidly structured in a way designed to control workers in a nineteenth-century cotton mill. The modern head will appoint highly skilled teachers who will benefit, when freed from management layers, to be more autonomous and able to respond to the needs of their learners. This has changed the way schools operate, even the way they look and feel. This change has been swift and overarching and might surprise even the youngest of the readers of this book! Those looking for a simple structure to slot into will need to think more imaginatively about their mission in teaching and the role they wish to play in leading initiatives for successful student outcomes.

Critical synthesis

The following is taken from Transformational Leadership *by Lynn Balster Liontos (1992)* (http://www.vtaide.com/png/ERIC/Transformational-Leadership.htm)

'The problem, explain Douglas Mitchell and Sharon Tucker (1992), is that we have tended to think of leadership as the capacity to take charge and get things done. This view keeps us from focusing on the importance of teamwork and comprehensive school improvement. Perhaps it is time, they say, to stop thinking of leadership as aggressive action and more as a way of thinking – about ourselves, our jobs, and the nature of the educational process. Thus, "instructional leadership" is "out" and "transformational leadership" is "in"'.

Research the link above, and any related resources you can find, to consider what transformational leadership is and how it has evolved.

The reference dates from 1992 – do you recognise a move from instructional management to transformational management where you teach? Do you recognise good practice in transformational leadership in your day-to-day working in schools?

If yes, reflect on its impact. If no, analyse why not.

The teacher as a leader of a professional team

The reasons for change are disparate and complex. It is difficult to separate and identify cause and effect. Change does not happen in isolation. Once it was clear to the developed world that their economic and natural resources were in decline and that development of their human resources was central for success, the role of schools came into sharp focus. There was the perceived need to reskill teachers. Headteachers were challenged to measure teachers' performance in their schools and enhance performance through rewards and sanctions. Since the 1988 Education Reform Act, subsequent initiatives linked inspection with performance management, target setting and league tables. In 1997 Tony Blair won the election for Labour on the platform of 'Education, education and education'. In 1998 the Green Paper, 'Teachers: Meeting the Challenge of Change' made no secret of Labour's ambitions and determination.

Once schools have placed teaching and learning at the centre of their planning, the role of the teacher is clear. What had been the case was that teachers had become 'too many things to too many people' (See Chapter 4 Every Child Matters: a holistic view of the school). From the 1960s the role of the teacher has widened, responsibilities have mushroomed! In an attempt to be 'child-centred' and to compensate for social and economic deprivation, some have argued that teachers had neglected their role as leaders of learning. Their time, it was thought, was being spread too thinly across the competing roles of counsellor, behaviour manager, surrogate parent, social worker and others. Imaginative staffing solutions are now being used by headteachers as a response to these diverse and perceived needs in children without necessarily allocating teacher resources to them. Trade unions were not slow to see implications for pay and job specifications as heads were increasingly involved in performance management, departmental reviews, lesson observation and sharing professional judgements. Twenty-four tasks were identified as inappropriate for teachers. The result of all these influences was the creation of a set of new colleagues in school, the teacher becoming the leader of this team of professionals.

Most radical perhaps was the introduction of 'Student Support Officers' (SSOs) working with pastoral year leaders. Now, of course, the idea is commonplace and you will find many variations on the theme of SSO in the schools you work in. Heads were enabled to free the year leader to focus on achievement and learning outcomes. With their SSOs, year leaders would be charged with identifying under-achievement and designing strategies with which to affect improvement. Evidence (often in the form of data) would inform action and measure success. This information would be managed by the new data-handling office and delivered to the year leader by the SSOs. In many schools this has resulted in a culture shift – a 're-engineering'. The pastoral role is envisaged as becoming more strategic for more of the time, targeting resources on specific students for a specific purpose. This replaces the hackneyed cliché of the well-meaning and rather harassed year tutor reacting to the random irritations of teachers coping with naughty children in 'their' year group! Being more proactive in measuring outcomes and designing bespoke improvement programmes responding to student needs feels professional, strategic and almost scientific! Schools are looking and feeling very different. Year leaders are now more likely to know about the level of achievement of their students both absolutely against national targets and also in terms of contextual value added. They will have clear answers to questions about student performance and how this is being improved for all children in the year group. 'Inclusion meetings' comprising learning mentors, SSOs, TAs and SEN staff are informing tutor meetings with data and agreed individual and group action plans for targeted students. All this information is, of course, shared with the learner to motivate and speed progress.

Replacing year tutors, SSOs are able to pursue behaviour and other support issues without the hindrance and distractions of a teaching timetable. They are available to 'man the office', responding to children and parents for a greater proportion of the schoolday and at other times. They are also able to complete the many bureaucratic tasks required of year leader officer performing some of these during teacher holidays. These officers are often young graduates (not QTS) with the time and energy to 'walk the corridors' with a commitment to working with young people. In my experience, and perhaps unsurprisingly, many decide later to enrol for QTS courses.

When training or as an NQT, you will need to be aware of the staff available to you in supporting your work. You will already be aware of the Professional Standards for Qualified Teacher Status (*www.tda.gov.uk/teachers/professionalstandards/standards/attributes/relationships/qts.aspx*). Q20 requires teachers to be aware of the varied roles of their colleagues in school. Q32 and Q33 lay emphasis on a 'team of professionals', identifying and responding to children's needs and the leading role of the teacher in coordinating this team and ensuring excellent communication between the members.

There can be no doubt that this aspect of a teacher's role in being aware of the work of fellow professionals and leading the team is vital for the schools of the twenty-first century to flourish. While on school-based training, you will become aware of the relationship between your work and the support available via some or all of the following:

- Learning mentors
- Special educational needs team members (learning support)
- Student support officers
- TAs (teacher assistants)
- HLTAs (higher level teacher assistants)
- ICT technicians
- D&T, science, music, performing arts and other specialist technicians
- Librarians
- Cover supervisors (largely replacing supply teachers).

This support can make all the difference if managed well through good communication and planning. The challenge for the teacher is to involve support professionals in conversations about individual students and their learning. Teacher-support officers need to be fully informed of every aspect of your planning and clear as to expectations before, during and following lessons. If this is not the case, then support can be fragmented and disjointed and cause confusion. Consistency and clarity of purpose for student and leaders of learning will be the result of a more collaborative, 'joined-up' approach.

Once another adult is in the room, the atmosphere and 'dynamic' will be changed. Your job is to ensure this is an enhancement. They will become involved in aspects of the lesson. You need to plan this involvement for optimum impact on student outcomes by deploying the facilitator's strengths and minimising the effects of their limitations.

Case study

Each of the following case studies is a genuine example from initial teacher training in the UK. The situations have all happened to teachers – some may even have already occurred in your own experience. Read through the case study scenarios and then reflect on the questions below each one.

During a trainee's final placement he became aware that on the class list supplied by the SSO a member of his Y8 group has a visual impairment. He was informed by his Head of Faculty that a trained member of the SEN team would be available for some (but not all) of his lessons with this group. The trainee urgently wanted to seek help and support but was unsure whom to contact. His mentor was supportive but not known as an expert in SEN, and the school's management structure had not been fully explained and he didn't know who was responsible for SEN within the school.

- Suggest a strategy for managing this situation for the best outcome for the student, the trainee and the school.

As part of a whole-school initiative to raise attainment, the senior learning mentor of your school is attached to your Y10 group where there are several boys identified as under-achieving, largely due to behavioural issues. You have been having difficulties with individuals in the class and finding it problematic to settle them and focus them on tasks. They are not seriously disruptive but do involve you in 'fire fighting' to maintain order.

- Who in the school might you have raised this issue with since identifying it?
- How would you feel about a senior member of staff being in lessons with you?
- What would be your strategy for handling this situation?

During a whole-school briefing a deputy headteacher at your school announces a major change to the curriculum. Subject areas are to be merged and there is to be a shift in emphasis towards vocational courses and work-based learning. It is clear from conversations after the meeting that very few staff knew of the changes, including middle managers. The deputy headteacher announces a very tight deadline and states that some training days have been organised and one of the assistant headteachers will be responsible for coordinating the changes.

- What models and styles of leadership and management appear to be evident in the school?
- If you were one of the middle managers how would you feel about this model of change?
- If you were the headteacher of the school how might you have promoted the change in a more participative manner?
- If you were the assistant headteacher now in change of the initiative how would you approach the change and what resistance might you expect?

The future

The focus for school management will continue to be effective learning and teaching monitored through measures of student outcomes. The Ofsted concern with a school's 'capacity to improve' is already resulting in change. Clearly, if the belief is that a poorly performing school does not have the capacity to improve from within, external help is required. 'Clusters' of schools (now termed 'families') offer opportunities where expertise can be co-opted by one school from another. Leaders in 'Outstanding Schools' receiving a grade 1 for inspection are being appointed as NLEs (National Leaders in Education) and allocated to spend a number of days a week working with the leadership teams and staff of less well-performing schools in the area or further afield. It will be interesting to see how these so-called 'Super Heads' go about the task of managing change in a very different environment from the school they will continue to lead part time. What influence will their part-time absence have on their 'home' school? Will it encourage development and growth among the deputies and assistants left with gaps to fill, or will it confirm the Ofsted view that the school leader is key to school performance? Will the host school leaders resent the 'interloper' or welcome a fresh view and additional proven leadership talent? Will the NLE simply apply their tried and tested 'formula' or assess the needs of this very different school anew?

I believe that headteachers will increasingly look to appoint leaders of specific projects within the school for a focused period of time. These strategic leadership posts will

**Many schools are changing their appearance
and enhancing their facilities. What is changing
in terms of what is done inside and how is it
managed?**
Source: Archimage/Albany

reflect school priorities as indicated through the processes discussed earlier. Money will
follow priority as indicated by student performance. Improvement will be rewarded both
in terms of school income and career progression for teachers. A 'market drive' is likely
to continue in our schools into the near future. Headteachers will be keen to demonstrate to Ofsted that their schools have developed what was always good in the school
and have responded to areas for development through the School Improvement Plan
and can evidence targeted improvements through student attainment data.

For several years 'teaching and learning' working groups of schools have led change
and innovation in schools. These are developing into what are sometimes called 'innovations groups' and will continue in the future looking at learning styles, VAK and ICT.
The headteacher might invite staff to join the 'Blue Sky' group or the 'Change Team'.

Leaders in learning will be active in these groups. Their goal is for teaching to be innovative and varied and highly responsive to the identified needs of the students they
teach. They might decide to focus their CPD on Master's-level modules in innovations
in learning and teaching. As a trainee or NQT, you might wish to establish yourself in
these groups as a leader of learning. The drive at the moment is towards teaching becoming a 'Master's profession'.

Curriculum change is constant. At present the most coveted student outcome is students who have 'learned to learn'. You will come across schools where a 'foundation year' has been designed in Y7. Often this will focus a few specialist teachers to welcome and successfully induct Y6 students from their primary schools. Projects or themes will 'carry' the knowledge and skills content of the curriculum. The aim is a carefully planned transition enabling students to settle quickly into a new environment (the 'big' school) and adjust to new expectations. Learning new skills of enquiry and using new teaching and learning facilities and materials available in the school will be central in trying to produce a more autonomous learner able to access information and find their way around a large organisation. This transitional Y7 leaves only two years to cover the KS3 agenda.

Some schools are reporting excellent outcomes resulting from 'vertical'-form groups comprising students of all age groups in the school. Younger students are provided with role models willing and energetic in passing on their experience. Older children respond positively to their responsibilities as senior students. Similarly, look out in schools for work with single-sex groups in certain subjects and for the innovative use of larger spaces in the teaching of large groups for parts of the curriculum.

Some schools are introducing GCSE work in Y9 in targeted subjects. Imaginative timetable scheduling is enabling schools to offer identified Y10 students time in college on vocational courses with minimum disruption to students' GCSE 'diet'. 'Fun' or 'Free and Easy' Fridays or a two-week timetable model are working in some schools to offer a more varied experience to children. Schools are increasingly working with partners to develop their own vocational programmes or are working collaboratively. The 14–19 agenda and the new Diplomas are already influencing curriculum design.

What is clear is that there are now many 'types' of schools serving children and their families in communities around the country. The distinction between state schools and independent schools remains useful, but the boundaries are a little more blurred than in the past. A clear understanding here will help you in deciding the kind of school you might wish to start and develop your career in.

Local Authority (LA) secondary schools dominate in number. These can be foundation schools, community schools, voluntary controlled schools, voluntary aided schools or special schools. The organisation of these schools varies according to the degree of LA and/or governor ownership of the land and buildings; the funding of the school; the employment of staff; adherence to the National Curriculum and design of the admissions policy. Roles of the governing body of a school have changed dramatically in recent years. Building Schools for the Future (BSF) is the biggest ever school-buildings investment programme (at time of writing). The aim is to rebuild or renew nearly every secondary school in England. PFI (the Private Funding Initiative) has altered the way an LA school utilises and manages its buildings and grounds.

Secondary schools not maintained by LAs include independent schools, city technology colleges, city academies and special schools not maintained by the LA. The motives and genesis of each are as diverse and varied as the opinions about their place in our educational system. They all employ teachers and are engaged in teaching and learning.

The existence of the 'Bog Standard Comprehensive', surely one of Alistair Campbell's least distinguished sound-bites of 2001, was also disputed by the then Education Secretary, David Blunkett. The influence of types of school on issues such as student learning, parental choice, curriculum organisation and place of employment is profound.

Practical task

Find out about the types of school outlined here. Design a table to distinguish these schools in terms of:

- Ownership of the grounds and buildings
- Governance of daily activity
- School funding
- Employment of staff
- Provision of services, e.g. Psychological and SEN
- Adherence to the National Curriculum
- Admissions policy.

Issues for the future in our schools are likely to focus around those 'hard to reach', bottom 10 per cent of our children where targeting of resources seems to have made little difference to their achievement during recent years. Widening participation initiatives seem to have made little impact where some postcode areas, family occupations and socio-economic groupings are concerned. Governments have continued to look to education as the 'great leveller' and promoter of social justice and mobility. It is hard to deny the cry for equality of opportunity in education, but it is clearly difficult to deliver.

Challenge your thinking

Building Schools for the Future (BSF) has had many visual effects on the school landscape – new buildings, enhanced resources and stunningly visual open spaces. This has a downside, though. The following is a quote from a report by PricewaterhouseCoopers LLP (2008).

Suggestions for the future

- Schools say that the BSF programme costs them significantly more in staff time than their Local Authority provides in funding. Frequently, however, schools do not have documentary evidence on costs, and provide estimates based on the proportion of time reportedly spent. Local Authorities should work with schools to put in place appropriate cost modelling systems to ensure current and future participants understand the scale of investment required and are able to track it through the various stages of the process. It would be helpful as part of this process to examine the relative merits of current approaches tried by schools, such as whether it is more cost effective to appoint dedicated resource (e.g. an operations manager) or to distribute responsibility across the SLT.
- Schools going through the programme (particularly refurbishment projects) may face considerable disruption in terms of the day-to-day running of the school. Schools that have not already done so should ensure their input to BSF explicitly includes remitting someone to monitor and document the impact on staff and student morale and on student attainment.
- Case study evidence suggests that the disruption caused by building works has the potential to have a greater impact in lower performing schools than in other schools.

In line with the key performance indicator on minimising disruption, it is important that LAs and construction partners work particularly closely with these schools to put in place measures to minimise the impact on teaching and learning.

- Whilst head teachers should be encouraged to see the programme as an opportunity for professional development of their staff, adequate support should be provided to staff to ensure that any increased workload does not have a negative impact on teaching and learning.
- Good practice needs to be disseminated locally to schools on managing the additional workload involved, in order to ensure that members of staff (particularly at SLT level) are not disproportionately loaded. LAs should take the lead in this, involving other stakeholders as appropriate.

(PricewaterhouseCoopers LLP, 2008: vi)

Consider the implications of being a headteacher of a school undergoing major refurbishment as part of BSF funding.

- What key issues would concern you, despite the potential advantages?
- What would you do to prepare staff and students so they can help to minimise disruption during building?
- As a leader, what would be your priorities before, during and after a major BSF build?

Summary

School leadership has changed in recent years and there is the near certainty of further change. A recent University of Manchester report on school leadership for the NCSL revealed:

'There are significant changes in leadership and management roles and the responsibilities of those working in schools: head teachers have been drawn into significant cross-boundary leadership activity, connecting at a strategic level with governors, other services, the wider community and local and national agencies. They have needed to develop skills as negotiators, facilitators and brokers within often diffuse relationships with minimal history and competing agendas. This has provided a range of opportunities and challenges for other senior and middle-level leaders in schools.'

(Chapman *et al.*, 2007)

Schools operate in a 'performance culture' (Gleeson and Husbands, 2001). Leaders are looking for NQTs to lead learning and make profound contributions to fulfilling the mission of the school. There will be new staffing structures with rewards and incentives for highly performing teachers and a 'fast track' through the NCSL (National College for School Leadership) for those with leadership potential. Increasing use is already being made of ICT, and there is a culture of ambition and performance. As a trainee teacher or NQT, have no doubt that you will be able to grasp these opportunities. Your enthusiasm, energy and personal commitment and vision will be advantageous from the moment you take up your first post. Begin to identify those areas of your professional practice where you wish to make your mark. It is my earnest hope that readers will be excited by the challenges and opportunities ahead and that school-based training will enable you to develop your interest as a leader in learning.

References

Barker, Bernard (2005) *Transforming Schools – Illusion or Reality*, Stoke on Trent, UK, and Sterling, USA: Trentham Books.

Bennett, N., Crawford, M. and Riches, C. (ed) (1994) *Improving Educational Management Through Research and Consultancy*, London: Paul Chapman in association with the Open University.

Bush, T. (1995) *Theories of Educational Management*, London: Harper and Row.

Chapman, C., Ainscow, M., Bragg, J., Gunter, H., Hull, J., Mongon, D., Muijs, D. and West, M. (2007) *Emerging patterns of school leadership: Current practice and future directions*: NCSL at *http://www.nationalcollege.org.uk/index/leadershiplibrary/leadingschools/leading-change/understanding-your-school-context/modelsofleadership.htm*

Dalton, I., Faweett, R. and Wast-Burnham, J. (eds) (2001). *Schools for the 21st Century*, London: Pearson Education.

Davies, Brent and Ellison, Linda (1997) *School Leadership for the 21st Century*, London and New York: Routledge.

Day, C. and Harris, A. (2009) 'Effective School Leadership National College for School Leadership', *http://www.nationalcollege.org.uk/media/416/99/effective-school-leadership.pdf*. Accessed October 2009.

DfES (2004) *Every Child Matters: Change for Children*, London: DfES. Also available at *http://www.everychildmatters.gov.uk*.

Gleeson, Dennis and Husbands Chris (eds) (2001) *The Performing School – Managing, Teaching and Learning in a Performing Culture*, London and New York: Routledge Falmer.

Glickman, C., Gordon, S. and Ross-Gordon, J. (2001) *Supervision and Instructional Leadership: A Developmental Approach*, Boston, MA: Alleyn & Bacon.

Hammer, M. and Champy, J. (1993) *Re-engineering the Corporation: A Manifesto for Business Revolution*, New York: Harper Collins.

Harris, A. (2004) 'Distributed Leadership and School Improvement: Leading or Misleading', *Educational Management and Administrative and Leadership*, 32(1): 11–24.

Liontos, L. B. (1992) *Transformational Leadership*, available at *http://www.vtaide.com/png/ERIC/Transformational-Leadership.htm*

PricewaterhouseCoopers LLP (2008) *Department for Children, Schools and Families Evaluation of Building Schools for the Future – 2nd Annual Report*.

Web resources

http://www.ncsl.org.uk/

http://www.everychildmatters.gov.uk/

http://www.ofsted.gov.uk/

http://www.tda.gov.uk/teachers/professionalstandards/standards/attributes/relationships/qts.aspx

http://www.dcsf.gov.uk/14-19/index.cfm?sid=3&pid=224&ctype=None&ptype=Contents

http://www.vtaide.com/png/ERIC/Transformational-Leadership.htm

Chapter 13

Collaborative working

Learning outcomes

By the end of this chapter, you will have an understanding of:

→ Collaborative on-line networking tools to promote the sense of community associated with collaborative working

→ How synchronous and asynchronous on-line tools can be used to encourage and conduct collaborative working practices

Introduction

The aim of this chapter is to introduce you to the benefits of collaborative working with your peers on your course and on into your teaching career. Collaborative working can take many forms, and in this chapter you will find descriptions of the different types, and also definitions of collaboration, coordination and cooperation, so that you can easily distinguish between them.

The chapter also describes some of the skills needed to undertake collaborative work effectively and stresses the importance of evaluating collaborative team working. Specific examples of collaborative working through the use of ICT are described, and the relative merits of synchronous and asynchronous tools are discussed.

Collaboration versus cooperation

The purpose of this section is to ensure that you are fully aware of the differences between collaboration and cooperation, and where the boundaries lie so that you are also sensitive to where both these things stop and where plagiarism begins (see Chapter 3 Academic writing and reading).

Practical task

Write down your own definitions of collaboration and cooperation before you read any further in this chapter. Then compare your definitions with those given here. Were you close?

Collaboration can be thought of as a situation in which specific types of interaction between people may be expected to occur, and through which learning mechanisms are triggered. Such situations might be the formation of groups within your PGCE classes, or your own social network on the course. Your tutor is likely to set up simulations of these types of situation to encourage you to collaborate with your peers on the course in order to produce specific pieces of work, such as presentations, wikis, teaching resources, lesson plans, and so on. The learning that goes on is, in reality, not linear. By that I mean that it can occur at any point, at different levels and at different times for each person in the group. It is unlikely to be the same for everyone.

Collaboration also involves the construction of meaning through interaction with others, through the commitment to a shared goal. It is often, in this sense, synergistic. When you collaborate with your peers, you work together towards a common goal, be that work on a particular assignment where you all agree to take notes and then pool them, or work in class on a particular activity the tutor has given you.

Collaborative or cooperative learning strategies consist of social interactions between students based on equal partnership in the learning experience, as opposed to fixed teacher–learner roles (Agada, 1998). Collaborative processes bring together individuals of differing backgrounds and help them to work towards a common goal or goals. There is a wide variety of processes that can be defined as 'collaborative', but each demand specific skills from participants. These skills will be discussed later.

There is sometimes confusion between what is meant by *collaboration, coordination* and *cooperation*. Winer and Ray (1994) summarised this and their definitions are presented in Table 13.1.

So there are clear differences between collaboration and cooperation – for example, collaboration involves longer-term, more intensive relationships with a common mission. Cooperation is much shorter term, ad hoc, informal and with the individual still retaining authority: but with some sharing of resources and information. What is also important here is to realise when you have strayed from cooperating into plagiarism. This might be because, for example, you copied notes taken by another member of your group, or based the structure of your essay on someone else's, or even used exactly the same references for an assignment. While this might not have been intentional, and is often easier to do when electronic copies of work are being passed around a group, you do need to be aware of crossing the line. (See Chapter 3 Academic writing and reading.)

Stop and reflect

Think about how you may have collaborated or cooperated with others in the past, perhaps for your first degree or at work.

- Evaluate your role during collaboration and during cooperation.
- Can you differentiate between the two?
- Analyse possible opportunities for collaboration and cooperation on your present course.

Table 13.1 Cooperation, coordination and collaboration

Cooperation	Coordination	Collaboration
Short term	Longer term	Long term
Informal relations	More formal relations	Long-term relationships
No clearly defined mission	Understand mission	Commitment to common mission
No defined structure	Focus on specific effort or programme	Results in a new structure
No planning effort	Some planning	Comprehensive planning
Partners share information about the project	Open communication channels	Well-defined communication channels at all levels
Individuals retain authority	Individuals retain authority	Collaborative structure determines authority
Resources are maintained separately	Resources and rewards are shared	Resources are shared
No risk	Power can be an issue	Greater risk – power is an issue
Lower intensity	Some intensity	Higher intensity

Having defined collaborative working we now move on to look at ways in which you can take advantage of collaborative working within your peer group. This can either be in face-to-face sessions or through the use of information and communications technology (ICT). The advantage of ICT-based collaborative working is that it will help you to continue to benefit from collaborative working while on school placement when you may be isolated from your peers. In either case, collaborative working requires collaborative skills.

These collaborative skills include social and communication skills, problem-solving abilities and negotiating skills. For effective collaborative work there has to be rapport, absolute integrity, empathy and complete trust. An effective strategy for collaborative working, as it is for group working of any kind, is to spend time reflecting and discussing group processes. Question how the group is working together and evaluate how the collaborative team is developing.

It is useful to reflect on group working processes when collaborating. Discussing how the group is working together can be as important as getting on with the task. In fact, if the group isn't working well together, the task may never be done unless group processes can be repaired.

A key model commonly referred to in team working, especially management teams, is that developed by Meredith Belbin (1981). Belbin researched 200 teams conducting business management games. Following observations Belbin identified nine team types. He concluded that almost always people have a mix of these types, but most of us have a dominant and sub-dominants. The types are:

1 Chairman – keeps progress going, a clan form of leadership
2 Shaper – leads by shaking things up and challenging
3 Plant – innovator and imaginative: not practical
4 Monitor/evaluator – an analyser: hard-headed and evaluates alternatives
5 Resource investigator – explores resources outside the group: good communicator
6 Team worker – negotiates and facilitates within the team
7 Company worker – good at carrying out the plans: hard working and self-disciplined
8 Completer-finisher – ensures work delivered on time: sense of urgency, work to deadlines
9 Specialist – person with expertise in one field who is needed by the team. Weakness is that they tend to focus only on the aspect in which they have expertise.

Stop and reflect

Study the Belbin team types above.

- Analyse which type most closely matches your approach to team working.
- Which type least closely matches your approach to team working?
- Reflect on a recent team working situation. Can you match the team members to team types? Were any team types missing? If so – did this have an impact on the effectiveness of the team?

There have been a number of other team types proposed, and this approach is not without its critics, but it can be a useful way to attempt to analyse collaborative groups. Another approach is to see group working as a developmental process – much in the way that a relationship can develop by passing through phases. This was proposed by Tuckman (1965) and is famous for its classification of the phases of group development. Tuckman stressed that groups needed to pass through the phases in order to come to terms with the complexities of the social interactions and to reach agreement about the social situations within the group. The phases are:

- *Forming.* Individuals seek acceptance by other group members and conflict is avoided. The group members busy themselves with day to day routines but are gathering information about each other. Not much work is done at this stage unless group leaders are assertive.

- *Storming.* At this stage the group starts to address the real issues and the task. They may disagree with each other and get to grips with how the group will work and who will lead it. This phase can be noted for conflict and some groups never leave it. Groups can get through with common sense and tolerance. Once through this phase, and with experienced group workers this can be a very short phase, the group has more trust and sense of purpose.

- *Norming.* Group members give up their own individual ideas and preferences and share one goal. The group is a team and each member takes responsibility.

- *Performing.* This is now high-level team working with autonomous members swiftly and effectively getting on with the task with little need of supervision. Decision-making processes are rapid and each person has a voice.

The idea of groups and teams going through essential phases of development is an important one for teachers. Learners are often placed into groups to carry out tasks, but are rarely encouraged to form teams or discuss how the team is welding together for more efficient working. Although occasional reforming of groups in lessons for a variety of reasons is expected, it is worth considering the value of allowing learners to work in the same group for longer and to monitor group processes. Interestingly, Truckman added a fifth stage to his model in 1977. This stage he called *Adjourning*. During this phase the groups breaks up. Members can find this stressful and upsetting as they break off friendships and move out of a close-knit and supportive group. Not surprisingly this phase is also known as 'mourning'.

This next section will provide you with ideas of how to apply on-line collaborative group working in your own learning, but also may influence your classroom practice: in other words, the approach you adopt with your own students when you teach in schools. Collaborative working is not age-dependent and students of all ages and academic levels respond well to the different ways of working collaboratively in groups. Try it – this is, after all, teacher training – if you can't try these things now, when can you?

Collaborative on-line group work

One way to ensure that you and your peers undertake some form of collaborative working is for your tutor to give you a *mandatory* group task that can *only* be done on-line, for example, while on placement. They could ask you to populate wikis on a website, or create a number of Web pages, or prepare presentations via discussions on a VLE that you access as part of your course.

This type of exercise has three purposes:

1 It promotes collaborative networking and community between trainees in the group.

2 It enables you to experience first-hand, and thus hopefully understand, how this type of activity can be used to promote a sense of community on-line.

3 It enables you to appreciate how on-line activities can be used for virtual collaborative group work, and thus apply it for use with your own coursework and assignments, independent of your tutor's requirements.

As an example of this, your group would be split into small groups for the purposes of the collaborative on-line assignment. The number and size of the groups depends on the number of the whole class, and your tutor might find it appropriate to create the groups in such as way so as to encourage collaborative working between trainees who would not normally work together.

Each group would be required to collaborate via electronic on-line means such as:

- Discussion boards on the institution's VLE – using specific threads to communicate progress and share the work

- Email, MSN messaging, for example – to swap notes and communicate with others

- Mobile phone texting – to keep in touch on progress

- Social networking sites such as Facebook – to upload and share information and photographs.

This list is not exhaustive, and by the time this book goes to print, it is likely that more will have been added – such is the speed of change in ICT.

The type of work you might be given for such collaborative activity could be to produce a fraction of an item, such as a scheme of work comprising several successive lesson plans, or to populate a set of subject-based wikis, such as the range of qualifications at levels 4 and 5 for a specific subject, on a website (possibly within the institution's VLE). The idea is, in the examples given, that when all the separate parts are added together, they make a complete, seamless product. This product could only be produced by the effort of all members of the group collaborating with each other, and in this case, by doing so on-line, while on placement.

Access to each group is restricted to the members of that particular group only, and individual members within each group have permission to upload files, send emails and add messages to a discussion board, and so on, within the group. Your tutor might also assign the role of 'project manager' for the exercise to one particular trainee. Their job would be to ensure that the group is working effectively, and that progress is being made at an appropriate rate – depending on any deadlines set, and that this is being communicated to all members of the group.

Ideally, the work set for this type of exercise should be practical and relevant to your course of study. Independent of the work set, you need to ensure that the end result is achievable in the time given, and that it is measurable in terms of outcomes, and benefits. Given that each group might only have to produce a small part of the end product, this should not be too arduous a task for any single one of you. These principles apply not only to work your tutor might set for this type of collaborative working, but also for any collaborative working you chose to do yourselves as a group or groups.

If, while reading this, you are thinking, ' mmm, this sounds like a good way to cut down my work ...', think again. Since this is collaboration on-line, it is incredibly measurable. First, your tutor, and indeed, possibly others in your group, are able to access materials, resources, messages and so on. If you don't participate in any communications, or upload files, as part of the work, you will be noticed. It is very easy to determine not only who is participating in the on-line collaboration, but also how they are participating. At one extreme you could be adding simple short messages only, at the other, you could be adding longer more discursive messaging with documents uploaded for others to share. All is visible on-line, and people who collaborate generally do not suffer 'idlers' lightly or for long. Your tutor will also be aware, particularly if this is an assessed exercise, of just how much effort you have put in, and will evaluate you accordingly.

Having produced something on-line through collaboration with your peers, you may be asked to present the final product during a face-to-face session at your institution. Such a presentation might include:

- Accessing the on-line work to examine the amount and type of activity that was done by members of the group
- Analysing the product of the collaboration for its fitness for purpose
- Evaluating the exercise as a group in terms of the intended benefits to the individual members.

The type of questions to be asked when evaluating this type of activity include whether or not you all found it useful as a means to understand on-line collaboration, and whether or not you all found it easy to collaborate on-line. Finally, you might ask whether or not you would do it again, and if you will use this type of activity for your own teaching practice.

Stop and reflect

Evaluate the different types of group work you have been given so far on your course. Do you think they could have been done as on-line collaborative activities? Would it have made it easier to do them this way?

Practical task

For the next piece of face-to-face group work you are given, determine how you would go about doing this on-line if you and your peers were on school placement. Write down just how you would do this, and what technology you would use to do it with.

Synchronous and asynchronous technology for teaching and learning in schools

This section describes, with examples, the use of some synchronous and asynchronous technologies. Synchronous technologies involve people communicating together at the same time – all are logged in and all can communicate, rather like a conference call on the telephone. With asynchronous technologies, you can log in and post a contribution at any time that suits you. You may have to wait for responses but you can also check these at any time convenient to you. Each person in the group will be checking, but at different times. No coordination is needed.

Synchronous tools

It is possible to set up a pre-arranged time at which you and your peers can meet virtually, in real time, within the on-line space that is provided by a VLE, or MSN messaging. Having set up the time for the session, and having also informed everyone involved of when and how to participate, you would each click on the 'Join' button to enter the virtual 'chat room'. In the chat room there would be others present, and some might join at various times during the session. The idea is that you could discuss topics related to your course outside face-to-face sessions, possibly while on school placement – for example, as a means of keeping in touch with *all* your peers *in real time*. You type in comments, questions and so on, and these can be seen by all participants as threads of conversations to which you can chose to respond or not. This is a useful means by which all interested parties involved in any on-line collaborative work can be updated at once. It is a good way to progress any on-line collaborative work without having to send out multiple emails, or add messages to discussion boards, as all the group can participate in real time together.

This technology gives you an opportunity to 'meet up' with your peers in real time, and can facilitate the continuation of the community spirit that was engendered during face-to-face classroom sessions. It might also be possible for you to arrange one or more of these types of sessions in your placements, and so continue collaboration throughout school placement.

There are many advantages to using this type of technology to maintain a sense of community and mutual collaboration between trainees. Not least is the reduction in the sense of isolation that can be felt once you leave the face-to-face sessions and are separated geographically from your peers during school placement. In large institutions school placements for any one single subject group can cover an area of 100 miles, with trainees spread out to all points of the compass within it. This means that it is unlikely that some of you will be able to meet up during placement *unless* it is via electronic means such as the ones described here.

This type of session is not only useful for the collaborative activities described above. Such sessions can also be useful for more informal type of collaboration that typically occurs within the type of learning communities that often form on teacher-training courses (McConnell 2006). You might find, for example, that it is good to meet all together in this way to discuss different sorts of topics. This to be done on an informal basis, and with no end product in mind other than wanting to feel you are not alone, and that others are in the same boat, or simply to get ideas for resources, planning and lessons you are taking on placement. Such discussions might include:

- Your aspirations and plans for the future, job applications and interviews
- Your relationships with others in school – keeping it professional, of course
- Sharing thoughts on how you are coping with the course and the assignments you are required to produce.

This list is not exhaustive, but it does give an idea of what you might want to talk about – things that are uppermost on your minds, your main worries and concerns. So, if the chat session is organised with these things in mind, then you should get a great deal of value from participating in it. This is something a tutor might arrange for you anyway, and something you might want to ask them to do if you feel it would benefit you and your peers.

One of the main advantages of this type of session that can be developed by your tutor is that it demonstrates, very visually (in that it is there as a list of conversation threads), what would be useful as discussion board topics for your group. One way to progress the ideas presented in the synchronous chat session is to replicate them on the discussion boards. In this way, the benefits to you and your peers from the synchronous session continue beyond that session throughout the course. You can then become responsible for taking topics forward and for collaborating asynchronously to progress any ideas discussed in real time. You might even want to suggest this to your tutor using the ideas given below:

- Get them to set up discussion boards for particular popular threads from the synchronous session, such as relationships with other teachers and students in your school, strategies for coping with assignments, work–life balance, plans for the future, resource sharing, and so on.
- You and your peers could instigate new threads on already populated boards to continue the lines of thought from the synchronous session. For example, on a board set up for assignments, you could start a new thread that further developed ideas from the synchronous session, or answered questions from that session in more detail.

There are a number of practical considerations to take into account when taking part in, or even requesting, this type of activity with your group:

- Any technical difficulties with the access accounts or central server may result in not all the group being able to access the session. Your ability to participate may depend on whether or not you have the appropriate software to access the session from home or from the school in which you are placed.
- There will never be a best or most convenient time for this type of live session, as it is not possible to please all of you all the time. Thus having set up an initial session, the time slot should be reviewed and the group asked about what times would be best for them. This should ensure that maximum participation is achieved.
- One other problem to be aware of for this type of session is that of time lag – the gap between typing a message, and it is being viewed on screen by other participants. This can lead to some mismatched, if interesting, threads. It can make the messaging appear disjointed and unsynchronised, particularly when an answer to one question appears after other questions have been asked. The time delay can affect the flow of text to such an extent at times that it resembles a 'Two Ronnies' sketch!

Practical task

Ask your tutor to set up this type of session for your group and give it a go. Work out a list of topics you would like to share and collaborate on during the session beforehand, then try it and see if it works for you. If it does work, think about how you might continue the discussions asynchronously to collaborate further.

Independently of how well the session is set up – and this applies to face-to-face as well as on-line sessions – some of you will get more out of it than others. Some of your peers will decide not to participate at all, as they may prefer more one-to-one communication with peers. Even if only a small number of you participate and get something out of the session, however, it is worthwhile doing. Having this type of synchronous session, while possibly not as good as face-to-face classroom interactions for some, is better than nothing at all for most people. It gives you real-time access to each other on a grander scale than can be achieved through email or texting alone during times when you are in school.

Stop and reflect

Think about the composition of your group. How well do you think this type of session would work? Reflect on the characters in the group and evaluate how well this type of session would work for each person. Overall, is your judgement that it would work well enough to make it worthwhile?

Critical synthesis

Research the following resources:

● E-moderating *by Gilly Salmon (2000) Kogan Page, London.*

● The e-Assessment Handbook *by G. Crisp (2007) Continuum, London.*

Having analysed the texts, consider how you might deploy e-learning assessment, teaching and learning activities in place of more traditional approaches.

How could e-learning be used specifically to encourage collaborative activities in class and beyond, such as group work.

Asynchronous tools

In this section, the use of discussion boards (or forums) is explored as a means for asynchronous communication and collaboration between trainees in the group.

Discussion boards within a VLE provide a very simple and effective means by which you can communicate with each other to share ideas and experiences, at a time when it is convenient for you. Discussion boards are 24/7 – they can be accessed at any time, and generally from anywhere (over the internet). They also provide an added advantage of being able to be read only – that is, unlike synchronous tools such as the chat session previously described, those of you who wish to take advantage of the information exchange of the boards can do so without having any (immediate) pressure to participate yourselves.

Discussion boards are usually accessed from the home screen for the site via the Discussion Board or Forum button. Any number of discussion boards can be set up. However, it should be borne in mind that, the more boards there are for a limited number of you within your group, the more likely it is that the messaging will become diluted. A typical PGCE group in a large institution is likely to have between 15 and 25 trainees, depending on the subject. In addition to this, not all of you will choose to participate, and so, if there are endless boards to add messages to, and only a limited number of active messengers, the boards run the risk of being underused. Once people see that they are not being used, the chances of any new messengers adding to them decreases significantly (Hramiak, 2007). Having a few highly relevant boards is probably the best way to increase the chances of success of this feature of the VLE, and thus increase the benefits to you as trainees.

Although it is stating the obvious, the more you use the discussion boards, the more you each get out of them. Collaboration is easy on discussion boards, as files and experiences can be shared, ideas can be explored, and so on. It is advisable, therefore, to set up and use boards that are particularly pertinent to the way that your course progresses. These could reflect your face-to-face sessions, or be build up to augment specific school experiences. Some tried-and-tested ideas for boards where you can share experiences and ideas specific to your course are:

● A discussion board for specific assignments–these could be set up to reflect the deadlines for the work, so that the messaging is pertinent to the work being undertaken at that particular time
● A discussion board for getting your first job in teaching
● Discussion boards for the different school placements – this can be two for some courses and three for others
● A social discussion board.

As the academic year progresses, it is helpful to maintain the discussion boards in parallel with the progress of the course. For example, the board relating to the first assignment or placement could be removed (or archived) after trainees move onto their second one, and a board added at the appropriate time for job applications, and so on.

Practical task

Make a list of the types of discussion boards you would find useful for collaboration with your peers on your course.

● How you would use them to collaborate?
● Are they different from the ones your tutor has set up?

As with synchronous sessions, it is up to you whether or not you feel you should participate in the boards, or whether you should just observe the messaging within them. If the intention is to try to replicate on the boards, as far as possible, the sense of community with the class you felt was present during your face-to-face sessions, then you would generally join in to a lesser or greater extent with the messaging. You would become a part of the on-line classroom community in much the same way as you were part of the face-to-face classroom community, thus transferring your presence to the on-line situation as far as is possible.

The boards are there to encourage you to share your experiences and collaborate in and out of your institution – and to do this independently of where you are all placed in schools. This can take many forms and, if the community that existed in face-to-face classroom sessions is successfully transferred to an on-line situation such as this, the boards can be literally 'swamped' with good ideas, help and assistance, shared experiences and thoughts in relation both to your course and to school placement.

Case study

A group of trainees at two northern universities were given blogging space as part of their course and encouraged to use it specifically for reflection. Individuals were encouraged to go on to the blog after school and describe their experiences in placement, often doing this daily. As a group, the blogging became a more collaborative activity in both institutions, as trainees began to see how useful it was to read the blogs of others, and to write their own for others to see. Their development as reflective practitioners speeded up as they became better reflective 'bloggers', and their sense of isolation on placement was also reduced as a result of this community of learners coming together on-line. Thousands of views were indicated on the system for hundreds of entries by less than 20 trainees, indicating the usefulness of the blog for all.

- What advantages do you think this 'community of learners' offered to the individual members?
- What professional, ethical and child-protection advice would you give to people adding reflections on their work in school to such a blog?
- Reflect on how useful you would find such a collaborative blog activity. What might be some of the barriers to you engaging with one?

Challenge your thinking

Tim Roberts and Joanne McInnerney (2007) have tackled the issue of on-line group work and collaboration by reviewing a number of articles on the issue. Despite the benefits of computer-supported collaborative working (CSCW), they have identified seven problems with this approach:

'Amongst the problems that are thought to be inherent to this method of teaching, the seven most commonly found in the literature are the following:

Problem #1: student antipathy towards group work
Problem #2: the selection of the groups

> *Problem #3: a lack of essential group-work skills*
> *Problem #4: the free-rider*
> *Problem #5: possible inequalities of student abilities*
> *Problem #6: the withdrawal of group members, and*
> *Problem #7: the assessment of individuals within the groups.'*
>
> (Roberts and McInnerney, 2007: 257)

- Do any of the problems match your experiences of undertaking any form of collaborative work, let alone on-line?
- With the increasing move to on-line support in schools, colleges and universities do you think the seven problems above will act as a serious barrier to implementing these strategies?
- Select three problems and design some possible solutions.

Summary

The practical suggestions for on-line collaboration described in this chapter show that collaborative working can be very effective in that there are ways in which ICT can be used for your ITT by working with others towards common goals.

Previous research recommends that members of a group, such as trainee teachers, have equal access to the shared electronic resources, so that a sense of community is created between the learners in the group, giving them opportunity to structure the on-line experience for themselves. Research that has explored the 'connectedness' of the students who engaged with the VLE for the purposes of study reports that there is a heightened sense of feeling connected as part of a wider learning community (Thurston, 2005). The forming of the sense of community is deemed to be a necessary initial step in on-line collaborative learning (Wenger, 1998).

This said, however, any activities that promote collaborative working with trainee teachers and, indeed, any collaboration that trainees create for themselves has to be fit for purpose. Collaboration is not all things to all people. It can be likened to making a loaf of bread. When you make this from scratch, you do not empty all the cupboards and mix everything together in the hope that it works. You take only what you need and then mix those things together. Also, as with a loaf of bread, although each of you may take a slice from the same loaf, what you do with that slice will be very different for each of you.

For collaboration to be successful, you need a clear definition and description of the purpose, rationale and benefits of its use, prior to actually using it, in order to ensure that you are getting the most out of it.

References

Agada, J. (1998) 'Collaboration Across Boundaries: Theories, Strategies, and Technology: Teaching collaborative skills in library and information science education, (LISE) ASIS Midyear '98'. Proceedings *http://www.asis.org/Conferences/MY98/Agada.htm*

0

Belbin, M. (1981) *Management Teams,* London: Heinemann.

Hramiak, A. (2007) 'Initial Evaluation and Analysis of Post Graduate Trainees' Use of a Virtual Learning Environment in Initial Teacher Training', *Electronic Journal of E-learning,* 5(2). Retrieved from *www.ejel.org*

McConnell, D. (2006) *E-Learning Groups and Communities,* Maidenhead: Open University Press.

Roberts, T. S. and McInnerney, J. M. (2007) 'Seven Problems of On-line Group Learning (and Their Solutions)', *Educational Technology & Society,* 10(4): 257–68.

Thurston, A. (2005) 'Building on-line communities', *Technology, Pedagogy and Education,* 14(3): 353–70.

Tuckman, B. W. (1965) 'Developmental sequence in small groups', *Psychological Bulletin,* 63, 384–99.

Wenger, E. (1998). *Communities of Practice: Learning, Meaning and Identity,* Cambridge: Cambridge University Press.

Winer, M., and Ray, K. (1994) *Collaboration handbook: Creating, sustaining and enjoying the journey,* Saint Paul, MN: Amherst H. Wilder Foundation.

Chapter 14

Personal, Social, Health and Economic education and Citizenship

Learning outcomes

By the end of this chapter, you will have:

→ An understanding of the place of citizenship and personal, social, health and economic education within the secondary school curriculum

→ An understanding of some of the issues relating to provision of these subjects within the secondary school curriculum

→ Considered your responsibility in relation to these subjects and issues that might arise from this

→ Looked at Social and Emotional Aspects of Learning (SEAL) and considered the relationship between this framework and PSHEe

Introduction

This chapter will give you an overview of the place of Personal, Social, Health and Economic education (PSHEe) and Citizenship within the secondary school curriculum. These are subject areas that teachers frequently find themselves involved with, often with very little specialist training. Many attend one lecture or seminar on these subjects during their teacher training courses and then suddenly find themselves responsible for teaching them in their NQT year. This can often lead to the uncomfortable feeling of not being in control or, worse, resentment leading to a lack of preparation and effort on the part of the teacher. This is a shame as these are important subjects which, if approached with understanding and enthusiasm, can offer rich opportunities for the development of students in encouraging them to engage with the wider community locally, nationally and internationally.

The National Curriculum: spiritual, moral, cultural, mental and physical development

The 1988 Education Reform Act demanded that each school provided a broadly based and balanced curriculum which:

'a) *Promotes the spiritual, moral, cultural, mental and physical development of students at the school and of society, and*

b) *Prepares such students for the opportunities, responsibilities and experiences of adult life.'*

(Great Britain, 1988)

Stop and reflect

Before we go any further, pause to analyse how your own subject helps to achieve the above aims. Where are the opportunities for spiritual, moral, cultural, mental and physical development in your own specialism? In what ways do you help to prepare students for the 'opportunities, responsibilities and experiences of adult life'?

While most subject areas could appropriately and convincingly argue that they contribute to these aims through their part of the 'broadly based and balanced curriculum', most teachers would agree that these are not in the forefront of their minds when they are planning and delivering lessons, where the focus has to be determined by the constraints of time, curriculum and assessment. However, it is important to remember that the curriculum was intended to be, and should be, more than simply gathering facts, forming opinions and passing examinations. Schools have a responsibility to prepare students for the 'opportunities, responsibilities and experiences of adult life' and this involves more than ensuring that students leave with a list of academic qualifications.

When the most recent version of the National Curriculum was published in 2007, even greater emphasis was put on a holistic view of the curriculum. The whole curriculum was underpinned by three, clearly identified aims. It states that:

'The National Curriculum has three statutory aims. It should enable all young people to become:

- *successful learners who enjoy learning, make progress and achieve*
- *confident individuals who are able to live safe, healthy and fulfilling lives*
- *responsible citizens who make a positive contribution to society.*

These statutory aims should inform all aspects of teaching and learning and be the starting point for curriculum design.'

(QCDA [on-line]. Last accessed 19 February 2010 at: *http://curriculum.qcda.gov.uk/ key-stages-3-and-4/aims-values-and-purposes/aims/index.aspx*)

This has given rise to schools being forced to review their curricula. Individual subjects are now expected to demonstrate how they can contribute to the achievement of these aims, and a reduction in the prescription about the amount of subject content that must be covered has allowed schools to achieve these aims in more flexible ways. Another important aspect of the new curriculum has been the inclusion of seven cross-curriculum dimensions:

1 *identity and cultural diversity;*
2 *healthy lifestyles;*
3 *community participation;*
4 *enterprise;*
5 *global dimension and sustainable development;*
6 *technology and media;*
7 *creativity and critical thinking.*

(QCDA [on-line]. Last accessed 19 February 2010 at *http://curriculum.qcda.gov.uk/key-stages-3-and-4/cross-curriculum-dimensions/index.aspx*)

With all of this to be taken into account it may be the case that on your placement you are encountering new curriculum structures, with more emphasis on cross-curricular themes and project work.

Practical task

Read more about the aims of the curriculum and the cross-curriculum dimensions at *www.curriculum.qcda.gov.uk*. Pay particular attention to the ways that schools might use the cross-curriculum dimensions. Then, with reference to your own subject, try to come up with ways that your own subject might link with others to add the aims and cross-curriculum dimensions.

Personal, Social, Health and Economic education (PSHEe) and Citizenship

Prior to these most recent changes, the inclusion of PSHEe and Citizenship in the curriculum was one of the key ways in which schools have addressed the need to offer a 'broadly based and balanced curriculum' and prepare their students for adult life. There are clearly areas in which individual subjects contribute to this, but PSHEe and Citizenship potentially offer schools the opportunity for developing a holistic approach to this aspect of the curriculum.

Personal, Social, Health and Economic education

PSHEe has been included in the National Curriculum since its inception but it originally had a non-statutory programme of study. Nevertheless, many schools chose to teach it as it helped them 'to fulfil their legal responsibilities to promote the well-being of students, provide advice and guidance on sex, relationships and drugs, as well as offering careers education and work-related learning' (QCDA, 2009). However, Sir Alasdair Macdonald was asked by the government to conduct an independent review of the proposal to make PSHEe statutory. Following the publication of his report in 2009, the decision has been taken to make PSHEe a statutory part of the curriculum from September 2011. However, the journey to this point has been a long and interesting one.

One of the key things that should be noted immediately about PSHEe is the fact that it goes under a variety of different guises. No other subject has such a wide variety of possible names and is so routinely called something different from one school to the next. In this book we are using the title PSHEe as Personal, Social, Health and Economic education as this is the title used for the subject in the National Curriculum published in 2007 and in Macdonald's Review (2009). It would be impossible to write an exhaustive list of all the titles that have been given to the subject, but here is a selection:

- PSE: Personal and Social Education
- PSHE: Personal, Social and Health Education *or* Personal, Social, Health and Economic Wellbeing
- PSME: Personal, Social and Moral Education
- PSMRE: Personal, Social, Moral and Religious Education
- SPACE: Social, Personal And Careers Education
- PHSCE: Personal, Health, Social and Citizenship Education
- PSHEe: Personal Social, Health and Economic education.

Initially it was the title Personal and Social Education (PSE) that was most common. This was used in National Curriculum guidance following the Education Reform Act (1988) and many schools timetabled it as a discrete lesson with that name. However, over time the title given to the subject has evolved, demonstrating the change of emphasis in some schools. For example, we can see from the list above that areas such as health and careers have been given more prominence in some contexts. For most of the period we are considering however, the title PSHE has been used widely by the vast majority of schools and Ofsted (2005 and 2007).

Stop and reflect

Think back to your own time at school. Did you have a lesson that would be the equivalent of PSHEe? If so, what was it called? What was the nature of the topics covered within that lesson?

An understanding of the way in which the shift in the title of the subject can highlight a shift in priority and focus can be seen if we consider the publication of the new National Curriculum Framework in 2007. Here we see the title evolve further to include the term 'Economic' and the non-statutory programmes of study published by the QCA have been subdivided. For each key stage there are two programmes of study. One deals with *'Economic wellbeing and financial capability'* and covers careers education, work-related learning, enterprise and financial capability. It also clearly supports the fifth outcome of the 'Every Child Matters' agenda (see Chapter 4). The other programme of study, *'Personal wellbeing'*, provides a context for sex and relationships education (SRE) and drugs education.

Practical task

Download the non–statutory programmes of study for PSHE from the National Curriculum website *http://curriculum.qca.org.uk* for both *Personal Wellbeing and Economic Wellbeing and Financial Capability* for Key Stages 3 and 4. Consider the following:

- What are the aims of PSHEe?
- If you were asked to teach PSHEe at Key Stage 3, what are the content areas in which you would lack confidence?
- Are there any contentious issues for you? Are there any topic areas where your views might be at odds with those of your students?

PSHEe: the issues

Although we have noted that there is great potential within PSHEe for the development of students' knowledge, understanding, skills and attitudes we cannot ignore that fact that in the past it has often been seen as a 'Cinderella' subject. The non-statutory nature of the curriculum has meant that the approaches in schools have been varied and this has led to inevitable problems. For example, an Ofsted report reviewing secondary education published in 1997 made the following observation:

'Personal and Social Education (PSE) is a timetabled part of the curriculum in Key Stages 3 and 4 in most secondary schools. It is provided in a very wide range of ways, through combinations of timetabled PSE courses, tutorial periods, National Curriculum subjects,

assemblies, extra-curricular activities and residential experiences. Despite its importance, however, the teaching of PSE is too often unsatisfactory and the status of courses with pupils is often low.'

(Ofsted, 1997)

While more recent Ofsted publications report improvement in the quality of PSHE programmes and suggest that national developments are likely to extend their role in the curriculum (Ofsted, 2007: 2), they have also highlighted additional issues:

- It is seen as a subject where students gain knowledge and understanding, rather than being a place to develop attitudes and values.
- Some schools have included other subjects (such as Citizenship) in PHSE. In many of these schools curriculum time for PSHE has been adversely affected.
- The PSHE curriculum is not broad enough.
- Some schools do not provide the subject in any form.
- PSHE recruits few teachers with directly relevant 'subject' qualifications. The quality of teaching by specialist teachers is better than that of non-specialist teachers.
- There is too little assessment of students' subject knowledge or progression. (Ofsted, 2005: 1–2)

Stop and reflect

Teach or observe a PSHEe lesson. When reflecting on the lesson, ask yourself the following questions:

- How do students feel about PSHEe? Did they enjoy the lesson?
- What knowledge gains have been made during the lesson?
- Have they had the opportunity to develop their attitudes or values?
- How was their learning and progress assessed?

PSHEe: the future

We have reached an interesting point in the development of this subject. In October 2008 it was announced that the government wanted to make PSHEe statutory and launched a review to explore the best way of achieving this (Macdonald 2009: 7). The review was asked to explore some of the concerns raised by this change. These concerns included:

- Pressures on the curriculum
- The role of governing bodies in determining their own approach to SRE
- The parental right of withdrawal from SRE
- The wider implementation issues (e.g. models of delivery and workforce development). (Macdonald, 2009: 7)

On all key issues the government accepted the recommendations of the review and in November 2009 it was announced that PSHEe would be a statutory subject within the National Curriculum from September 2011.

It has already been noted that most schools opted to include some form of PSHEe in their curriculum prior to this change of status. However, this may necessitate a review of provision in some schools as they work out how best to incorporate the content of the statutory programmes of study from September 2011. There is a move to look at training provision for specialist PSHEe teachers but the fact remains that, due to flexible approaches to curriculum provision and the unique nature of the content of the PSHE programmes of study, it may still be the case that non-specialist teachers will be asked to be involved with PSHEe provision.

PSHEe on your timetable

We have already looked at the programmes of study for PSHEe, however the content can be delivered through a wide variety of models. Where it is not delivered through a discrete timetabled lesson, it may be delivered through form-group time, in a cross-curricular model or through a series of 'off timetable' days. There are a number of possible approaches and you will have opportunities to experience and evaluate the strengths and weaknesses of some. To help in this process, it would be a good idea to discuss with colleagues and the people on your course the models that they have worked with so that you understand the variety of approaches and the relative merits of each. However, it is worth noting that one feature of many PSHEe programmes is the use of specialists from outside the school to deliver lessons. Health professionals, people from local businesses, police officers and many others may be invited to speak to groups of students about particular areas of the curriculum. This has obvious advantages for students, but also means that teachers do not have to be experts in every aspect of the curriculum.

Even though Ofsted acknowledge that it is better when PSHEe is taught by specialist teachers than non-specialist teachers (Ofsted, 2007: 3) there are still many schools where, for different reasons, this is not possible. Therefore, it is highly likely that, at some point in your career, you will be asked to teach PSHEe. You might be asked to join the PSHEe team, and deliver discrete lessons to particular classes, or you may be asked to deliver the subject to your own form group. This will cause more anxiety for some NQTs than others. For example, specialists in Religious Education, Citizenship and English may be more used to leading classroom discussion or handling sensitive issues than their colleagues from other subject areas. Don't be afraid to seek advice from more experienced colleagues. Even if there is no specialist team in the school, Ofsted report that the leadership and management of the subject is generally good (2007: 3); if you are asked to teach it there will be people in your school to offer support.

Social and Emotional Aspects of Learning (SEAL)

In the non-statutory programmes of study for Personal Wellbeing, reference is made to the fact that this area of the curriculum provides an opportunity to focus on the development of skills identified in the framework for Social and Emotional Aspects of

Learning (SEAL). SEAL is a framework that has been used in primary schools and was introduced into secondary schools in 2007. It is defined in a DfES publication in the following terms:

'What is SEAL?

Secondary SEAL is a comprehensive approach to promoting the social and emotional skills that underpin effective learning, positive behaviour, regular attendance, staff effectiveness and the emotional health and wellbeing of all who learn and work in schools. It proposes that the skills will be most effectively developed by students and staff through:

- *using a whole-school approach to create the climate and conditions that implicitly promote the skills and allow these to be practised and consolidated;*
- *direct and focused learning opportunities (during tutor time, across the curriculum, in focus groups and outside formal lessons);*
- *using learning and teaching approaches that support students to learn social and emotional skills and consolidate those already learnt;*
- *continuing professional development for the whole staff of a school.*

(DfES, 2007: 4)

The social and emotional skills that SEAL aims to develop are based on a five-fold categorisation development by Goleman (1996: 283–4) as shown in Table 14.1.

It is argued that individuals who have good skills in these areas will be more effective and successful learners, work well with others, manage their emotions, persist in the fact of difficulty and understand and value the differences and commonalities between people (DfES, 2007: 4–5).

Make a special note that the inclusion of references to SEAL in the programmes of study for *Personal wellbeing* in PSHEe serve as a reminder of the original vision for the subject (in whatever form it takes). SEAL, through its emphasis on the preparation for coping with the social and emotional demands of adult life, appears to provide a way of bring us back to the aims of the National Curriculum which gave rise to the development of PSHEe. In return PSHEe can provide a place within the curriculum for learning and developing some of the skills that SEAL seeks to promote; invaluable following the introduction of another initiative to an already crowded curriculum. However, as already discussed, the secondary curriculum needs to offer students more than instruction in a series of subjects; it also needs to promote the personal and social development of students. Whatever our subject specialism, we all have a part to play in that.

Table 14.1 Goleman's five fold categorisation model

Personal	Self-awareness
	Managing feelings
	Motivation
Social	Empathy
	Social skills

Critical synthesis

In his article, Learning for well-being: personal, social and health education and a changing curriculum, *Crow identifies four points in his conclusion for consideration:*

- *The connection that PSHE makes with the role schools play in supporting, developing and protecting their children and young people is key.*
- *Schools need to embrace the concept of learning for well-being and to develop and shape a curriculum that prepares its students for life.*
- *PSHE can no longer turn its back on assessment.*
- *PSHE should become a compulsory subject within the curriculum.*

(Crow, 2008: 50)

PSHEe will be statutory from September 2011, but what of his other points? Read the article for yourself and then critically reflect on his arguments in the light of your own experience of PSHEe. Do you see any progress in other areas too?

Citizenship

Another subject that in itself can help curriculum planners address the overarching aims of the curriculum is Citizenship. The subject was introduced to the National Curriculum in 2000. It was included in the KS1 curriculum in 2001 (via the non-statutory Personal Social and Health Education (PSHE) framework) and then it became a requirement in Key Stages 2 and 3 the following year. In 2004 it was made a statutory subject at Key Stage 4.

Background

In 1998 the government's Advisory Group on Citizenship, headed by Professor Bernard Crick, published its report *Education for Citizenship and the Teaching of Democracy in Schools.* This report was asked to deliver two main outcomes:

1 a statement of the aims and purposes of citizenship education in schools
2 a broad framework for what good citizenship education in schools might look like, and how it can be successfully delivered – covering opportunities for teaching about citizenship within and outside the formal curriculum and the development of personal and social skills through projects linking schools and the community, volunteering and the involvement of students in the development of school rules and policies. (QCA, 1998: 4)

The report concluded that citizenship education should be a statutory entitlement in the curriculum. Although the recommendation was that the curriculum time given to the subject at each key stage could be distributed as blocks or modules, as part of existing tutorial time or as a discrete lessons, it was recommended that individual schools should decide how best to proceed for themselves (QCA, 1998: 22). The report also recommended that schools should consider the relationships between citizenship education and other whole school issues (such as school ethos) (QCA, 1998: 23).

Following these recommendations it was decided that Citizenship would be introduced as a statutory subject on the school curriculum at Key Stages 3 and 4 (at Key Stages
1 and 2 programmes of study are published by the QCA but they are non-statutory). This
was a phased introduction with all schools given until September 2002 to have citizenship education included as part of the Key Stage 3 curriculum and until 2004 to fulfil the
requirements for Key Stage 4.

Definitions of citizenship

Before we can go any further we must approach the difficult issue of defining the term
'Citizenship'. The term has several different meanings:

- *A legal and political status.* In this sense 'citizenship' is used to refer to the status of
  being a citizen; being a member for a particular political community with the associated rights and responsibilities.
- *Involvement in public life and affairs.* In this sense the term refers to the behaviour and
  actions of a citizen – active citizenship.
- *An educational activity.* In this sense the term refers to the process of helping people
  learn how to become active, informed and responsible citizens. Citizenship in this
  sense is also known as *citizenship education* or *education for citizenship*. It encompasses
  all forms of education, from informal education in the home or through youth work
  to more formal types of education provided in schools, colleges, universities, training
  organisations and the workplace. (Huddleston and Kerr, 2006: 2)

Here we are concerned with the third of these definitions. However, the content of citizenship education is necessarily concerned with the concept as defined in the first two
definitions.

Citizenship: a National Curriculum

The publication of the National Curriculum for Citizenship in 1999 highlighted three
key principles for the subject. It intended to help students in:

- becoming informed citizens
- developing skills of enquiry and communication
- developing skills of participation and responsible action. (DfEE/QCA 1999: 6)

These principles were to provide headings and structure for the organisation of the
programmes of study in this first version of the citizenship curriculum (DfEE/QCA
1999: 14–16). However, each of them also points to a significant aspect of the citizenship curriculum. Firstly, the fact that the subject can hope to help students become
'informed citizens' indicates that there is a body of knowledge associated with the
subject. Citizenship is not simply about discussing in an abstract way the nature of 'citizenship'. There are things that students are expected to learn to help them develop into
citizens. They need to understand the nature of the society in which they live and their
role, rights and responsibilities within that society. However, the second principle also

points to the discursive nature of the subject. Students should not simply be given knowledge; they should be given the opportunity to discuss, evaluate, research and develop personal opinions. Finally the third of these principles highlights the active element of the subject. Opportunities should be given for active engagement, not just abstract thought in a classroom context.

The National Curriculum published in 2007 reviewed and re-structured the existing curriculum. Whilst changes have been made to the curriculum, the principles considered above still clearly underpin citizenship education. In addition to the subject content outlined in the new curriculum (QCA 2007c: 32–33) that must be accessed by students, they must also have the opportunity to develop skills of 'Critical thinking and enquiry' and they should be able to express and explain their own opinions, communicate an argument and represent the views of others (QCA 2007c: 30). In addition students must also be able to take 'informed and responsible action' and they must be given opportunities for participation 'in both school-based and community-based citizenship activities' and to 'participate in different forms of individual and collective action, including decision-making and campaigning' (QCA 2007c: 31, 34).

Practical task

- Download a copy of the programmes of study for Citizenship at Key Stages 3 and 4 from the National Curriculum website (*http://curriculum.qca.org.uk*).

- Compare these with the PSHEe programmes of study that you have already downloaded (or you can do this on-line using the subject comparison tool on the website).

- In what ways is the content of the citizenship curriculum similar to the PSHEe curriculum and how is it different?

- Now analyse the citizenship programmes of study alongside those for your own subject. Where are the overlaps (if they exist) with your own subject area (consider skills as well as knowledge when thinking about this question)?

Active citizenship

One of the main challenges for citizenship teachers is in delivering the 'active' strand of the citizenship curriculum. This was a key element of the citizenship curriculum from the start. In his report Crick stated that:

> '"Active citizenship" is our aim throughout … it is obvious that all formal preparation for citizenship in adult life can be helped or hindered by the ethos and organisation of a school, whether students are given opportunities for exercising responsibilities and initiatives or not; and also whether they are consulted realistically on matters where their opinions can prove relevant both to the efficient running of a school and to their general motivation for learning.'
>
> (QCA, 1998: 25)

The national curriculum states that students must have opportunities to participate in both school based and community-based activities (QCA 2007c: 34). This is generally easier to accommodate inside the school than in the community. For example, the running of a democratic school council in many schools offers the opportunity for the 'student voice' to be heard and the process offers a valuable learning opportunity. However, finding or creating opportunities for students to work with people outside the school setting is not always easy. Talk to the member of staff with responsibility for Citizenship in your school. Find out how they provide opportunities for participation, especially outside the school environment. However, be aware that often schools will cite ongoing charity work or school events to which members of the community are invited as 'active citizenship'. Ofsted, while finding these activities 'laudable', point out that they do not fulfil the intentions of the National Curriculum (Ofsted 2006: 17–18).

Citizenship on the curriculum

Citizenship provides us with a very interesting case study. It is rare to have the opportunity to chart the progress and development of a curriculum subject. At its inception Citizenship, although facing some obvious challenges, had much to commend it. The difficulties of turning an ideal into reality were relished as an opportunity by some and met with scepticism and resentment by others.

The first decision that had to be made by schools was how the subject was going to feature on the school curriculum. The subject was to be introduced into an already crowded timetable and, as already noted, the recommendation of the Advisory Group on Citizenship was that the subject might not be best served by discrete lessons on the secondary school timetable. It was suggested that schools be allowed to choose a model that suited them for the introduction of the subject (QCA 1998: 22).

There is a variety of possible models for the organisation of citizenship education with the school timetable. In the CPD handbook *Making Sense of Citizenship* four main ways of delivering the citizenship curriculum are identified:

- Citizenship as a stand-alone subject
- Citizenship through other subjects
- Citizenship through the tutorial programme and assemblies
- Citizenship through suspended timetable events. (Huddleston and Kerr, 2006: 44)

Some would, of course, argue that if Citizenship is going to gain creditability and develop its own identity, the best model is to deliver the subject as a stand-alone subject. However, this was not the model adopted by many schools. Although there is a growing body of teachers who are trained to teach Citizenship, at the time the subject was introduced there were not enough for every school to employ a specialist. Therefore, the reality is that many schools have developed an approach to the subject that uses a combination of the above approaches to deliver the requirements for Citizenship. In fact, some would argue that this is a better approach and is necessary if the active citizenship elements of the curriculum are going to be successfully delivered. While some of the subject content may be best delivered in dedicated discrete lessons, some topics may be best approached through one-off suspended timetable events.

Stop and reflect

Ask yourself the following questions:

● How is Citizenship taught in your placement school? (If you don't know you need to find out.)

● Have you/will you be asked to teach Citizenship in your placement school?

● Evaluate your own position in relation to the Citizenship curriculum. How confident would you be if you were asked to teach aspects of the citizenship curriculum?

All of this again points to the fact that teachers of any subject specialism might find themselves teaching Citizenship. This is especially true if (in common with PSHEe) your school delivers citizenship education through the tutorial programme or as part of a cross-curricular project. Alternatively you might be asked to deliver aspects of the citizenship curriculum though your own subject area or to help with the organisation and management of suspended timetable events.

Those who are asked to teach Citizenship as a non-specialist need to ensure that they are familiar with the programmes of study, address the gaps in their own knowledge and ensure that they fully understand the aims and principles that underpin the subject. This is a national curriculum subject and, just as you would expect a non-specialist teaching your own subject to approach the task with commitment and enthusiasm, our citizenship colleagues should and do expect us to approach their subject in the same way. This is not always easy, and Ofsted recognised this in their report *Towards consensus? Citizenship in secondary schools*:

> '*Most teachers of citizenship are "non-specialists"; many work far from their normal comfort zone both in subject knowledge and teaching approaches, especially with regard to controversial and topical issues … If the teaching is perceived by students as dull or irrelevant, then citizenship lessons can be counter-productive.*'

(Ofsted, 2006: 1)

However, despite acknowledgment of the difficulties faced by non-specialist teachers of Citizenship, it is also noted that:

> *… the quality of teaching is also influenced by the very different attitudes towards the subject held by staff, including some unhealthy scepticism.*

(Ofsted, 2006: 31)

The report highlights the necessity of good subject knowledge for quality teaching and learning in citizenship and comments that good lessons are also characterised by high levels of student participation, good use of visits and visitors (although the role played by the teacher in briefing and interventions determines the success of such ventures), the use of good and topical resources, and the development of activities designed to motivate and inform students (2006: 35–38). All of this is clearly a challenge, especially in a subject area that is not your own. Nevertheless our professionalism demands that we rise to meet this challenge and make the most of opportunities that we are given through the citizenship curriculum.

Two distinct subjects

One problem for PSHEe and Citizenship is that, due to the way the latter has been introduced and is being taught in schools (that is, often combined with the former so that the two subjects are delivered simultaneously), sometimes both students and teachers lose sight of the difference between the two subjects. It is perhaps helpful here to make clear the distinction between the two. Put simply, PSHEe concentrates on the individual, where Citizenship is more concerned with public policy. For example, the issue of smoking is one that might conceivably appear on both a PSHEe and a Citizenship scheme of work. In PSHEe, however, the focus would be on factors such as the effects of smoking on the body (health education) or discussion about the peer pressure that might lead to someone trying cigarettes (personal and social education). However, Citizenship might concentrate on arguments relating to bans on cigarette adverts or on arguments for and against the ban on smoking in public places. PSHEe focuses on the impact of smoking on the individual, but Citizenship focuses on the impact on the community.

Practical task

While we must remember that PSHEe and Citizenship each have a unique body of knowledge, there are several areas in which the two subjects might overlap. Complete the table below, indicating the area of interest for each subject within that topic.

Topic	PSHEe	Citizenship
Money	Personal budgeting and money management	Sources of public money and who decides how it is spent
Diversity		
Handling conflict		
Employment		
Drugs education		

Assessment in PSHEe and Citizenship

There is no space within the confines of this chapter to discuss assessment in PSHEe and Citizenship in any depth. However, we should note that this has been an issue in both subject areas (Ofsted, 2007: 18; Ofsted, 2006: 39–40). There are issues in both subjects with the challenge of trying to assess and chart progress in attitudes or skills which cannot easily be contained and defined. For example, whilst it might be possible to test a student's knowledge of the workings of the British parliament, it is not so easy to quantify their success in the area of active participation. That said, assessment is essential for planning for future learning and therefore cannot be avoided.

Ofsted have highlighted assessment as the weakest area of PSHEe teaching (Ofsted, 2007: 18). It is likely that some teachers struggle as the subject has no attainment levels against which they can check their judgements. However, Ofsted do highlight areas which could be addressed by schools seeking to develop assessment in the subject. These include the following:

- Determine students' current knowledge and understanding before a new topic is taught.
- Plan for assessment as a key element of teaching and learning.
- Involve students in assessing their own progress.(Ofsted, 2007: 18)

We should note that these are all key elements of the Assessment for Learning approach (see Chapter 9).

In Citizenship the situation is perhaps made slightly easier by the inclusion of attainment targets, in line with other national curriculum subjects, following the 2007 curriculum review. In common with other subjects schools are expected to keep a record of each student's progress, include Citizenship in their annual report to parents and assess each student's attainment at the end of Y9. Ofsted, in their most recent report on Citizenship, noted that accurate assessment in Citizenship was still presenting a challenge (2010: 9). The report, *Citizenship Established?*, comments that the schools where assessment of Citizenship is most effective are those that 'had comprehensive arrangements that included well-planned assessments, good marking and records, a range of modes of assessment, and thorough and informative reports to parents' and that schools who were offering accreditation (e.g. a short course GCSE qualification in Citizenship) generally had more developed approaches to assessment. However, in schools that did not have core citizenship programmes or where Citizenship was taught by tutors or across the curriculum it was noted that assessment was the weakest (2010: 21–2). Non-specialist teachers have to be mindful of the fact that Citizenship is a National Curriculum subject with national attainment targets. Everyone teaching Citizenship, regardless of whether or not they are a specialist, has a responsibility to be familiar with these levels to ensure they create meaningful assessment opportunities and help their students to make progress.

Practical task

Anyone teaching citizenship will need to be familiar with the attainment targets for citizenship. To help familiarise yourself with the levels, look at the attainment targets for the end of Key Stage 3 (you have already downloaded them). Look at levels 4, 5 and 6 and re-write each level into 'student-speak'. For example, your re-write of level 4 might start like this:

'I can look at more than one source of information about current issues or controversial problems, and I can discuss the rights of the different people involved. I can also explain why there is conflict in the situation, explain why people disagree about a topic and give you my own opinion....'

Case study

It was announced in November 2009 that from 2011 lessons in gender equality and preventing violence in relationships will be compulsory in the PSHEe curriculum (BBC, 2009). However, this announcement provoked criticism from some parents who were angry at what they saw as interference in how they bring up their children and argued that schools should use their time to focus on reading and writing instead.

Are there other aspects of both the PSHEe and Citizenship curricula that could be criticised in this way? Talk to your colleagues and talk to parents to help you reflect on this issue. Do you think that the content covered in these programmes of study is important or at times are we venturing into areas that should be left to parents? Does it help provide a broad curriculum that prepares students for the challenges of adult life or should the curriculum time be used differently?

Challenge your thinking

The citizenship curriculum has generated a great deal of debate – ranging from those who see it as an essential part of our educational system in producing future active citizens able to play a vital part in society, to others who have a more guarded view and see potential problems of a centralised Citizenship controlled by government. Some even identify the possibility of indoctrination – especially in the field of political values (Garrett, 2000). After all, in recent times mention of homosexuality in schools as part of sex education was frowned on.

● How valid are fears that the citizenship curriculum reflects the norms and assumptions of those designing the curriculum?

● Is there a chance that only a narrow view of UK citizenship may be reflected in terms of the norms and values proposed?

Summary

In this chapter we have explored the nature both of Personal, Social, Health and Economic education (PSHEe) and of Citizenship within the secondary school curriculum. These are important subjects which, if approached with understanding and enthusiasm, can offer rich opportunities for the development of students. As stated in the chapter, schools have a responsibility to prepare students for the 'opportunities, responsibilities and experiences of adult life', and this involves more than ensuring that students leave with a list of academic qualifications.

No other subject has such a wide variety of possible names as Personal, Social, Health and Economic education and it is called different things in different schools. The subject has evolved greatly over time, but has received greater prominence and importance with the move to address the Every Child Matters agenda. However, it is still sometimes seen as a 'Cinderella' subject with low status and a shortage of appropriately qualified teachers.

The chapter moves on to discuss aspects of SEAL and the relationship between citizenship and PSHEe. A key issue mentioned is the problem of PSHEe and Citizenship being taught in schools in a combined way so that the two subjects are delivered simultaneously. This means that sometimes both students and teachers lose sight of the difference between the two subjects. The chapter makes clear the distinction between the two – PSHEe concentrates on the individual, where as Citizenship is more concerned with public policy.

References

BBC (2009) *School lessons to tackle domestic violence outlined* [on-line]. Last accessed on 19/02/10 at: *http://news.bbc.co.uk/1/hi/8376943.stm.*

Best, R., Lang, P., Lodge, C. and Watkins, C. (eds) (1995) *Pastoral Care and Personal-Social Education: Entitlement and Provision,* London: Cassell.

Citizenship Foundation, *http://www.citizenshipfoundation.org.uk/main/page.php?286.* [Accessed 21/08/09.]

Crow, F. (2008) 'Learning for well-being: personal, social and health education and a changing curriculum', *Pastoral Care in Education,* 26(1): 43–51.

Department for Education and Employment and Qualifications and Curriculum Authority (DfEE/QCA) (1999) *Citizenship: The National Curriculum for England* [on-line]. Last accessed on 19 February 2010 at: *http://curriculum.qca.org.uk/uploads/Citizenship%201999%20programme%20of%20study_tcm8-12053.pdf.*

DfES (2007) *Social and Emotional Aspects of Learning for Secondary Schools* [on-line]. Last accessed 19 February 2010 at: *http://nationalstrategies.standards.dcsf.gov.uk/node/157981*

Garrett, D. (2000) 'Democratic citizenship in the curriculum: some problems and possibilities', *Pedagogy, Culture and Society,* 8(3): 323–46.

Goleman, D. (1996) *Emotional Intelligence: why it can matter more then IQ,* London: Bloomsbury.

Great Britain (1988) *Education Reform Act 1988,* Chapter 40, London: The Stationery Office.

Huddleston, T. and Kerr, D. (eds) (2006) *Making Sense of Citizenship,* London: Hodder Murray.

Macdonald, A. (2009) *Independent Review of the proposal to make Personal, Social, Health and Economic (PSHE) education statutory* [on-line] Last accessed 19 February 2010 at: *http://publications.dcsf.gov.uk/default.aspx?PageFunction=productdetails&PageMode=publications&ProductId=DCSF-00495-2009*

Office for Standards in Education (Ofsted) (1997) *Secondary Education 1993–97 – A Review of Secondary Education Schools in England* [on-line]. Last accessed 19 February 2010 at: *http://www.archive.official-documents.co.uk/document/ofsted/seced/chap-7o.htm*

Office for Standards in Education (Ofsted) (2005) *PSHE in secondary schools* [on-line]. Last accessed 19 February 2010 at: *http://www.ofsted.gov.uk/Ofsted-home/Publications-and-research/Browse-all-by/Education/Key stages and transition/Key-Stage-3/Personal-social-and-health-education-in-secondary-schools*

Office for Standards in Education (Ofsted) (2006) Towards consensus? Citizenship in secondary schools. [on-line] Last accessed 19 February 2010 at: *http://www.ofsted.gov.uk/Ofsted-home/Publications-and-research/Browse-all-by/Education/Curriculum/Citizenship/Secondary/Towards-consensus-Citizenship-in-secondary-schools/(language)/eng-GB*

Office for Standards in Education (Ofsted) (2007) Time for change? Personal, social and health education [on-line]. Last accessed 19 February 2010 at: *http://www.ofsted.gov.uk/Ofsted-home/Publications-and-research/Browse-all-by/Education/Curriculum/Personal social-and-health-education/Primary/Time-for-change-Personal-social-and-health-education/(language)/eng-GB*

Office for Standards in Education (Ofsted) (2010) Citizenship Established?: Citizenship in Schools 2006/09 [on-line]. Last accessed on 19 February 2010 at: *http://www.ofsted.gov.uk/Ofsted-home/Publications-and-research/Browse-all-by/Documents-by-type/Thematic-reports/Citizenship-established-Citizenship-in-schools-2006-09*

Qualifications and Curriculum Authority (1998) Education for Citizenship and the Teaching of Democracy in Schools [on-line]. Last accessed 19 February 2010 at: *http://www.qcda.gov.uk/4851.aspx*

Qualifications and Curriculum Authority (QCA) (2007a) Secondary National Curriculum. PSHE: Economic wellbeing and financial capability. Programme of study for Key Stages 3 and 4. [on-line]. Last accessed 19 February 2010 at: *http://curriculum.qca.org.uk/key-stages-3-and-4/subjects/key-stage-3/personal-social-health-and-economic-education/Economic-wellbeing-and-financial-capability/index.aspx*

Qualifications and Curriculum Authority (QCA) (2007b) Secondary National Curriculum. PSHE: Personal wellbeing. Programme of study for Key Stages 3 and 4. [on-line]. Last accessed 19 February 2010 at: *http://curriculum.qca.org.uk/key-stages-3-and-4/subjects/key-stage-3/personal-social-health-and-economic-education/personal-wellbeing/index.aspx*

Qualifications and Curriculum Authority (QCA) (2007c) Citizenship: Programme of Study for Key Stage 3 and Attainment Target [On-line]. Last accessed on 19 February 2010 at: *http://curriculum.qcda.gov.uk/uploads/QCA-07-3329-pCitizenship3_tcm8-396.pdf*

Qualifications and Curriculum Development Agency (QCDA) (2009) PSHE Education in Secondary Schools [on-line]. Last accessed 19 February 2010 at: *http://www.qcda.gov.uk/14702.aspx*

Qualifications and Curriculum Development Agency (QCDA) Aims, Values and Purpose [on-line]. Last accessed 19 February 2010 at: *http://curriculum.qcda.gov.uk/key-stages-3-and-4/aims-values-and-purposes/index.aspx*

Qualifications and Curriculum Development Agency (QCDA) Cross Curriculum Dimensions [on-line]. Last accessed 19 February 2010 at *http://curriculum.qcda.gov.uk/key-stages-3-and-4/cross-curriculum-dimensions/index.aspx*

Chapter 15

Vocational and work-based learning in the school environment

Learning outcomes

By the end of this chapter you should be able to:

→ Define work-based learning (WBL)

→ Identify the implications of work-based learning for current KS4 qualifications

→ Explain the implications for the student teacher of the Diploma qualifications

→ Clarify some of the practical issues surrounding work-based learning

→ Explain what your role may be within this expanding area of work-based learning

Introduction

Work-based and work-related learning is nothing new. Although something of a buzz phrase at the moment, we have been doing it throughout history and continually through our working lives. It is easy to point at the old apprentice system where a youth would work with a master craftsman until he had reached a standard at which he could be trusted to take the mantle on himself. You, of course, have recently, or are currently, undergoing a long period of work-based and work-related learning in conjunction with your educational establishment and teaching placement schools to enable you to achieve your QTS status. In this chapter we will be looking at what work-based and work-related learning means in schools today, and what the implications may be for you as a new member of the school community.

'Learning from work' and 'learning for work'

Initially we might view work-based learning (WBL) within two parameters. First, we might consider the learning gained by the learner **from** the workplace. This might be any kind of learning, as long as it has been gained within the context of the workplace. It might be something to do with mathematics, literacy, ICT, geography, for example, or it might be work-related, e.g. using a tool, writing a technical report, calculating the price of a product. Second, we might consider learning **for** work. This might be any kind of learning, often referred to as 'employability', which helps the learner in preparing for and understanding how to function effectively within the workplace, but it might be learnt anywhere – for example, in school or in the workplace (see Table 15.1).

The aim of *employability* is to encourage learning (understanding, skills, qualities and attitudes) which enables the individual to gain/maintain/obtain/sustain and change (again and again) employment as the need arises and to realise their career potential. 'To be employed is to be at risk, to be employable is to be secure'(Hawkins, 1999).

The most important thing for the learner is not the experience of work but the learning that comes out of this experience. If we are to help learners become more effective 'workers' then the key is to enable them to become more effective learners: that is, to increasingly:

- develop autonomy
- learn about learning
- develop core/key skills
- develop self-managing skills (including planning, evaluation and action planning skills)
- be open to experience.

Therefore, the aims of work-based learning, of employability and of the school curriculum are completely congruent with each other. This means that good learning, teaching and assessment activities and practices (effective learning environments) are central to work-based learning. Work-based learning is also about the transfer of learning – from

Table 15.1 Learning from work/learning for work

Parameter	Learning context (place)	Type of learning
Learning from work	Workplace	Any
Learning for work	Anywhere	Employability

the school setting to the workplace and vice versa – so that the learning gained in one context is transferable to, and strengthens, reinforces and enriches, the other. In relation to the workplace this might be called 'employability', in the education setting it might be referred to as 'lifelong learning'. I hope, by now, that you see that work-based learning is not (only) about vocational or job seeking skills or simply work experience (even if it is called this!).

Practical task

- Critically evaluate a student who is on a work placement (and if it helps think of a particular student and a particular placement).
- List what you expect that learner to learn while on placement, that they could also learn at school.
- Now list what you expect the learner to learn because they are in a workplace setting (and that you would not expect them to learn in the school setting).
- List how you expect the learning gained from the work placement, by the learner, will positively impact on that learner's behaviour and attitude when they return to school after the placement.
- Analyse how the placement experience might make the above happen by design, rather than by chance.

Work-based learning within the school environment

In this section, we will consider what work-based learning means within schools. In some eyes, work-based learning seems to be a rebranding of the careers lessons which they may have undertaken as part of their own secondary education experience. Obviously, there is still a role for the careers lesson, but the depth to which things are now covered is much more than a box file with a few pamphlets and a talk with a careers teacher as to the possible options which may be open to you. This said, where work-based learning fits into the working life of the school depends very much on the school, since some place a higher level of importance on this area than others. Work-based learning is high on the agenda for schools at the moment due to the larger issue of the role of vocational education within the secondary and post-sixteen sector. The principal vehicle for vocational education at the moment is the Diploma, and the previous government invested heavily in its design and inception. However, the question must be asked as to why we need to invest so heavily in vocational education in the first place and what is wrong with a purely academic approach to education?

There are two main drives behind the increased interest in a higher profile for vocational education. First, the issue of student engagement is one which has been high on the agenda for some time. This has been particularly true since the early 1980s:

'increasing disaffection and disengagement with education by some groups of young people … . has led successive UK governments from the 1980s onwards to reassess strategies to post-14 curriculum.'

(Haynes, 2008)

If we accept that students learn in different ways, it is reasonable to expect that a considerable number of students will not be turned on by an education system that looks towards a graded system which is targeted towards enabling students to access higher education. It is hoped that bringing vocational education into the mainstream will cause more students to be set on routes which seem appropriate and meaningful to them.

The second principal driver is the desire of industry to reduce the perceived skills shortages within the current education system. Many comments have been made about the employability of school leavers and its wider social implications:

'the key aims of the 14–19 reform agenda were to broaden the skills acquired by all young people to improve their employability, bridge the skills gap identified by employers, and overcome social exclusion.'

(DfES, 2002)

'we believe firmly that the educational system should produce reliable basic material on which employers can build at their own expense to provide vocational skills.'

Education and Skills Survey (CBI, 2008)

It would appear, therefore, that raising the profile of vocational courses and their inclusion in mainstream education would be generally desirable. Students would be gaining 'real' qualifications in subjects that might not be within the traditional secondary education brief, such as construction and the built environment, retail business and hospitality. It is also important to note that the involvement of industry in helping to create these qualifications should help to give them the status which they have previously lacked.

The widespread introduction of vocational courses via diplomas would involve the creation of a three-track system: the traditional, CGSE, A-level 'academic' route; the Diploma, occupying the broad middle stream; and a third, smaller stream of work-related learning leading towards modern apprenticeships and the workplace. This could benefit the individual child in following a route which is more appropriate to their individual needs and aspirations, but a major issue for the future will be how these routes are valued, especially by students, parents, employers and higher education. Will the Diploma qualification be seen as the academic equivalent of the traditional GCSE/A level? At the moment, it would be a reasonable guess that most people see vocational routes as lower in status than the more traditional academic routes.

'General education is selective and aimed primarily at entry to higher education, with the result that the dominant image of vocational learning in the 14–19 phase is a route for those who cannot succeed within this regime. Thus, vocational education in the schools system is seen by young people and their parents as a lower status option.'

(Hodgson and Spours, 2008)

The success of vocational qualifications, and of the Diploma in particular, may depend upon the possibility of changing this prevailing feeling about the hard value of such qualifications. Until the system is accepted, and is in place and widely available, it will not be possible to answer this question fully.

Since 2009 schools have been required to enable students to access any one of ten Diplomas, and have had to invest greatly. Some of the issues in the introduction of the Diplomas will be discussed later in this chapter, but at the forefront of these is the question of the ability of the schools to deliver the courses in terms of their individual teacher skills and the resources available to them. Do teaching staff have the background to make learning experience of their students realistic in terms of the application of skills in the workplace?

14–19 Diplomas

In this section we will look at the 14–19 Diplomas in more depth, investigate the subjects available and review a model for delivery. As indicated earlier in this chapter, there has been a long-standing understanding of the need for vocational education as a viable alternative to the more traditional, academic routes. Industry has been increasingly vocal in expressing its concerns about the quality and appropriateness of the qualifications gained by secondary-level students. This was combined with a concern that the traditional academic routes were not engaging or relevant to a considerable number of students. The 2005 White Paper 14–19 Education and Skills identified the reforms needed to address this problem. Its objective was to create qualifications which would improve a student's life and social skills as well as their academic ability, thus preparing them for a world where the workplace is constantly evolving. The principal difference between these and other previous vocational courses was the direct involvement of industry working in partnership with government and educationalists in the design of the new 14–19 Diplomas.

The issue of the Diplomas is still a contentious one, with many schools holding back from committing fully to the Diplomas because of uncertainty about their future. A wholesale embrace of the Diplomas will represent a huge investment in terms of staff and funding. While the Brown government committed itself to the roll-out and widespread adoption of this qualification, the current government have stated that they will not support the full roll-out as intended. At the time of writing this is still unresolved. The issue of how to deliver the courses is also still under review, as schools are expected to work in partnership to deliver the courses rather than deliver them individually. The issues that this raises will be discussed later in this chapter. However, it is reasonable to assume that the Diplomas will continue in some form, and it is important to have a good understanding of the subjects available and the structure of delivery.

The Diploma has been identified as an alternative to the traditional academic GCSE/ A level route or the vocational apprenticeship schemes. It is also intended that the Diplomas will provide a recognised route into higher education, should the student wish to follow this option. The basic idea behind all of the Diplomas is that they will provide a mix of theory and practical experiences within their subject. Consequently, students can expect to learn through work-related scenarios as part of their studies rather than learning about subjects generically and applying them to real-life situations later.

Currently, it is the intention to roll out a range of diploma options by 2011. These are being released in phases. In 2008 there were five Diplomas:

1 Society, Health and Development
2 Creative and Media
3 Construction and the Built Environment
4 Engineering
5 Information Technology.

Following that in 2009 were options such as:

1 Business, administration and finance
2 Hair and beauty
3 Hospitality
4 Manufacturing and product design.

Further options planned for 2011 include:

1 Retail business
2 Sport and active leisure
3 Travel and tourism.

The remaining three subjects will be started in September 2011 unless the political will to do so has evaporated:

1 Humanities and social sciences
2 Languages and international communication
3 Science.

Each of the Diplomas is offered at three levels. The foundation and higher levels are aimed at the Key Stage 4, 14–16 year old students, and the advanced intended as an alternative to traditional A-levels. In terms of academic value, successful completion of the foundation route will give a student the equivalent of 5 GCSEs at grade D-G level. The higher level will be the equivalent of 7 GCSEs at grade A*-C, and the Advanced Diploma will have the equivalent value to 3.5 A Levels, although the grade equivalency has not yet been stated. There is also a progression diploma option which is the equivalent of 2.5 A levels.

It is expected that, especially with the foundation and higher levels, Diplomas will run alongside other qualifications. Consequently, students will be expected to take GCSEs alongside their diploma course. It is also an option for students of advanced Diplomas there is to elect to take A-level courses in addition to their Diploma.

Structure and delivery of the Diploma

The general structure in terms of guided learning hours and the majority of the content of the generic learning section have been established for each of the Diplomas. In this section we will be looking at these issues along with the role of functional skills within the Diplomas.

As with each qualification, guided learning hours are stated for each Diploma. For the different levels of Diploma, the structure and guided learning hours are as shown in Table 15.2, Table 15.3 and Table 15.4

Table 15.2 Foundation Diploma – 600 guided learning hours

Principle Learning	Generic Learning	Additional and Specialist Learning
240 GLH 50% Applied Learning	Level Functional Skills in English, Maths, ICT 120 GLH	120 GLH
	Level 1 project 60 GLH	
	Personal Learning and Thinking Skills 60 GLH	
	Work Experience Minimum 10 Days	

Table 15.3 Higher Diploma – 800 guided learning hours

Principle Learning	Generic Learning	Additional and Specialist Learning
420 GLH 50% Applied Learning	Level Functional Skills in English, Maths, ICT 80 GLH	180 GLH
	Level 1 project 60 GLH	
	Personal Learning and Thinking Skills 60 GLH	
	Work Experience Minimum 10 Days	

Table 15.4 Advanced Diploma – 1080 guided learning hours

Principle Learning	Generic Learning	Additional and Specialist Learning
540 GLH 50% Applied Learning	Level Functional Skills in English, Maths, ICT (No GLH at Level 3)	360 GLH
	Level 3 Extended Project 120 GLH	
	Personal Learning and Thinking Skills 60 GLH	
	Work Experience Minimum 10 Days Exception of SHD – 20 days level 3	

Functional skills and personal learning and thinking skills

One of the main initial concerns voiced about the Diplomas has been that, within a shifting marketplace, students will be restricting themselves unnecessarily by taking a qualification which is aimed at only one area of the economy – for example, Construction or Hair and Beauty. Although this is a reasonable criticism, since gaining the qualification will require a considerable effort focused on that one area, it would not be fair to assume that the students of the course are restricted solely to that career option for their future. The main reason for this is that the courses have been designed with transferable skills at their heart. Employers have identified that pure academic skills are not enough to make a student employable; they also need to have a number of generic skills. These six areas are grouped together within the Personal Learning and Thinking Skills (PLTS). All students of the Diploma will also be expected to take a core qualification in English, Maths and ICT, the level of this being appropriate to the level at which the qualification is being taken. The aim of this is to ensure that students reach a minimum standard, and they will not be able to secure their Diploma without passing these three Functional Skills.

The skills identified within the personal thinking and learning skills are independent enquiry, creative thinking, reflective learning, team working, self-management and effective participation. These are seen as important in making a student a strong, independent learner, but also one whose skills would be highly valued in the workplace (see Table 15.5).

Assessment of the Diploma

The Diplomas are assessed by a combination of examination and coursework. However, it is clear that students have to pass all components of the course to achieve the Diploma. So, for example, if a student fails to pass their functional skills in any one of the

Table 15.5 Personal learning and thinking skills framework

Independent enquirers	Creative thinkers	Reflective learners
Focus: Young people process and evaluate information in their investigations, planning what to do and how to go about it. They take informed and well-reasoned decisions, recognising that others have different beliefs and attitudes. **Young people:** • identify questions to answer and problems to resolve • plan and carryout research, appreciating the consequences of decisions • explore issues, events or problems from different perspectives • analyse and evaluate information, judging its relevance and value • consider the influence of circumstances, beliefs and feeling on decisions and events • support conclusions, using reasoned arguments and evidence.	**Focus:** Young people think creatively by generating and exploring ideas, making original connections. They try different ways to tackle a problem, working with others to find imaginative solutions and outcomes that are of value. **Young people:** • generate ideas and explore possibilities • ask questions to extend their thinking • connect their own and others' ideas and experiences in inventive ways • question their own and others' assumptions • try out alternatives, or new solutions and follow ideas through • adapt ideas as circumstances change.	**Focus:** Young people evaluate their strengths and limitations, setting themselves realistic goals with criteria for success. They monitor their own performance and progress, inviting feedback from others and making changes to further their learning. **Young people:** • assess themselves and others, identifying opportunities and achievements • set goals with success criteria for their development and work • review progress, acting on the outcomes • invite feedback and deal positively with praise, setbacks and criticism • evaluate experiences and learning to inform future progress • communicate their learning in relevant ways for different audiences.

Team workers	Self-managers	Effective participators
Focus: Young people work confidently with others, adapting to different contexts and taking responsibility for their own part. They listen to and take account of different views. They form collaborative relationships, resolving issues to reach agreed outcomes. **Young people:** • collaborate with others to work towards common goals • reach agreements, managing discussions to achieve results • adapt behaviour to suit different roles and situations, including leadership roles • show fairness and consideration to others • take responsibility, showing confidence in themselves and their contribution • provide constructive support and feedback to others.	**Focus:** Young people organise themselves, showing personal responsibility, initiative, creativity and enterprise with a commitment to learning and self-improvement. They actively embrace change, responding positively to new priorities, coping with challenges and looking for opportunities. **Young people:** • seek out challenges or new responsibilities and show flexibility when priorities change • work towards goals, showing initiative, commitment and perseverance • organise time and resources, prioritising actions • anticipate, take and manage risks • deal with competing pressures, including personal and work-related demands • respond positively to change, seeking advice and support when needed • manage their emotions, and build and maintain relationships.	**Focus:** Young people actively engage with issues that affect them and those around them. They play a full part in the life of their school, college, workplace or wider community by taking responsible action to bring improvements for others as well as themselves. **Young people:** • discuss issues of concern, seeking resolution where needed • present a persuasive case for action • propose practical ways forward, breaking these down into manageable steps • identify improvements that would benefit others as well as themselves • try to influence others, negotiating and balancing diverse views to reach workable solutions • act as an advocate for views and beliefs that may differ from their own.

Source: www.qcda.gov.uk.

three areas of Maths, English and ICT at the level appropriate for the qualification, they will not be able to secure the Diploma. The functional skills section of the Diploma is assessed by examination, which is marked externally. Other parts of the principal and generic learning sections are marked internally and moderated externally to ensure standards are accurate and appropriate.

It is reasonable to question how a student is assessed for the personal thinking and learning skills section of the Diploma. These are not assessed separately, but are threaded through the qualification and evidence gathered within their principal learning areas and the project. The project itself has to be appropriate to the specific qualification the student has opted for and assessed locally. The work experience section of the Diploma is not assessed.

Students taking the Diploma are also required to undergo an advanced and specialist learning section. These are separate GCSE qualifications studied by the student. So, for example, a student may take the Diploma in travel and tourism and then take French GCSE in this further section. Although this section is marked externally, the student must pass it at grade C or above in terms of the Higher Diploma or at G or above in the Foundation Diploma.

As regards the grading students achieve, the level 1 Diploma is worth the equivalent of 5 D–G grades at GCSE, although these are reported to the student as grades A*, A, B. The level 2 qualifications have the equivalency of 7 A*–C GCSEs and are reported to the student as A*, A, B, C, and the level 3 Diploma is worth 3.5 A Levels. Students taking the Advanced Diploma score a maximum 490 UCAS points. Any students taking a diploma who do not meet the criteria in all of the sections are awarded a U.

Information, advice and guidance

Although the Diplomas are in their early stages and, in some instances, have yet to be launched, the support provided behind the scenes in terms of information, guidance and advice is vital. It is important to understand that the Diplomas represent a move away from some of the more traditional qualifications which have been delivered in isolation within the individual schools. The success of the Diplomas depends upon the collaboration of the various schools delivering the various courses, the support of the local authority and the inclusion of local industries who are active in the work-experience section of the Diploma as well as helping with case studies and appropriate group visits. It is also important to remember than not all schools and colleges are delivering all of the Diplomas, and that, although some act as the lead school for certain courses, they may not be able to lead on them all. The implication of this is that students from different schools are moving between the different sites in order to complete their Diploma. The issues surrounding this will be discussed later in this chapter; however, it is clear that this is a logistical headache which needs careful planning and organising.

A good example of a group that is already active can be drawn from the East Midlands where Ripley Heanor Learning Community (LHRC) is currently supporting both existing vocational courses as well as helping with the roll-out of the Diplomas. The group itself is made up of six mainstream schools, one special school, a further education college, a training provider and the Connexions service. This group is responsible for providing resources, activities and events such as Key Stage 3 option evenings where students and parents can discuss what courses are available to them and the production of a prospectus and local community website giving information about the Diplomas and Key Stage 4 apprenticeships. Obviously, despite the fact that the Diploma contains transferable skills, the selection of the appropriate qualification is important for any student. It will become increasingly important for teachers to not only deliver the courses at Key Stage 4, but be able to provide the appropriate guidance and support for students in Key Stage 3 as they come up to the selection of their options.

Delivery models for the Diploma

Although it is still early days in the development of Diplomas, there are already a few models for delivery from those areas where they are already being awarded. One example would be that of Chorley and South Ribble Learning Community who are currently delivering the Engineering Diploma to a number of students.

Case study

The learning community of Chorley and South Ribble Learning Community comprises 21 institutions consisting of one special school, one short-stay school and one college of further education. The remaining 18 institutions are 11–16 schools. The level 2 Engineering Diploma qualification is delivered at three schools, each one leading for a group within the learning community. Students from the different schools within the learning community attend host schools on their diploma days. As part of the Diploma, students work on projects which are based on industrial scenarios arrived at in cooperation with the learning community's industrial partners (Leyland Trucks, BAE Systems, Springfield Fuels and ImechE) who are active not only in providing case studies and projects for the students to work on, but also in providing visits to the workplace and staff for talks at the school. Although the students are only halfway through their course, it is hoped that this model will enable the students to see a clear pathway as the theory in the classroom is directly related to their project work and experiences outside the classroom. The use of case studies and projects helps to drive the learning and, it is hoped, improve engagement.

The model of delivery described in the case study above is typical of those being delivered at the moment. A consortium combining schools, further education colleges and industry work together to produce materials, case studies and projects directly related to the qualification being sought. The decision on which institution acts as the lead will depend upon the skills and facilities available. Many schools have now been assigned a local specialist status in, for example, engineering or computing, so it would be reasonable to assume that they take the lead role within a consortium. In some instances, the lead institution may not be a traditional school, but a local college or external provider.

Whatever the lead institution is, it is responsible for delivering the principal learning, both practical and theoretical, as well as the individual project. The aspects of PLTS are assessed within the project and principal learning, and evidenced within the work that the students undertake. The functional skills and additional and specialist learning take place at the student's home institution.

An example of the delivery of vocational education

In this section a model for the delivery of work-based learning used in a school ('School X') in the north of Sheffield is considered. In this case the school places a great emphasis on the importance of work-related learning and, as a result, introduces it at Key Stage 3 via specific careers days in Y8 and Y9. At Key Stage 4 a large number of students take BTEC qualifications while also experiencing careers lessons during the normal week. The reason why this school and model have been selected is down to their practical experience of the delivery of vocational courses. Many of the issues which they have in delivering the BTEC courses will also be relevant for the delivery of the diploma qualifications and such schools may find it easier to migrate to the diploma qualifications.

Work-based learning at KS3

As indicated earlier, School X places a great deal of importance on the issue of work-based learning, dedicating curriculum days to the area at different points within the school year. The content of these days are delivered by a combination of dedicated staff, form tutors and external visitors. During these days students will be taken off timetable and receive sessions which are targeted at informing the students what work may mean to them and start to explore such things as what qualifications they may need to enable them to target specific jobs and careers. This may involve sessions with careers staff and specialist speakers who come into the school from outside.

There may be information-gathering sessions for the students where they are expected to find out information about specific jobs and careers via the internet, which they may then be expected to turn into a presentation, for example. They may also experience career-identification software packages such as KUDOS where students are given a range of possible career options based on the responses they give to questions posed by the programme.

In some cases it will help to guide students in their selection of qualifications at Key Stage 4, while for others it may simply stimulate them into thinking for the first time about what the future may hold for them. In this situation, you, as the tutor, may be expected to support the sessions and become involved in aspects of guidance, but the sessions will more than likely be led by experts, both internal and external.

Work-based learning at KS4

In Key Stage 4, the whole issue of work-based and work-related learning gains momentum. In this model the students are given a dedicated careers lesson a week which will be delivered by a specialist teacher. A typical scheme of work for this session will place a heavy initial emphasis on the use of careers-identification software such as KUDOS which may have been already used at Key Stage 3. From here, students will be taken through a route which will include units on business enterprise, health and safety at work, the application and interview process, writing personal statements and completing both paper-based and on-line applications.

During Y10, students will also undertake a two-week work placement within the local community based in local industries and services. Needless to say, this is a huge operation and a logistical nightmare for many schools to take part in and usually requires coordination with other schools as well as potential employers to reduce the issue of competition for limited placements and ensure a quality of provision.

In this situation the school will ensure that each student is visited while on placement. This will involve all teaching staff in the school, since time on the timetable will be freed up as students are out of school at those times. The visit will involve an interview with the placement provider as well as the student on the placement and will normally follow a prescribed format.

The timing of the placement is intended to reduce the disruption which it will inevitably cause. In this instance the work-experience block occurs in the two weeks prior to the Easter break. This allows the students to return and reflect on their experience as well as to conduct a number of activities.

In Y11 students will be expected to participate in a mock interview day where a range of local employers and services come into the school to give the students the experience of a formal interview, but also provide a detailed feedback on their application, personal statement and interview performance. This highly valuable experience is then used to inform rewriting of personal statements, CV and application forms.

Linking work-based learning to the curriculum

The delivery of careers lessons is, however, only one aspect of work-based and work-related learning which students can expect to experience. As indicated earlier, government concerns about student engagement and the appropriateness of the curriculum to deliver the needs of industry in terms of its future workforce have resulted in a raised profile for vocational courses, in particular the 14–19 Diplomas. In the Sheffield school

Practical Task

Critically consider the following questions in the light of government policies regarding the 14–19 curriculum, and write down your thoughts based on your own experiences and reading.

- What do you think that a student should gain from following a vocational course?
- What do you think about a student possibly making a career choice at 14?

An example of a student on a work-based learning route
Source: Education Photos

discussed later in this chapter, a range of BTEC qualifications have been on offer for the students, which have proved increasingly popular amongst the student body.

The positive way in which successfully run vocational courses are received by students is further supported by a number of studies:

> 'These new work-related courses and experiences for 14–16 year olds have proved very popular with those learners who have experienced them (for example Ofsted 2005; Golden et al. 2005; Steer and Grainger 2007). In the Steer and Grainger study, which examined the impact of a locally devised "Raising Enjoyment and Achievement Programme" in Wolverhampton, learners stated that they had experienced a wide range of activities, many of which took place outside the school context. For the most part, the activities had a clear purpose and focus, learning was at the right pace, they were given regular feedback on their progress and they benefited from the considerable individual attention.'

> (Hodgson and Spours, 2008)

This would seem to imply that, although there are a number of practical issues to consider, with a different method of delivery, vocational courses can prove very popular and motivational to students who may not have been so keen on traditional, academic courses.

Although the delivery of vocational courses is not new, and some schools are very experienced in their delivery, there are a number of key issues which should be considered that may be different for many schools, especially when we consider that they may have, up to this point, delivered only academic courses.

Critical synthesis

Evaluate the Level 2 Diploma by comparing it with a similar qualification at this level, such as the OCR National Award (or compare the Level 3 Diploma with the GCE). Do you think there is parity of esteem between the Diplomas and these more traditional types of qualification?

Try to critically analyse just how far education has come from the Tripartite System of the 1940s to where we are today (see McCulloch, 1994, for further reading).

Issues in the delivery of vocational courses in schools

The implications for the widespread use of vocational qualifications within the secondary educational system are considerable. The success of the delivery of the diploma qualification, for example, depends upon the cooperation of a range of schools and providers to coordinate their efforts. For example, School X may provide a diploma in Business studies and School Y may provide one in Engineering, but not one in Business studies. The assumption is that students from Schools X and Y may travel between each other to undertake their qualifications, which, on paper, seems fine. However, there are problems which immediately leap to mind, and these were identified and emphasised by the work of Gill Haynes publishing in the *Journal of Education and Work*. During this research, head-teachers gave the following concerns centred on the practical issues of logistics and staff.

Logistical issues

1 Harmonisation of timetables across participating schools and the college: weekly and termly, including length of teaching periods.
2 Transportation of students to other learning sites – organisation and funding.
3 Procedural matters:
   * induction of students to new learning sites
   * behaviour management
   * monitoring student attendance
   * dress codes
   * responsibilities for writing reports on the students' progress
   * contingencies for staff absences.
4 Health and safety issues, where courses involve work placements.

Staff matters

1 Professional development of college staff: for example, some are not qualified to teach 14–16 year olds; others may need 'refresher' courses.

2 Staff pay and conditions – college staff pay and conditions of work are different from those of their colleagues in schools.

3 Monitoring of the quality of teaching and learning.

Seventy-three per cent of headteachers responded 'yes' to a question asking whether their school had experienced problems with vocational courses delivered at other institutions.

The seven most frequently mentioned problems are listed below in order of the frequency with which they were mentioned:

1 *Teaching quality* – perceived by the school to be at a lower level than at the students' home institution

2 *Behaviour management* – schools commented on college/training providers' inability to cope with KS4 students

3 *Timetabling difficulties*

4 *Communication problems* between school and college/training provider

5 *Travel to learn* – cost/supervision of students

6 *Reporting procedures*

7 *Attendance/punctuality* of students.

(Haynes, 2008)

It is clear that there are a number of issues which need to be resolved, but there may also need to be a leap of faith by schools if this system is to work. Obviously a huge amount of money has been invested in the development of the diploma system, and the government would appear to be committed to its implementation. However, if schools continue to work separately in terms of their timetable, and the basic issues of travel and people management are not resolved, the successful roll-out of the diploma qualification could prove very difficult indeed. Consequently, in order for the wide-scale implementation of the Diploma to be a success, the first requirement must be that schools start to work together, rather than acting as independent establishments, as has been the case historically.

The role of external partners

Vital to the success of any vocational course are the practical skills it gives to its students. Central to this must therefore be the role which industry plays, not only because of the ten days of work experience, but also in the course content and delivery. In some European countries, for example Germany, there is a tradition of social partnership within education. This means that there is an expectation that industry will be actively involved in education. This is not the case in Britain.

> 'At the heart of the problem of vocational learning and the work-based route lies the issue of employer engagement and the nature of employment in modern Britain. First and foremost, there is no strong tradition of a social partnership approach to vocational education'
>
> (Hodgson and Spours, 2008)

Despite the continued drive for vocational education from the early 1980s onwards, the role of industry has been one of voluntarism. This did not change with the Brown and

Blair governments of the 1990s and post-2000, and the expectation is more one of voluntary support and involvement. Obviously industry has been involved in the development of the courses, but there is no obligation on industry to take a more active role. This, therefore, becomes a real problem for the success of the diplomas, and at a time of economic recession, involvement in education may not be one of the highest priorities for struggling industries. Also, as these links are not formalised, there is some scepticism about the strength of the links between industry and the Diploma in particular. Hatcher sums this up in the following statement:

> 'the indications so far of tenuous links with employers, largely classroom-based teaching with only ten days required work experience, and a lack of credible resources and staffing raise doubts about the diplomas.'

(Hatcher, 2008)

Delivering vocational courses

This does not mean that the implementation of vocational qualifications in schools cannot be done successfully. The delivery of the BTEC qualification where the school is in effect farming out the delivery of the qualifications to external providers has proved particularly successful. For example, School X in Sheffield has implemented the BTEC successfully, offering its students Retail, Hair and Beauty, Health and Social Care, Catering, Beauty Consultancy and Sport. Approximately 50 per cent of the students in Key Stage 4 are currently on this course and it becoming an increasingly popular for those students who may not have enjoyed as much success in the traditional academic courses which had been offered by the school.

The success of the courses appears to be down to the effective identification of students for the appropriate course at the appropriate level combined with the delivery style and content where the students see that it is relevant to them in the medium to long term. Students go off site, out of the normal uniform into a more 'adult' environment and mix with students from other schools. To get a place on the course, students have not only to undergo an interview with an appropriate member of staff at the school, but also need to get permission slips from their parents, who in turn have to confirm that they are comfortable with their child making their own way to and from their placement. This might put some of them off. The providers will also receive a profile of the student as well as details of their school attendance and, while on placement, their behaviour, attendance and so forth are monitored and recorded for the school to check. The students can also expect their placement provider to be visited by a staff member from school.

Practical task

Critically analyse what the expectations of work experience may be for the student, their parents, and also the school and the employers. Reflect upon the implications that this may have for the both the work experience placement and the qualification which the student opts for.

The students themselves will be expected to make their own way to their provider, by whatever means is available to them and to stay for a full day. A typical day may involve a theoretical, class-based activity in the morning with a more practical, hands-on session in the afternoon. The groups themselves will be made up of students from a number of schools, enabling an element of mixing which would not normally be available to them and encouraging individual development in communication skills. In terms of assessment, the students will not be required to conduct a summative examination at any stage, but will be assessed by coursework assignments and practical assessment, both of which will prove popular with the students.

Built into this whole experience will be ten days of work experience for the student. Usually, the work-experience placement will be connected to the qualification which they will be taking, giving them a better understanding of the potential workplace in which they may later find themselves. In some placements, however, this may not be the case and the student may find themselves in a different type of establishment. This can cause some concern for the student. However, this does not mean that a positive learning experience for the student cannot take place.

At the start of this chapter we looked at learning from work and learning for work and the issue of employability. The very fact that the students will find themselves within the workplace will enable them to develop transferable skills and this may make them more employable in the long run. For example, the interpersonal skills which are needed when answering the phone to a business customer may be a totally new skill for some students.

Practical task

List those transferable skills which a student on a work placement may develop as a consequence of their experience. Evaluate their use to you as their classroom teacher – try to determine just how transferable the skills really are.

Implications for you as a teacher

The implications of WBL for the classroom teacher depend very much on the direction which the school takes when acting upon the whole issue of work-based learning. For some, it may mean direct and active involvement with the delivery of courses, such as Diplomas. If this is the case, then a range of issues will come into play, such as the changing content of your classroom in terms of the students in it and the content you will be delivering.

Most of the causes for concern have already been identified earlier in this chapter, such as the movement of students between schools, and the delivery and assessment of courses using personnel from a number of schools. As the Diploma is only just getting underway, it is difficult to take these issues much further as we have not seen how they will work in reality. Some may be real and need resolving, others may not. As a professional teacher, you will have to address them when they present themselves.

However, if we look at the likely involvement of a normal teacher in a normal school, the current involvement does tend to revolve around work experience, and your role as a form tutor when it comes to writing references.

During work experience you may well find yourself performing quality-assurance visits, speaking to employers and the student who is on placement there, checking that all is well and writing a short report. If you are a form tutor, you may be involved further. This may, for example, involve you assisting students in creating their CV and personal statements. You will almost certainly be expected to write an individual reference for each student within your form where you will have to comment on the school life of the student concerned, which is a considerable responsibility.

Stop and reflect

If we accept that the effective implementation of qualifications such as the Diploma will become part of our lives as teachers and that this may involve collaboration with other schools, reflect upon the following issues:

- How do you feel about teaching students from other schools?
- How do you feel about the possibility of teaching across different locations?
- How do you feel about practitioners rather than teachers delivering courses?

Challenge your thinking

The debate about A levels and vocational qualifications, especially the famous (infamous?) Diplomas, is not recent. Look at this extract from a newspaper article:

'Custodians of education's most sacred cow, the A level, have been mobilised to defend the "gold standard" against what they see as its deadliest rival – the overarching post-school qualification.

Tory backbenchers and pressure groups such as the Campaign for Real Education are leaning on ministers to dissuade them from sanctioning the creation of an advanced diploma or national certificate which would credit holders with a broad range of achievement, from A level to vocational study.

They are worried that the overarching award, an idea which has been floated by Sir Ron Dearing in the interim report on his review of qualifications for 16–19 year-olds, may be an educational "Trojan horse" out of which might emerge a series of A-level reforms.

(Tony Tysome, *Times Higher Education Supplement*, 24 November 1995)

Reflect on the article.

- Do you think that A levels will ever be replaced as the main university entrance qualification?
- What skills and experiences do Diplomas offer that A levels do not offer?
- How would you convince a university admissions tutor at a traditional university that one of your students who has successfully completed a vocational diploma should be given a place on the course of their choice?

Summary

This chapter intended to give you a greater understanding of what work-based learning may mean for you as a newly qualified teacher. Obviously, the most likely implications for you will revolve around the successful roll-out of the 14–19 Diplomas. It is clear that there are a huge range of issues and practical considerations which need to be discussed and resolved, but that challenge needs to be embraced rather than shied away from.

If work-based learning and, in particular, the 14–19 Diplomas are to be effective, a number of things are clear. First, schools need to work collaboratively rather than in isolation and competition. Second, bodies outside direct education need to be involved and be prepared to dedicate the time and resources to it. Finally, we need to think what schools are. Are they buildings or just a location where part of our students' education takes place?

References

CBI (2008) 'Taking Stock: CBI Education and Skills Survey 2008'. Available on-line at *www.cbi.org.uk/pdf/eduskills0408.pdf*. Accessed November 2010.

DfES (2002) '14–19 Extending opportunities, raising Standards'. London: DfES.

Hatcher, R. (2008) 'Academies and diplomas: two strategies or shaping the future workforce', *Oxford Review of Education*, December, 665–76.

Haynes, G. (2008) 'Secondary headteachers' experiences and perceptions of vocational courses in Key Stage 4 curriculum: some implications for the 14–19 diploma', *Journal of Education and Work*, September 2008, 333–47.

Hodgson, A. and Spours K. (2008) *Education and Training 14–19: curriculum, qualifications and organization*, London: Sage.

Kitchener, D. (2008) 'Inclusion or Selection? The 14+ Education and Training Reforms', *Forum*, 397– 408

McCulloch, G. (1994) *Educational Reconstruction: The 1944 Education Act and the Twenty-first Century*, Ilford: Woburn Press.

Web resources

The following websites provide a great deal of useful and up to date information on the diplomas.

Diploma website: *http://yp.direct.gov.uk/diplomas/*

Direct government: *www.directgov.co.uk/en/EduactionAndLearning/14To19*

Qualifications and Curriculum Development Agency: *www.qcda.gov.uk*

Specific Diploma courses

Business, Administration and Finance: *www.baf-diploma.org.uk*

Construction and the Built Environment: *www.cbediploma.co.uk*

Creative Media: *www.creativeandmediadiploma.com/*

Engineering: *www.engineeringdiploma.com*

Environmental and Land-based studies: *www.diplomaelbs.co.uk/*

Hair and Beauty: *www.habia.org/diploma/*

Hospitality: *www.hospitalitydiploma.co.uk*

Humanities and Social Sciences: *www.humanitiesdiploma.co.uk*

ICT: *www.e-skills.com*

Languages and International Tourism: *www.tandtdiploma.co.uk*

Manufacturing and Product Design: *www.manufacturingdiploma.co.uk*

Public Services: *www.diplomainpublicservices.co.uk*

Retail Business: *www.diplomainretailbusiness.com*

Science: *www.sciencediploma.co.uk*

Sport and Active Leisure: *http://saldiploma.skillsactive.com/*

Travel and Tourism: *www.tandtdiploma.co.uk/*

Diploma support

www.diploma-support.org

Learning communities

www.ripleyhenoric.org

www.countydurham14-19.co.uk

BTEC Nationals: *www.qca.org.uk*

Chapter 16

Pastoral care and the role of the form tutor

Learning outcomes

By the end of this chapter, you will have:

→ An understanding of the possible structures for the pastoral system within a secondary school

→ An understanding of the responsibilities that a form tutor might be given and have considered the rewards of undertaking this role

→ Considered what teenagers are going though during the years they are in your pastoral care and reflect on some of the issues that form tutors might face in carrying out their roles

Introduction

'One looks back with appreciation to the brilliant teachers, but with gratitude to those who touched our human feelings. The curriculum is so much necessary raw material, but warmth is the vital element for the growing plant and for the soul of the child.'

(Carl Jung)

All teachers are more than simply teachers of a particular subject. As Jung points out, the curriculum offers essential material that all students must know, leading to qualifications that will affect the rest of their lives. However, during the years that students spend in secondary school, so much more will happen to them. They will move from being children to adults and experience both the biological and emotional experiences of adolescence. They are likely to experience their first love and their first heartbreak, and face big decisions about the rest of their lives. For others the experience will be much more dramatic as they face bereavement for the first time or cope with the break-up of their family. All of this will impact upon them, their personal development, their attitude, their motivation and their academic achievement. As teachers who see them for a few hours a week in the context of a particular subject area, most of this is unlikely to concern you (unless events outside school are particularly serious and their impact cannot be ignored). However, students will need support of a more personal kind. They need someone who is looking out for them, coordinating responses to difficult situations, and keeping an eye on the 'bigger picture'. That person is usually a form tutor and, quite soon, it will be you.

Stop and reflect

Did you have a form tutor when you were at secondary school? Did you have more than one? Was your relationship with your form tutor different from the relationship that you had with your subject teachers? On reflection, evaluate how important this relationship was to you.

The development of pastoral education

The National Curriculum requires that all young people should be helped to become:

- Successful learners
- Confident individuals
- Responsible citizens.

In addition to the role that different subject areas are expected to play in helping achieve these aims, there is also a requirement that the school curriculum plans for the personal development of students. It is expected that this will be built into the curriculum in a structured way. It states that:

'An effective curriculum will include a planned and coherent approach to personal development and ECM and be reflected in the ethos and values of the school. Every member of the

school staff can contribute to personal development and therefore to the wellbeing of each young person in the school.'

(National Curriculum (2007) [on-line]. Last accessed on 18 February 2010 at:
*http://curriculum.qca.org.uk/key-stages-3-and-4/personal-development/
Personal-development-in-the-curriculum/index.aspx*)

All schools require some way of organising the pastoral care of their students. This is traditionally done through a system of houses or year groups with students divided into groups under the guidance of a tutor. Approaches such as these have evolved over a period of time, probably from roots in the public school system (Marland 2002), but have developed into the myriad approaches that we see today. However, there is no formal guidance on the best way to approach or structure a pastoral system and curriculum within a school. The idea of putting each student under the care of a form tutor was given some of its earliest support in the Norwood Report, published in 1943.

'Each form of pupils would be the special care of one master, whose interest and work it would be to watch over the general development of his pupils in all spheres of school life … because he saw more of his pupils than other masters, he would know more of them as boys and they would know him as a man as well as a teacher; he would be in a position to advise about many aspects of their school life because he had seen their life from their point of view.'

(Norwood, 1943: Part 3, Chapter 1)

The Elton report further emphasised the need for effective pastoral systems and a structured use of tutorial time in its recommendations. It said that headteachers should 'base their pastoral systems on the strengths of the traditional integrated academic, welfare and disciplinary role of the teacher' and that they should 'identify clear aims for the use of tutorial time' (Elton, 1989: Recommendations 37 and 38).

The modern curriculum has continued to recognise the importance of the development of the whole child. Emphasis on Every Child Matters (see Chapter 4) and the requirement that we should promote the spiritual, moral, cultural, mental and physical development of learners while preparing them for the opportunities, responsibilities and experiences of adult life (Great Britain, 1988; QCA, 2007) means that all schools have to address this aspect of the curriculum. This inevitably means that all staff will be involved, at least in the role of form tutor, or perhaps in a pastoral-management role.

Pastoral care and the pastoral system

It is perhaps worth thinking about the distinctions between the pastoral care and pastoral systems. Best notes that these terms are sometimes used interchangeably and that teachers, when asked to describe the pastoral care, will actually describe the pastoral structures within their school (Best, 1995: 5). He points out that 'to care' is a verb, therefore it is something that we do; as such it cannot necessarily be defined by a structure. The concept of pastoral care is also a British one; it is not found in all education systems around the world (Best, 1995:3). We must also be clear that in this chapter our focus is on pastoral *care* rather than the pastoral curriculum (i.e. the aspects of personal development that schools might actively seek to address through subjects such as PSHEe). It is true that schools have developed systems for organising and managing this, and we will consider these. However, we are concerned with thinking about the importance of these structures in helping us to *care* for students.

The organisation of pastoral care

Pastoral systems can be organised differently from school to school. There are three main structures that might be employed.

The horizontal system

Some schools structure their pastoral system by caring for the students in year groups. Each year group is divided into forms of 25–30 students, each looked after by a form tutor. All the tutors and students in their year group are supervised by a head of year. In this model it is common for the tutor to stay with their group from Y7 to Y11. Heads of year will also usually follow the year group throughout Key Stages 3 and 4. Sometimes exceptions are made here, though – for example, sometimes the head of Y7 is static as they specialise in liaising with primary schools and managing the transition from Y6 to Y7. In this situation each year group and their tutors pick up a new head of year in Y8 who will then be with them until the end of Y11.

Where the school has a sixth form the tutor may also follow the group into Y12 and Y13 under the leadership of a head of post-16 education. However, some schools prefer to have a team of specialist sixth form tutors who have experience in guiding students through the university, further education and job application processes.

The advantage of this system is that the whole form group are going through the same experiences at the same time. Therefore, the support can be tailored to meet the needs of the whole group (for example when making curriculum choices at the end of Key Stage 3 or preparing to take external examinations). However, the difficulty of this is that it can also create 'flash-points' in the year. For example, reports for every student in the form need to be checked and sorted at the same time and on parents' evening the tutor might have to see 30 sets of parents/guardians in addition to the parents/guardians for the students for whom they are a subject teacher.

The vertical system

In this system form groups are made up of 4–5 students from each year group from years 7–11 (or 7–13 where applicable). The school may still have heads of year to oversee the concerns of students in each year group at key moments, alternatively each form will belong to a house and a head of house will take responsibility for all students in their house.

The personalisation agenda has, in recent years, been responsible for encouraging many schools to re-organise their pastoral system using a vertical structure. In schools where the emphasis is now on encouraging students to attempt qualifications when they are ready, rather than at a particular age, a pastoral system where students are used to mixing with students from other year groups can be very valuable in changing the ethos. It means that neither the curriculum nor the pastoral system is based on age.

Other advantages of this system are that it creates an 'extended family' within the school, with older students within each form group supporting and mentoring the younger members of the form (Kent and Kay, 2007). Some schools also feel that it has reduced instances of bullying. It also has a practical advantage for form tutors that, at key points (such as parents' evenings, when choosing Key Stage 4 or post-16 courses or a report-writing time) they only have a few tutees in each year group. However, it does mean that the tutor is involved in every parents' evening and reviewing reports for every year group. It can also make the sharing of information more complicated. If a message needs to be given to every student in a year group, every single tutor in the school is involved, rather than the 6–8 form tutors who would need to remember (and could easily be reminded) in the horizontal system.

Critical synthesis

The Specialist Schools and Academies Trust maintains that:
When done well, a VT [vertical tutoring] system offers an effective way to run a school because it is about improving relationships between all members of the school community – teachers, students and parents – and focusing these relationships on learning. It can provide the staffing flexibility that enables teachers to focus on teaching, and provides students and parents with a tutor who will know them throughout their time at school.

SSAT [on-line]. Last accessed 19 Feb 2010 at:
https://www.ssatrust.org.uk/pedagogy/PersonalisingLearning/
Pages/verticaltutoringevents.aspx

Explore some case studies (available on-line) of schools that have moved from horizontal to vertical tutoring systems and research this issue in relevant literature. Synthesise the arguments and opinions that you encounter to help your reach an informed judgement about the pros and cons of the horizontal and vertical systems.

The house system

This is not necessarily a separate structure that could be employed to manage pastoral care, as it could be used alongside either a horizontal or vertical system. This is when each form group is also attached to a house. The existence of several different houses can then add another dimension to school life as houses compete against one another in sports and other events. This is an idea that has its roots in independent boarding schools when students were organised into houses to create a sense of family and community (Marland, 2002: 5).

Some schools (although not all) disbanded their house systems when adopting horizontal pastoral systems. Where a school with horizontal form groups has a house system, either a whole form will be a member of one particular house or individual members of the form will each belong to different houses. The house system is still very popular in schools that adopt a vertical pastoral system. It gives all the members of each form, regardless of their year group, a common identity and common goals.

Practical task

Find out how the pastoral system is organised in your placement school. You should know about the structures of the system. For example:

- Is the system is horizontal or vertical? Is there a house system instead (or as well)?
- Are their heads of year/house and do they have deputies? What are their responsibilities?
- Who are their line managers?
- Evaluate the effectiveness of the system in the light of any stated aims.

The responsibilities of the form tutor

The form tutor is likely to be the only person who has daily contact with the students in their form. For many of these students, just 'being there' is important. The tutor can be an important constant in what would otherwise be a large and impersonal school. Also, the routine established by the tutor can be important in helping students to start each day in the right frame of mind.

The role is a subjective one and the exact nature of it can vary from school to school. Every teacher carries out the role differently because they all bring their own personality and style to it. However, we should consider what is required to do this role well.

Giving out information to a form in group in school
Source: Pearson Education Ltd/Ian Wedgewood

When asked to describe a 'good tutor' the following list was drawn up by a group of Y12 girls. They said that a good tutor:

● Listens to you

● Is not judgemental

● Does not raise issues about things you have done in the past

● Is someone you can relate to

● Listens to the troubles you are having with your subject teachers

● Organises a way of sorting out your differences with the subject teacher

● Is someone who will listen but will also advise

● Can advise on different aspects of life (not just school things)

● Supports you

● Gives you reassurance

● Is knowing they are there and will help you. (Carnell and Lodge, 2002b: 13)

Stop and reflect

What is your initial response to the list above? Is there anything about the role that you are uncomfortable about? Analyse your response to see if it gives rise to any potential problems or tensions?

From the list we can immediately see that the students are describing someone with whom they have a very different relationship from the one they have with their subject teachers. There is an expectation that they will not only care about what their tutees are going though, but also offer them practical and useful advice. They are also looking to them for reassurance and consistency. Particularly interesting is the idea that they expect their tutor to 'not raise issues' about the things that have happened in the past. From their tutor, students need someone who will deal with things (disciplining them when necessary), but then move on and let them have a fresh start; they need someone who is on their side.

The actual responsibilities of the form tutor will vary from school to school and from system to system. However, below we shall consider some of the things that you may be expected to do.

Administration

Most schools set aside time each day for a form tutor to spend with their group. This might be at the beginning, in the middle or at the end of the day. In some schools it will be no more than 10–20 minutes; in others a timetabled tutor period takes place once a week and some do a combination of the two. The purpose of a short daily period is usually in part to help share information across the school (e.g. give out notices or collect information) in addition to the obvious taking of the register (usually done electronically).

Home–school liaison

The form tutor is normally the main link with home for individual students. Through parents' evenings and regular contact (written contact, meetings or telephone calls) the form tutor usually knows the parents and guardians of the students in their form better than any other member of staff. For parents and guardians who have concerns about any aspect of school life, the first person they contact will be their child's form tutor. These parent–tutor relationships, in some cases built up over many years, are very important for some students and their parents. The form tutor becomes the 'human face' of the school and, with home and tutor working together, students experiencing difficulties can be supported and kept on the 'straight and narrow'. It is true that many teachers, even those who are experienced, do not always find working with parents easy. However, Marland and Rogers comment that:

> 'No tutor will ever regret the effort, time, care and generosity she gives to students' families. There will be disappointments and misunderstandings with some families, but even here the tutor will feel happier for genuinely having tried.'

(1997: 96)

Academic tutoring

Form tutors are not specialists in every subject area, but they are specialists when it comes to knowing the students in their form groups. For this reason form tutors are often involved in helping students to make academic decisions, such as choosing optional subjects for Key Stage 3 or Key Stage 4. However, the development of the personalised learning agenda means that this aspect of tutoring is becoming more important. Students faced with greater choices will need more support. There is evidence to indicate that that good tutoring is effective in supporting young people's learning. Lodge comments that 'tutors occupy a unique position in the school. This position gives them the potential to share a breadth of knowledge about the student and their experience of school in a dialogue about learning' (2002a: 36).

Monitoring

The 'breadth of knowledge' that a tutor will have about their tutees comes from the fact that tutors are often responsible for monitoring student progress. This may in part be an administrative task. For example, in some schools tutors often collate and check academic reports or other monitoring data. They may be asked to look for patterns or trends (e.g. if a student appears to be underachieving) and perhaps help with target setting. This gives them a good overview of how students are progressing and where their strengths and weaknesses lie. However, this monitoring role also extends to keeping an eye on how individuals are doing in more general terms. Marland (1989:14) has described the tutor as 'the heart of the school, the specialist whose specialism is bringing everything together, whose subject is the student herself, who struggles for the tutee's entitlement, and who enables the student to make the best use of the school and develop her person'.

Behaviour management

In addition to having an overview of their tutees' academic and personal progress, form tutors often have oversight of their tutees' behaviour around the school too. If a teacher has concerns about a student's behaviour or attitude one of the first things he or she might do is speak to the form tutor about it. In this way form tutors collect information and are often in a position to spot changing patterns of behaviour or attitude. This is another area where close links with home can be important. The tutor may be aware of changing home circumstances that help to explain the situation or may be able to seek support from home for dealing with poor behaviour or attitude.

Teach PSHEe/Citizenship

In some schools PSHEe and/or Citizenship is taught to students in form groups by their form teacher (see Chapter 14). This model has the advantage that some potentially difficult and emotional subjects (e.g. sex and drugs education) are taught to a group by a teacher who knows them all well. There are, of course, disadvantages to this model and these are discussed below.

Practical task

- Find out the responsibilities of a form tutor in your placement school. If you have not already been assigned a form, ask to be attached to one for the duration of your placement.

- Speak to the tutor of that form about the students within it to make sure that you are aware of any particular issues with individuals within the form.

- Also ensure that you know how the registration system works and, if form teachers deliver PSHEe/Citizenship in your school, make sure that you have the schemes of work covering the period of your placement.

In addition to all of the above there are responsibilities that are not so 'formal' but that are very important and form a crucial part of the secondary school experience. For example, it will often fall to the form tutor to coordinate charity events, assemblies and celebrations. At the end of Y11 there will be yearbooks and proms to be organised. There will be discos to be staffed and certificate presentations to attend. Activities such as these are not necessarily part of the 'job description' but they help tutor and tutees to 'bond' and they consolidate relationships through shared experience. The goodwill gained as a result of getting involved in activities such as these can also be hugely important in gaining cooperation in more difficult moments.

The extent to which any form tutor is expect to carry some (or all) of the above responsibilities will vary from school to school. However, in every context the relationship formed between tutor and tutee can be one of the most important and influential of a student's school career. There will be students who are unlucky and have several tutors during their secondary education. However, many schools have a model designed to ensure that, unless a teacher is promoted or leaves, each student can have the same tutor for most of their career. For some students this will be crucial as this relationship will become one of the longest and most constant in their lives to date. For others it will not be important in this way, but it will form the foundation of their secondary school career.

Issues for the form tutor

'We expect teachers to handle teenage pregnancy, substance abuse, and the failings of the family. Then we expect them to educate our children.'

(John Sculley)

Along with the many potential rewards of being a form tutor, come the inevitable challenges. Teachers often feel unprepared for taking on the role of form tutor. However, it is also difficult to imagine how initial teacher education courses could comprehensively prepare students for all that the role might possibly entail. We rely heavily on 'on the job' training, but there is little that can prepare you for dealing with the traumas of adolescence. However, it is worth considering some of the issues that might arise in an effort to address this.

Getting the relationship right

One key challenge for a form tutor is to establish the right relationship with their tutees. A tutor needs to be approachable; students have to feel that they can approach them for support with concerns and problems. However, a form tutor is not a friend; there are likely to be occasions when the tutor has to discipline a student and this cannot be compromised or affected by an over-friendly working relationship. However, be aware that the relationship a teacher has with their students can be different from the relationship that a tutor has with their tutees. This can cause problems when an individual is both subject teacher and a tutor to some students; the students in this situation also need to understand the difference between the class and form-time situations.

Workload

Being a thorough and dedicated form tutor can be a time-consuming activity. Where there is a student with particular problems, the time needed to support them will need to be found. The most extreme cases may require the tutor's attendance at meetings with other members of staff and external agencies. Less extreme cases can still require a tutor to drop everything to deal with the upset or angry student. If a student is standing in front of you in tears the situation has to be dealt with there and then – it cannot wait. Also the time needed to 'go the extra mile' (e.g. helping students to organise a prom or write a yearbook) has to be found in addition to the time required to meet existing commitments and demands. However some of the administrative tasks that had traditionally been associated with the role of the form tutor are no longer the responsibility of teaching staff as a result of the national agreement on *Raising standards and tackling workload* which came into force in 2003. Part of this agreement determined that teachers should not be expected to undertake routine administrative tasks that could be done by others, such as collecting money, collating reports, chasing student absence and analysing attendance figures. This relieves some of the administrative load, allowing tutors to concentrate on their tutees

Pastoral support

One of the major challenges for those new to tutoring is the potential for situations to arise where they will be required to offer advice and deal with emotional situations that are difficult and sometimes complex. Teachers are not counsellors; they do not have the necessary knowledge or training to be expected to fulfil this role, and the relationship between teacher and student is not the same as the relationship between counsellor and client. However, there is a need to be mindful of the fact that these situations can arise and it is, therefore, important that tutors are aware of the places and people that they can go to for support and that they understand the processes for dealing with child protection issues.

The challenge of PSHEe and Citizenship

This is discussed in greater detail elsewhere in this book (see Chapter 14). However we should note that, whilst for some the opportunity to discuss the issues raised in these subject areas will be seen as a great opportunity to get to know their students better, others will be anxious at the thought of talking about potentially sensitive issues with their form group.

Guidance

There no central government guidance on 'how to be a form tutor'. This allows schools to develop the role as they wish in line with their own pastoral systems. It gives schools the flexibility and freedom to support their students in the best way that they can. However, Ofsted do report on pastoral care, giving each school a grade for 'Personal development and wellbeing'. The current Ofsted framework asserts that inspectors should evaluate:

> 'the care, advice, guidance and other support provided to safeguard welfare, promote personal development and achieve high standards.'

> (Ofsted, 2005: 21)

Clearly much of this will be addressed through or underpinned by a strong and supportive pastoral-care system. However, there is no clear advice about the best way to achieve this and no definitive description of what makes a good form tutor. To find an answer to this question requires wider reading, support from a good head of year or head of house, and also some experience.

Stop and reflect

Reflect on how you feel about being a form tutor; consider in particular your skills in relation to the expectations that may be placed on you as a form tutor.

- Are there any aspects of the role that cause you anxiety?
- Where can you go for help and advice if you feel out of your depth?

Dealing with difficult issues

It is in their role as form tutor that most teachers will encounter some of the most demanding and difficult situations of their careers. What these are and the extent of them will depend very much on the individual. However some of the things that might need consideration are outlined below.

Personal values and experience

Some of the issues and situations faced by secondary school students may be things that the tutor themselves has never (and will never) face. It is difficult for anyone to be equipped in this situation to deal with the emotions involved. In addition to this is the fact that many students come from different backgrounds and, as a result, have different beliefs and values. Tutors need to be aware of these differences so that they can handle situations sensitively and appropriately (and ITE students need to be aware of them as this understanding forms part of the criteria for passing some of the standards for QTS).

Safeguarding

A child may make a disclosure (when they tell someone that they are being hurt in some way by another person) to any adult at any time. However, the close relationship that many tutors have with their tutees may mean that a student in trouble feels that they can approach their tutor if they are in difficulty. In a situation like this the most important thing is that the teacher must not promise confidentiality. They have to make the student aware that they may need to involve other adults to get them the help that they need. The disclosure should then be reported to the school's named member of staff who is trained to deal with child protection issues.

Every school has a child protection policy. It is important that you are familiar with the one in your placement school and know who the school's named person is.

Bullying

This is an ever-present issue in secondary schools. Tutors often have to deal with instances of bullying when members of their own form group are involved. Each school has its own anti-bullying policy and all tutors need to be familiar with this. If parents have to be involved then this contact may require involvement of the student's form tutor as part of their home–school liaison role.

Positives of tutoring

Carnell and Lodge highlight the unique position of the form tutor. They note that, over time, a tutor acquires various assets:

1 They have knowledge of the school

2 They have knowledge of the students

3 They have the potential to communicate this knowledge for others. (Carnell and Lodge, 2002a: 59–60)

They acknowledge that they may not have all of these assets all of the time, but this unique combination can be used to help learners understand their own learning (2002b: 13). This is what makes the role of the form tutor truly different. The knowledge a tutor has of their tutees as individuals can be used to help students make the right decisions and can be used to help others make good decisions for the benefit of students.

However, one of the main benefits of being a form tutor is the personal satisfaction that the role can bring. One tutor says of their experience:

> *'I enjoy watching them grow and develop through the shyness and uncertainty of Year 7, through teenage angst which starts in Year 9, to, hopefully, confident and capable Year 11s ready to move on in whatever direction life takes them.'*

(Lodge, 2002b: 35)

The opportunity to be a form tutor can bring a lot of hard work, but it can also be very rewarding. It is a fundamental part of the experience of being a teacher.

Challenge your thinking

In September 2002 the head of Y8 position became vacant at a large comprehensive school in a rural market town. The headteacher decided to appoint a youth advisor, rather than a teacher, to fill the vacancy. This move was intended to leave teachers free to teach, but many of the staff were not convinced that youth workers would understand the school environment, while others were concerned that the move would limit their own promotion prospects. Nevertheless, the pilot went ahead and, as other head of year positions became vacant, they were also filled with pastoral workers. By September 2005 every head of year in the school was a non-teaching member of staff.

Consider this case study and ask yourself the following questions:

- How do you feel about the situation? If you were a member of staff at this school how would you react?

- Would you feel relieved to have the fact that you have little specialist training in pastoral care recognised? Are you supportive of the idea as it recognises that you are, first and foremost, a subject teacher?

- Would you be disappointed? Are you looking forward to being a form tutor? Did you hope that one day you might pursue promotion by being a head of year?

Summary

In this chapter you have been able to review your understanding of the importance of the pastoral system and possible structures for the pastoral system within a secondary school. These include horizontal, vertical and house systems. The advantages and disadvantages of them are discussed.

The chapter then moves on to consider the wide range of responsibilities that a form tutor might be given. You have been encouraged to understand these roles and to appreciate not just the work load implications but also the rewards of undertaking this role. Within this section you were asked to think about roles such as administration, monitoring, behaviour management, home–school liaison, academic tutoring and teaching PSHEe. You were introduced to research that indicated that school students value pastoral tutors who listen, give advice, are not judgemental, reassure and gives support.

Finally, the chapter asks you to consider what teenagers are going though during the years they are in your pastoral care and reflecte on some of the issues that form tutors might face in carrying out their roles. You are given help and advice about dealing with difficult issues such as bullying and safeguarding, but the chapter ends with a mention of all of the positives of being a pastoral tutor.

References

Best, R. (1995) 'Concepts in Pastoral Care and PSE, 3-17', in Best, R. (*et al.*) (1995) *Pastoral Care and Personal-Social Education,* London: Cassell.

Best, Ron (2007) 'The whole child matters: the challenge of Every Child Matters for pastoral care', *Education 3–13,* 35(3): 249–59.

Carnell, E. and Lodge, C. (2002a) *Supporting Effective Learning,* London: Paul Chapman Publishing.

Carnell, E. and Lodge, C. (2002b) 'Support for Students' Learning: What the Form Tutor Can Do', *Pastoral Care,* December, 12–20.

Department of Education and Science and the Welsh Office (DES/WO) (1989) *Discipline in Schools. Report of the Committee of Enquiry Chaired by Lord Elton* (The Elton Report), London: HMSO and on-line: last accessed 18 February 2010 at: *http://www.dg.dial.pipex.com/documents/docs1/elton00a.shtml*

Great Britain (1988) *Education Reform Act 1988,* Chapter 40, London: The Stationery Office.

Kent, P. and Kay, A. (2007) 'Vertical tutoring and the personalisation agenda', *Secondary Headship.*

Lodge, C. (2002a) 'Tutors' and Students' Learning or Why do Schools have Tutors?', *Pastoral Care,* June.

Lodge, C. (2002b) 'Tutors Talking', *Pastoral Care,* December, 35–7.

Marland, M. (1989) *The Tutor and the Tutor Group,* Harlow: Longman.

Marland, M. (2002) 'From 'Form Teacher' to 'Tutor': The Development from the Fifties to the Seventies', *Pastoral Care,* 3–11.

Marland, M. and Rogers, R. (1997) *The Art of the Tutor: Developing Your Role in the Secondary School,* London: Fulton.

Norwood Report, The (1943) *Curriculum and examinations in secondary schools* [on-line]. Last accessed 18 February 2010 at: *http://www.dg.dial.pipex.com/documents/docs2/norwood08.shtml*

Ofsted (2005) *Every child matters: Framework for the inspection of schools in England from September 2005,* London: HMSO.

Qualifications and Curriculum Authority (QCA) (2007) *The Secondary Curriculum* [on-line]. Last accessed on 18 February 2010 at *http://curriculum.qca.org.uk/key-stages-3-and-4/index.aspx.*

Raising Standards and Tackling Workload (2003) [on-line]. Last accessed 19 February 2010 at: *http://www.tda.gov.uk/upload/resources/na_standards_workload.pdf*

Specialist Schools and Academies Trust (2010) *Why Vertical Tutoring?* [on-line]. Last accessed 19 February 2010 at: *https://www.ssatrust.org.uk/pedagogy/PersonalisingLearning/Pages/verticaltutoringevents.aspx.*

Chapter 17

Learning from others

Learning outcomes

By the end of this chapter you will have an understanding of:

→ The meaning of the term 'comparative education'

→ The use, and dangers, of international league tables of children's performance in mathematics, English and science

→ Some factors worthy of comparisons between education structures in a range of countries

→ The importance of learning from others and sharing expertise across international boundaries

Introduction

The aim of this chapter is to introduce you to key models and ideas related to comparative education and to provide approaches to help you to reflect critically on how the UK education system compares with that of other countries. This will help you to become aware of different approaches to education and how we can learn from good practice in other parts of the world.

What is comparative education?

Wendy Bignold and Liz Gayton (2009) state in their excellent book *Global Issues and Comparative Education:* 'any serious student of education has to pay attention to international perspectives'. Surely it makes professional sense that if we can learn from other teachers within our school we must be able to learn from teachers and educationalists across the world. This provides us with a rich and varied source of structures, approaches and philosophies to examine and reflect on. What could be better for the aspiring teacher?

Practical task

Think about your training experiences so far as a teacher:

- How many have involved observing other teachers or getting feedback from other teachers?
- Reflect on the experiences those teachers had during their training and careers.
- Is there a chance that their approaches and advice might be based on a view of education based on their experiences within one country and one education system?
- If the answer to the question above is yes, what advantages and disadvantages might this present for your training?

You will know from your experiences in schools that you can expect a variety of approaches as you move from subject area to subject area and teacher to teacher observing and reflecting on their practice – and yours. We each have our own views about what good teaching is and what education is for. Even within the UK there is a wide range of views, theories and working practices relating to education, each with its own advocates and with its own history. These views grow out of each individual's background, philosophies and experiences. However, a certain overall character or property of an education system can emerge that is largely shaped by the nature of the political and economic circumstances of the country. It would be hard to imagine a country ruled by a dictator having a free and open, adventurous and creative educational system. The differences between the education systems in different countries can be very marked and worthy of study. After all, we cannot always assume that we know best and cannot learn from others. Where would you rank as a reflective practitioner if that was your view?

Bignold and Gayton (2009) go on to explain that the study of different countries is known as comparative education. They go on to define comparative education as:

'...the comparison of education systems, processes and outcomes both in different countries and within a single country.'

(Bignold and Gayton, 2009: 1)

It isn't only researchers who are interested in comparative education. Governments are increasingly looking at education systems from other countries to compare their success to theirs and identify any areas of work and development that might be adopted in their own country.

'Governments are paying increasing attention to international comparison as they search for effective policies that enhance individuals' social and economic prospects, provide incentives for greater efficiency in schooling, and help to mobilise resources to meet rising demands'.

(OECD, 2007: 3)

The OECD (the Organisation for Economic Co-operation and Development) has increasingly become involved in comparative education studies and reports. In collaboration with its Centre for Education Research (CERI) the OECD has published a valuable range of reports comparing national statistics relating to expenditure on education, participation rates in formal education, school organisation, learning environments and student performance. Such reports, from OECD and other organisations, will be discussed later in the chapter.

Why learn from other countries?

Clarkson (2009) points out the dangers of regarding oneself as part of a particular team, group or nations. Within the groups are shared prejudices about other groups and nations. She goes on to make the very valid point that we even use the term 'culture shock' when confronted by the norms, practices and opinions of other groups. The more 'different' from us these groups are, the more culture shock is experienced. To overcome this fear, a common initial approach to comparative education is to be rigorous in collecting qualitative and quantitative information. Clarkson (2009) lists the most common areas or issues about which this information is collected:

- The nature of the curriculum
- Accountability and cost effectiveness
- Administrative practices, retention and attrition
- Achievement and national standards
- Children at risk
- Decentralisation and teacher autonomy
- Equality of opportunity, inclusion and multiculturalism
- Education and training of education professionals.

(Clarkson, 2009: 5)

The learners in both of these schools do well, despite them being very different
Source: Neil McAllister/Alamy   *Source:* Pearson Education Ltd/Ann Cromack. Ikat Design

It is important to note that comparative education should not be about grading the educational systems of different countries, but rather it should be a way to identify different approaches that might be relevant within one's own contexts. Superimposing another country educational system on the UK would not take into account the social, economic, historical and political contexts within which the system grew.

Case study

David is a member of a PGCE group comprising an interesting mixture of trainees from a variety of cultural backgrounds. Within the group are Muslims, Sikhs, Christians and atheists and a number of people who haven't declared any religious beliefs or lack of beliefs. The group also contains a fascinating range of ages and educational backgrounds. Some of the trainees attended very formal private schools in the UK, others studied at inner-city comprehensive schools. Four trainees were students at schools in a country where they sat in rows with over 80 in a class.

Behaviour management was strict with corporal punishment common. One person had attended a Catholic school and others were from countries with a very flexible and easy-going curriculum involving cross-curricular projects and a great deal of work outside the classroom. Some of the group started school when they were four years old, some attended once they were five years old and others were at least seven years old.

- How could the PGCE tutor draw on these valuable experiences to help the group to share ideas and good practice?

- What could David do to ensure he gains as much information about other educational systems as he could from his colleagues?

- Reflect on your experiences to date. Have you taken opportunities to find out about other approaches to education from those educated outside the UK or in very different schools to those you attended?

Issues relating to information comparing different international school systems

Shorrocks-Taylor (2000) outlined clearly some of the potential pitfalls in comparing information about the education systems in different countries directly. Though acknowledged as a valuable process, the comparisons have to be done with a view to potential errors and discrepancies. The main issues are summarised below:

● Most major studies have focused on a limited age range of school students. These are commonly 9–10 years old and 13–14 years old. Occasionally those nearer to school leaving age are used. The reasons given for using 9–10-year-old children is that, if studies selected or sampled younger children, there might be bias in favour of nations with a lower school starting age. It would be unfair to compare children who have just started school with those who have had two to three years of schooling.

● Very few studies are longitudinal (following children across the age ranges as they grow older). Most are cross-sectional. This means that the studies look at two age ranges at one point in time. As Shorrocks-Taylor points out, this does allow for some comparisons but not 'real insights into the factors affecting learning, and their long term influence' (Shorrocks-Taylor, 2000).

● There can be large variations in how the terms 'grades' and 'year groups' are defined between countries. For example, the relationship between the grade a child is in and their chronological age may vary in some countries. Some educational systems have vertical groupings where children in the same grade can vary in age by a few years. In some countries children are held back to repeat grades.

● It is important to set any international comparisons into context. It is important also to know about the types of schools involved. For example, are the children selected or sampled typical of the school or are they atypical? If it is difficult to obtain detailed information about schools within some countries, this will prevent such contextualisation from taking place.

● Response rates for some studies can be very poor. Small sample numbers from some nations can give a false impression of overall education issues and performance.

● Reporting very complex findings can be problematic and so many studies have simplified reporting – often in the form of easy-to-grasp charts and tables.

Edwards (2009) also points out the need for care in international comparisons:

'International comparisons of what secondary pupils from different countries achieve in literacy, mathematics and science are regularly undertaken by a number of agencies including the International Association for the Evaluation of Educational Achievement (IAE), the European Commission (EU) and the Organisation for Economic Co-operation and Development (OECD). These types of investigation may vary in terms of their scale and the nature of the evidence gathered but they are increasingly used to either justify the educational policies and practices in different countries or condemn them.

(Edwards, 2009: 48)

Other authors also quote the IES National Centre for Education Statistics to illustrate the point that policy makers and educators are increasingly tempted to use:

> *'international comparisons to assess how well national systems of education are performing. These comparisons shed light on a host of policy issues, from access to education and equity of resources to the quality of school outputs.'*

(Potts and Safle, 2008)

If valuable information is simply used to make political points or create newspaper copy, there will be a danger that those more directly engaged in education – teachers like you – do not have an opportunity to digest the real messages available from international comparisons. One can hope that comparative education is not reduced to yet more league tables – with the serious implications for those at the top and bottom of the tables and especially for those deemed to have fallen down the table.

Stop and reflect

Critically reflect on a league table system comparing literacy, science or mathematics performance between different countries.

- What might be some of the factors affecting literacy within each country?
- How might cultural beliefs about science impact on performance?
- How can mathematics performance be fairly compared across many different cultures?
- What is your view about the value of international comparisons represented in league tables?

What are international league tables and what do they tell us?

In recent years there have been a number of newspaper headlines highlighting the apparent fall in the UK's position in international league tables. Typical are:

> *'UK schools slip down global table.'*

(The *Guardian*, 2008)

> *'Britain nosedives in education league tables.'*

(The *Daily Telegraph*, 2007)

These headlines are accompanied by dramatic statements and claims such as:

> *'British teenagers have plummeted down an international education league table, sparking fresh fears that schoolchildren are failing to master the basics.'*

(Paton, 2007)

The analysis lacks depth but the figures are accurate if misleading:

> *'In reading, 15-year-olds in the UK dropped from seventh in 2000 to 17th, behind countries including Estonia and Liechtenstein. In maths, pupils fell from eighth to 24th – placing them below the international average.'*

> *'In science, secondary school students in the UK dropped from 4th to 14th.'*

'In maths, the UK actually scored below the international average for the first time, as it was overtaken by a number of other nations including Slovenia, Belgium, the Netherlands, Denmark and Austria. Taiwan was the top-ranked country followed by Finland and Hong Kong.'

(Paton, 2007)

The press coverage of the PISA tables has been fully discussed by Grek (2008). The coverage largely assumes the accuracy and value of the PISA studies and uses the tables to criticise the large spending on education by the UK government with such 'poor' results.

'... above all there is a single dominant reality evident in journalists' writing as well as in the reaction of policy makers, educators and politicians to the study; PISA is an event that no-one can afford to miss – it requires answers and demands actions. It has become the major international tool mobilising interest and debate on the relation of education with the knowledge economy agenda. No matter one's opinion of PISA, critical or approving, there is certainly one position no media, policy maker, politician or researcher can take – that is, ignore it.'

(Grek, 2008)

What are the tests and are they a fair comparison?

The tests are the performance tables produced as part of the OECD's Programme for International Student Assessment (PISA). They are based on independent tests taken by 400,000 secondary school students worldwide.

PISA assesses how far students near the end of compulsory education have acquired some of the knowledge and skills that are essential for full participation in society. In all cycles, the domains of reading, mathematical and scientific literacy are covered, not merely in terms of mastery of the school curriculum, but also in terms of important knowledge and skills needed in adult life. In 2003 an additional domain of problem solving was introduced to continue the examination of cross-curriculum competencies. Each period of assessment focuses on one of the areas of competence fields, though the others are tested as well. Recently the fields have been as shown in Table 17.1.

All students in the survey take pencil-and-paper tests, with assessments lasting a total of two hours for each student. For the PISA 2009 assessment, some participating countries/economies opted for an assessment of the reading of electronic texts. Test items are a mixture of multiple-choice items and questions requiring students to construct their

Table 17.1 **PISA competence fields**

Year	Competence field	Countries taking part
2000	Reading	32
2003	Mathematics	44
2006	Science	57
2009	Reading	63

own responses. The items are organised in groups based on a passage setting out a real-life situation.

The table below gives a summary of the most recent positions for countries in a league table drawn up from PISA performances. Reading results for 2009, published in 2010, are not included.

Table 17.2 **A league table of nations based on the most recently available data from PISA.**

Position in league table	Reading literacy (2000)	Mathematics (2003)	Science (2006)
1	Finland	Finland	Finland
2	Canada	South Korea	Canada
3	New Zealand	Netherlands	Japan
4	Australia	Japan	New Zealand
5	Ireland	Canada	Australia
6	South Korea	Belgium	Netherlands
7	UK	Switzerland	South Korea
8	Japan	Australia	Germany
9	Sweden	New Zealand	UK
10	Austria	Czech Republic	Czech Republic
11	Belgium	Iceland	Switzerland
12	Iceland	Denmark	Austria
13	Norway	France	Belgium
14	France	Sweden	Ireland
15	United States	Austria	Hungary
16	Denmark	Germany	Sweden
17	Switzerland	Ireland	Poland
18	Spain	Slovakia	Denmark
19	Czech Republic	Norway	France
20	Italy	Luxemburg	Iceland
21	Germany	Poland	United States
22	Hungary	Hungary	Slovakia
23	Poland	Spain	Spain
24	Greece	United States	Norway
25	Portugal	Italy	Luxemburg
26	Luxemburg	Portugal	Italy
27	Mexico	Greece	Portugal
28		Turkey	Greece
29		Mexico	Turkey
30			Mexico

Practical task

Study the league table above.

- As a teacher in the UK how does the table make you feel?
- What do the tables really show about the educational systems in the different countries?
- Write a short account explaining why the tables have limited use and where a source of error may have been introduced.
- Research what TIMSS is and consider what TIMSS tells you about international education.

More useful international comparisons

League tables have been used as a shorthand way of drawing crude comparisons of educational performance between countries. However, a great number of different factors impact on performance in any form of assessment. As was discussed earlier, there are differences in the social, economic, historical and political contexts within which the educational system sits. Simple, direct comparisons in the form of league tables are an oversimplification and can mislead.

In addition to the PISA tables there are some more substantial education comparison reports published. The OECD produces annual reports covering a very wide range of factors that make interesting reading. These reports highlight a number of indicators. However, the OECD itself points out that these indicators are not selected on purely educational grounds:

'First, the indicators need to respond to educational issues that are high on national policy agendas, and where the international comparative perspective can offer important added value to what can be accomplished through national analysis and evaluation.

Second, while the indicators need to be as comparable as possible, they also need to be as country-specific as is necessary to allow for historical, systemic and cultural differences between countries.

Third, the indicators need to be presented in as straightforward a manner as possible, while remaining sufficiently complex to reflect multi-faceted educational realities.

Fourth, there is a general desire to keep the indicator set as small as possible, but it needs to be large enough to be useful to policy makers across countries that face different educational challenges.

(OECD, 2007: 3–4)

Some key factors are presented below. These are all taken from the 2007 OECD report, *Education at a Glance* quoted above. This huge document contains hundreds of pages of text, tables and charts but these do help to set any comparisons of performance into a wider context.

Factor 1: Percentage of Gross National Product (GNP) spent on education

OECD countries spend on average 6.2 per cent of GNP on education. Countries spending above 7 per cent are Israel, Iceland, the USA, Korea and Denmark. The UK sits at nearly 6 per cent, with Greece the lowest at 3.4 per cent.

Factor 2: Average class sizes

Over the years there have been many studies and debates about the impact of class size on learning and teaching – and teacher workloads and stress. The OECD report sums this up succinctly:

> 'Smaller classes are often perceived to allow teachers to focus more on the individual needs of students and reduce the amount of class time teachers spend dealing with disruptions. Smaller class sizes may also influence parents when they choose schools for their children. In this respect, class size would be an indicator of the quality of the school system. Yet evidence on the effects of variations in class size upon student performance is very mixed.'

> (OECD, 2007)

In primary classrooms the average class size across the OECD nations is 32. For lower secondary this is 24. In Korea class sizes in primary schools are on average 33, in Luxemburg the average is 15. The average class lower secondary class size in the UK is 26 – slightly above the average.

Factor 3: Earnings and education

Evidence from the OECD countries shows that earnings increase with each level of education passed. Those who have attained upper secondary, post-secondary, non-tertiary or tertiary education enjoy substantial earnings advantages compared with those of the same gender who have not completed upper secondary education. Across all countries, individuals with tertiary-type A and advanced research education had earnings that were at least 50 per cent higher than individuals whose highest level of educational attainment was below upper secondary level of education.

Factor 4: Hours of instruction

> 'The amount and quality of time that people spend learning between early childhood and the start of their working lives shape much of their lives both socially and economically. Countries make a variety of choices about instruction, concerning the length of time devoted to instruction overall and the subjects that are compulsorily taught at schools. These choices reflect national priorities and preferences for the education received by students at different ages, as well as general priorities placed on different subject areas. Countries usually determine statutory or regulatory requirements of instruction hours. These are most often stipulated as the minimum number of hours of instruction that a school must perform. A central notion in the setting of minimum levels is that the provision of sufficient teaching time is a prerequisite for achieving good learning outcomes.

> (OECD, 2007)

- Average hours of instruction in OECD countries (ages 7–8) = 769 hours per year of compulsory instruction time.

- Average hours of instruction in OECD countries (ages 9–11) = 814 hours per year of compulsory instruction time.

- Average hours of instruction in OECD countries (ages 11–14) = 859 hours per year of compulsory instruction time.

- On average among OECD countries, the teaching of reading, writing and literature, mathematics and science comprises nearly 50 per cent of the compulsory instruction time of students aged 9 to 11 and 40 per cent for older students.

- The total number of instruction hours that students are intended to receive between ages 7 and 14 averages 6,898 hours among OECD countries. However, formal requirements range from 5,523 hours in Finland to over 8,000 hours in both Italy and the Netherlands. Interestingly, Finland tops many international league tables and yet has a relatively low number of hours of compulsory contact. Is this a case of quality not quantity?

Factor 5: The hours that teachers teach

The number of teaching hours per year in public primary schools averages 803 hours but ranges from less than 650 hours in Denmark, Japan and Turkey to 1,080 hours in the United States. The average number of teaching hours in upper secondary general education is 664 hours, but ranges from 429 hours in Japan to more than 1,080 hours in the United States.

The school year also varies considerably. Although teachers in Denmark teach for 42 weeks in the year compared with 35–36 weeks per year in Iceland, the total teaching time (in hours) for primary teachers in Iceland is greater than for teachers in Denmark and equal for upper secondary teachers.

The OECD report rightly points out that the proportion of working time spent teaching provides information on the amount of time available for other activities:

- Lesson preparation
- Assessment, marking and correction
- In-service training
- Staff meetings
- Out-of-class activities such as clubs and sport.

A high proportion of working time spent teaching may indicate that less time can be devoted to work such as student assessment and lesson preparation. Alternatively, these duties may be performed at the same level as teachers with a lower proportion of teaching time but conducted outside regulatory working-time hours.

For information, some examples of the percentage time spent teaching in lower secondary schools is given below.

- Scotland = over 60 per cent
- Spain 50 per cent
- Denmark = less than 40 per cent
- Japan = less than 30 per cent.

Practical task

Look through the factors that are reported above.

● Which do you think are most likely to have a direct or indirect impact on student performance and achievement?

● How valid are international comparisons that do not take into account these factors – such as the PISA league tables?

● List any other factors, not discussed above, that can influence differences between national educational systems?

● Out of interest – what percentage of your time is spent teaching? How much of your time do you spend on teaching-related duties?

● How might these figures change when you are in your NQT year?

Edwards (2009) considers in detail the direct comparisons between Finland and England in terms of the nature of the countries and perceived performance in international league tables. As you saw above the choice is an apt one – Finland tops most league tables and England is reported as lagging behind or even losing ground on other nations.

The first thing Edwards does is to make some interesting points about the two countries.

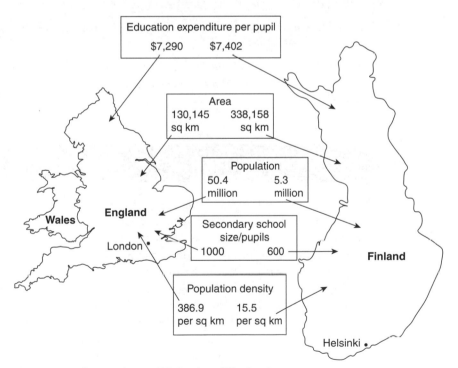

Figure 17.1 Comparison of Finland and England

Edwards then warns of the dangers on relying on the statistics of league tables. Dunn and Goddard (2002) also tell us that any statistical differences between nations cannot be solely assumed to be the result of differences in schooling. Other factors, such as what is learnt out of school, have to be considered. Increasing use of 'out of school learning', cram schools and what is referred to as 'shadow schooling' is popular in many countries to supplement school education. This has, in some cases, grown to such a scale as to rival formal schooling (Baker and LeTendre, 2005)

Critical synthesis

Read the following extracts from Education at a Glance 2008 *(OECD, 2008):*

'*Measuring the socio-economic status of students in higher education by their fathers' educational background reveals large differences among countries. In many countries, students are substantially more likely to be in higher education if their fathers completed higher education. They are more than twice as likely to be in higher education in Austria, France, Germany, Portugal and the United Kingdom than are students whose fathers did not complete higher education. In Ireland and Spain this ratio drops to 1.1 and 1.5, respectively.*'

'*There are large differences among countries in the degree to which students from a blue-collar background participate in higher education. Ireland and Spain stand out as providing the most equitable access to higher education, whereas students from a blue-collar background in Austria, France, Germany and Portugal are about one-half as likely to be in higher education as their proportion in the population would suggest.*'

Reflect on how significant the quotes are in terms of equity and access to education.

Study the data directly in the report – available on-line from: http://www.oecd.org/dataoecd/23/46/41284038.pdf.

● *How much trust would you place in published findings from this source?*
● *Research the OECD to discover more about how it is funded and organised.*

Are international comparisons of any use?

Do the limitations of international comparisons of performance mean that all international comparisons are meaningless? The answer is an emphatic no! Simple league tables based on tests given to samples of young people in different countries should be treated with caution, but other comparisons can be of great use. Differences in what countries spend on education, how schools are structured, the hours teachers spend teaching and preparing for teaching are all significant and worthy of comparison.

Many researchers have argued that we think and learn best through discussions with our peers. Students learn best from one another, with the support of teachers and parents. This approach is favoured by countries such as Sweden and Finland, where learning is guided by 'formative assessment' that informs teaching throughout the academic year. These countries do well in international comparisons, so it would seem that learners do not have to be regularly and formally tested to be good at tests. It appears that concentration on individual needs is more effective.

Comparisons of factors such as the average working week of teachers, the range of grades taught and the number of subjects taught can provide a useful context to any comparisons and allow us to reflect on our own conditions and practices. International conferences, research articles and internet communications and publications, exchanges and educational visits can all provide experiences and information to enhance our reflections on our practice.

Challenge your thinking

In September 2008 *The Times On-line* was one of many news sources to report on the OECD report of that year. Nicola Woolcock, in an article entitled 'Britain fares poorly in international schools league table', reported:

> 'British children start education younger and have a longer school day than most foreign students, an international league table published today indicates.
>
> Yet the United Kingdom comes almost bottom at keeping its teenagers in education beyond the age of 16, with only Mexico, Turkey and Israel doing worse.
>
> And comparatively few young British adults have achieved even a basic secondary education, according to the report by the Organisation for Economic Cooperation and Development (OECD).'

If the data are correct then it would seem that despite a greater **quantity** of education, the **quality** of British education is not high enough to encourage learners to remain engaged.

- What do you consider to be the value to society of having an increasing number of people in education post-16? Is the number of teenagers in education beyond the age of 16 something we should all work to increase?

- What drastic changes to the education system could be made to ensure that more young people are interested in studying further? Is raising the school leaving age to 18 the answer?

Summary

This chapter aimed to discuss the meaning of the term 'comparative education' and to consider the use, and often misuse, of international league tables of children's performance in mathematics, English and science. You should now be able to appreciate the potential errors and over-simplifications inherent in such comparisons. You should also be more aware of a wider range of factors that can be prepared, most easily through the regular reports of the OECD.

Learning from others is an essential part of professional development, and the wide variety of educational systems and approaches around the world offers rich sources for our reflections. Sources include OECD reports, international conferences, research literature, exchanges and visits. Remember that comparative education is about learning from others, not competing to top a league table.

References

Baker, D.P. and LeTendre, G.K. (2005) *National Differences, Global Similarities,* Stanford, CA: Stanford University Press

Bignold, W. and Gayton, L. (2009) (eds) 'Global Issues and Comparative Education', *Learning Matters.*

Clarkson, J. (2009) What is comparative education?' pp. 4–17, in Bignold, W. and Gayton, L. (2009)(eds) Global Issues and Comparative Education, *Learning Matters.*

Dunn, M. and Goddard, E. (2002) *Student achievement in England; results in reading, mathematical and scientific literacy among 15-year olds from OECD PISA 2000 study,* London: The Stationery Office.

Edwards, A. 'High schools and high stakes assessment', pp. 48–63 in Bignold, W. and Gayton, L. (2009)(eds) *Global Issues and Comparative Education, Learning Matters.*

Guardian, The (2008) 'UK schools slip down global table', Stephen Spain, Tuesday 9 September.

Grek, S. (2008) CES Briefing, No. 45, April 2008: *http://www.ces.ed.ac.uk/PDF%20Files/Brief045.pdf*

OECD (2007) *Education at a Glance: OECD Indicators,* OECD.

OECD (2008) *Education at a Glance: OECD Indicators,* OECD.

Paton, G. (2007) 'Britain nosedives in education league tables', *Daily Telegraph,* 4 December.

Potts, C. and Safle, J. (2008) *Characteristics of the 100 largest Public Elementary and Secondary School Diversity in the United States: 2007–8,* IES National Center for Educational Statistics, Washington: US Dept for Education.

Shorrocks-Taylor, D. (2000) 'International Comparisons of Pupil Performance: An Introduction and Discussion', pp. 13–28 in Shorrocks, D. and Jenkins, E.W. (eds) *Learning from Others* (2000), The Netherlands: Kluwer Academic Press.

Woolcock, N. (2008) 'Britain fares poorly in international schools league table', *The Times On-line,* 9 September. *http://www.timesonline.co.uk/tol/news/uk/education/article4714581.ece*

Chapter 18

Getting a job and keeping it

Learning outcomes

By the end of this chapter, you will be able to identify:

→ When to look for and apply for a teaching post

→ Where to look for vacant teaching posts

→ What kind of job to apply for

→ What to look for in a job advertisement and details of a post

→ How to write a good application for a post including:
   – completing an application form and writing a letter of application
   – using the job description, person specification and stages of the selection and recruitment process to improve the quality of your application

→ How to manage a job interview

→ What to do if you are not getting a job interview

→ How to keep your job once you are in post

When should you begin looking for your job?

Although teaching posts are advertised all year round, usually they relate to recruiting staff from 1 September, 1 January or from the end of the Easter school holidays, to coincide with the post commencing at the beginning of school terms.

Let us assume that you are seeking a post to begin teaching at the beginning of a new academic year. It will be in January when you will first spot advertisements for such teaching jobs. Although these might be few and far between at this time, the number will increase as the year progresses until the bulk of jobs are advertised from April through to June.[1] There will still be jobs advertised in July, which will include ones which have been re-advertised. Jobs advertised after the end of May cut-off point will not be suitable for teachers already in post,[2] but it will be a good opportunity for you, as an NQT, to apply (since, because you are not in post, you will be free to take up a job in September).

Where should you look for your job?

Although the *Times Educational Supplement (TES)* (issued every Friday) and the Tuesday edition of the *Guardian* newspaper are key places to look for vacant posts, jobs can be searched for on-line (on specialist teaching and general recruitment sites), including via the *TES* (*http://www.tes.co.uk*) and *Guardian* websites (*http://jobs.guardian.co.uk/jobs/education*), where you also might be able to register to have relevant job alerts emailed to you. Almost universally each local authority will publish a bulletin of vacant teaching posts, which can be accessed on-line or copies obtained from the LA: (*http://www.dcsf.gov.uk/localauthorities/index.cfm?action=authority*). Teaching jobs are advertised also in the local press, again often also accessible on-line.

What kind of job are you looking for?

If you are training in a shortage teaching subject or applying for a job at a time when there are many national vacancies in your subject, you will have more choice and can be more discriminating about what kind of job you want, at what kind of school, in what area, etc. So you can begin to prioritise what, whom and where you wish to teach:

- In a school or college?... public or private?
- KS3, KS4, A2, vocational, community, provision?

---

[1]This is because in April schools set their budget for the new financial year and thus know what staffing resources they have available. By the end of May teachers moving posts will have submitted their letters of resignation to begin a new appointment in September and so schools will be advertising posts during May and June to replace these staff.
[2]This is because teachers in post have missed the end of May cut-off point for submitting their resignation. Their next cut-off point is the end of September to begin a new post the following January.

- In a large, medium or small institution?
- Within a particular Local Authority?
- Within a particular part of the country or type of community, e.g. rural, urban, city, inner-city?
- A specialist area, specific subject or range of subjects?
- With a certain type of learner?

Even in times where you are faced with stiff competition to gain your first job you should still consider these questions and begin to prioritise the kind of jobs which attract you.

The advert

The advert, although often concise about the nature of the post, will generally say whether the job is considered suitable for 'NQTs' or more experienced teachers. In advertisements there is usually only enough space to offer a summary or overview of the school, the job and the kind of person that the school hopes to attract. Because of this you may wish to obtain further details about the post before you decide whether or not to apply for it. It may be only in the further details where there will be sufficient information about the post and school to enable you to make up your mind whether or not to apply.

The advert, however, will tell you something about the school and/or its learners, e.g. 'lively', 'vibrant'. Ask yourself what your overall impression of the advert tells you about the organisation and the kind of person who would be attracted to it and feel comfortable working in it. The advert will give you information about how to obtain further details. Increasingly you will be able to download further details of the job from the school's own website.

Practical task

Deciding which jobs to apply for

Look at editions of the *TES*, Tuesday *Guardian*, local press and on-line sources to investigate the different places where teaching jobs are advertised.

- What do the advertisements tell you about the kind of teacher required, the school, the job and the context in which you would be teaching?
- Could you make a decision from this information about whether a job is suitable for you?
- What additional information would you need to decide whether to apply for the post?

Use the experience to help you to prioritise what kind of jobs attract you (e.g. type or size of school, types of learners, learning provision offered, location, etc.). List the criteria which you might use to decide what teaching jobs you will apply for.

Further details and application form

When you send for further details about a post you may be sent a range of information. This might include:

- a copy of the (full) advertisement,
- a summary of the previous inspection report,[3]
- further information about the school, the area and the Local Authority.

Core information which you should receive is:

- Further details about the particular post being advertised
- An application form
- A job description
- A person specification (perhaps).

Further details about the particular post being advertised

The further details may include supplementary information about the department, for example, the range and level of provision taught and the achievement attained (for example, some quotes from a recent Ofsted report). It might include information about facilities and resources available, and the contribution it makes to the wider school, e.g. enrichment, out-of-school activities, and supplementary information about the school in general. Crucially, it might give information about whether visits to the school by prospective applicants are welcomed and, if so, the arrangements for doing so. If you are able to do so, and the opportunity arises, it is advisable to visit the school before you submit your application. First, the visit will help you to decide whether to apply for the post or not. Second, if you do decide to apply, you might be able to use what you learn from the visit to tailor and improve the quality of your application.

The application form

You may have a choice of application forms to complete. The different choices will ask for the same information, but sometimes you will be given the option to complete a paper copy of the application form, or an on-line version (e.g. in Microsoft Word or pdf format or in some other Web-based format). If you choose the latter options then normally you would submit the completed application form on-line, but whichever option you choose, you are advised to print out the application form after you have completed it so that you can see the layout of the form as the recruiters will see it when they print it out. Check that there are no big gaps or lost print (because the formatting is too wide for the width of the page or a text box is too big to fit on one page, etc.). Adjust the formatting and layout of the form so that, when you do submit/email it, the printed version of the form (the one that the recruiter will see) presents you as professionally as possible.

---

[3] If your pack does not include a copy of the previous school inspection report, you will be able to download one from *http://www.ofsted.gov.uk/oxcare_providers/list*.

Sometimes an Equal Opportunities Monitoring Form is enclosed with the application form. You will be invited to complete it and also perhaps be asked, if you submit a paper copy, to send the equal opportunities form accompanied with the application form in a separate envelope to the same address or to a different location (e.g. the Equal Opportunity Monitoring Section of the LA).

The job description

This is an outline, in varying detail, of the main roles and responsibilities of the post. Hence the list will cover areas such as:

- A requirement that you implement and work in accordance with school policies, processes and procedures
- How the postholder will contribute to the teaching of the subject
- Curriculum planning responsibilities
- A requirement to keep abreast of developments in the field
- How the postholder will be expected to contribute to the wider department activities
- Record-keeping responsibilities
- Expectations about attendance at meetings with other colleagues and parents
- Supervision and cover duty responsibilities.

It may also mention expected standards of behaviour and dress. Sometimes the responsibilities and duties above will be placed in the context of Part 12 of the Conditions of Employment of Teachers and the Professional Standards for Teachers (or a future updated version).

The person specification

It is the person specification that focuses on the experience, skills, knowledge and attributes that are needed for an individual to be able to carry out the duties and responsibilities described in the job description effectively. This is often written in the form of a table, covering headings such as qualifications, experience, skills and qualities. Generally for each of these headings there are 'essential' and 'desirable' requirements identified. For example, with respect to qualifications you would expect under 'essential' to see that the individual would be required to hold a qualification which confers recognised qualified teacher status in the UK, and it may also mention that the postholder should have a degree or equivalent and may say something about the classification of the degree. If the post relates to, say, Physical Education, then under 'desirable' certain coaching awards in a particular sport or sports (often linked to a current need of the school) might be identified. Sometimes it may also mention how these characteristics are to be assessed – for example, through the application form, through presentation, or through interview. If you are not sent a person specification with the further details of the post, then you would need to match your application with the job description and any other information included in the further details for the post. Alternatively, you could collect the person specifications of similar jobs and use these to inform your construction of your letter of application, alongside the other information sent with the further details of the post for which you are applying.

Practical task

Analysing the 'further details' of a job

Send off for a range of further details relating to teaching jobs which you might reasonably apply for. Note how they vary and what is common about these examples.

- What information does the 'further details' give you about the job that is important enough to help you to decide whether to apply for the post, and also important enough to require you to give further thought to the content of your application.

- How does this compare with the list of criteria you created to help you judge whether to apply for a vacancy? Record the areas you would need to write about in a letter of application to match the aspects that a selection panel would consider in making judgements about an applicant: e.g. qualifications, knowledge and understanding, skills, experience, expertise, personal and professional qualities.

Applying for the post

When you apply for a job you will be the applicant, and you will naturally think through the process from the point of view of an applicant. However, to make a successful application, you might also need to spend some time thinking through the process from the point of view of the recruiter(s). Let's look at these two processes Table 18.1.

Table 18.1 The recruitment process

The applicant		The recruiter
Where to look for jobs being advertised – LA local bulletins, local and national press, on-line		
Deciding which job to apply for		Identifying the need(s) of the school and deciding which job will best meet the need(s)
Sending off for details		Advertising the job, writing the job description and person specification
		Deciding the selection process, e.g. asking applicants to make a presentation?, work with a group of students?, meet staff? As well as interview(s)
Completing and sending off the application form. Applying on-line or off-line?		Sending out details and application form to prospective applicants
(Hopefully) being invited to and attending for interview		Perhaps long-listing and short-listing applications received

Table 18.1 (*continued*)

		Inviting short-listed applicants for interview and requesting references
		Involving short-listed applicants, in other selection activities, e.g. making a presentation, meeting staff, meeting students
(Hopefully) being offered and accepting the post		Deciding whether to make an appointment (offer someone the post)

Now, from what you have learned about the recruitment and selection process above how can you use this information to inform the quality of your application (thus putting you in the best possible position to be invited for interview)? When you are putting together an application, revisit the stages above to remind yourself about what the selection panel will be looking for and to consider what implications this has for your application. Use Table 18.2 below to help you make this connection.

Table 18.2 Linking your application to the recruitment process

The recruiter	What the applicant might think about?
Identifying the need(s) of the school and deciding which job will best meet the need(s)	• Does the school need a specialist in a particular area, e.g. a physicist or a good generalist in the subject – someone who can teach physics, biology and chemistry? • Are there any other subjects the recruiter is looking for from the applicant, e.g. also teach a little ICT, Technology? • Is the school looking for the applicant to teach a particular age range, e.g. Key Stage 3, A2?
Advertising the job, writing the job description and person specification	What are the key words used in the advertisement – and why has the recruiter chosen these: 'enthusiastic', 'experienced'?
Deciding the selection process, e.g. asking applicants to make a presentation?, work with a group of students?, meet staff? As well as interview(s)	The recruitment panel will wish to encourage the interviewees to demonstrate a range of knowledge and understanding, personal and professional skills, qualities, attitudes and values, and it is unlikely that using just one selection activity will be able to cover all this. So, what is it that the recruiter will be wanting/encouraging interviewees to demonstrate specifically if they are, for example, asked to make a presentation, work with a group of students, talk with staff, answer interview questions?
Sending out details and application form to prospective applicants	

(*continued*)

Table 18.2 *(continued)*

(Perhaps long-listing and) short-listing applications received	What will the selection panel be looking for when they read the applications. How are they expecting applicants to use their applications to demonstrate the skills, understanding, experience and qualities identified in the person specification and which will be required in order to carry out the job
Inviting short-listed applicants for interview and requesting references	
Interviewing short-listed applicants and undertaking other selection activities	The selection panel will have already collected evidence from the applications about the applicants. What will they want to explore further during the interview process? What will they want to check out after having read your application? What will they be interested in exploring further with you? What will they be wanting you to demonstrate which cannot be demonstrated through a written application?
Deciding whether to make an appointment (offer someone the post)	Do you want the post if it is offered to you?

Your application

When you decide to actually apply for a post then normally your 'application' will comprise a completed application form, a letter of application and a covering letter. The decision as to whether a selection panel will invite you to interview is likely to be based solely on the quality of your application form and letter of application – both on the quality of information contained in it and the quality of its presentation. Thus in order to submit a strong application you should submit both a completed application form and a letter of application. Do not be tempted to substitute either of these for a CV (Curriculum Vitae).

Your application form

Do not leave any gaps in the application form. If there are any gaps in employment or study then include these time frames and share why they are not applicable. If there are any questions or sections that you are not going to answer, include a statement as to why the question or section is not applicable to you. If you have a disability, it is possible that the school or LA have different versions of the application form – for example, large print or Braille, which might better suit your needs. Contact the Local Authorities Equal Opportunities or Disabilities Unit (or equivalent) for further advice.

Your letter of application

The purpose of a letter of application is give you the opportunity to show how your qualifications, experience and capabilities match the requirements in the person specification, to expand on information included in your application form and to share something about yourself as a person and your values, beliefs about of learning and teaching. In writing your letter of application:

- Give special attention to your opening paragraph. Make this a strong assertion which gives an overview of your very best abilities/experiences and how this makes you a strong candidate for the job. Later in your letter of application you must back up any claims you have made in this paragraph with evidence that justifies and substantiates these claims. This suggests that you should not just make a claim about your capabilities (e.g. I plan effectively all my lessons) but include well-chosen examples of your practice to illustrate these and show how you use these capabilities in a professional context (e.g. sharing what it is about your planning approach which would make the reader agree with the judgement that you plan effectively).

- Be very careful about using any kind of presentation or format which deviates from a more recognised type of letter of application, e.g. using coloured paper, photos, desk-top publishing newsletter-style formatting, different or unusual fonts and font sizes. You want your letter of application to stand out – but for the right reasons. You want to ensure that the reader is attracted to your letter of application and can read it easily, rather than being put off by it or finding it difficult to read and follow. Having said that, many letters of applications are very similar to each other – so give some thought to what you could do to set your letter of application slightly apart from the others. On the other hand, do not make your letter of application too formal. Do not write it as an essay, avoid long sentences and long periods of full prose. Use instead a positive, encouraging, vibrant style – aim for a style which you would like the selection panel to use to describe you!

- Be concise and ensure that your letter of application is easy to read and easy to follow. It should have a clear structure, perhaps using sub-headings to offer a clear logical order to and pathway through the areas you are writing about. Often reading it out aloud or asking another person to read it to you will help you to detect areas which you need to re-visit and improve.

- Do not write a standard 'template' and send this to every job for which you apply. Ensure that your letter of application is tailored to the job and personal to the school to which you are applying by using the requirements of the person specification (and other information in the further details) to target your letter of application to the specific needs and characteristics of the job and the school. For example, look at the most recent Ofsted report about the school. If, say, the school needs to improve student behaviour or pastoral support then use the letter of application to highlight your experiences and strengths in these areas. Generally it is better to use fewer well-chosen, key examples and link these to the school and the post than just to offer a long list of bullet-pointed examples. Shape the application to the actual school you are applying for – show empathy and make the school feel special.

- Don't just mention what you have been doing – share the skills, understanding, learning and qualities you used and developed as a result of this involvement.

- Link your application form and letter of application to the roles identified in the job description and the skills, attributes and qualities identified in the person specification (and perhaps the advert) – the closer the match between you and what the selection panel are looking for, the greater the chance of you being invited for interview

- Do not forget that skills are transferable – the selection panel might be looking for a good team worker, someone who can work on their own initiative, with the ability to work under pressure and to support others. You might not be able to evidence all of these while working in a school context, so you need to consider how you might be able to demonstrate them from other contexts in which you have worked, e.g. previous employment, part-time jobs, student union activities, voluntary work, etc.

- Check that the final version of your letter of application addresses the requirements of the person specification. Read your letter of application and ask yourself: will the reader form an opinion of you – what kind of person you are like and what you value? Does the letter of application communicate to the reader the kind of person that you want it to communicate?

- Be honest!

- Check for errors! Ask a friend to check for spelling and grammatical errors and provide feedback on how to improve clarity and layout.

- Try to keep your letter of application down to about two sides of A4. Do not be tempted to use small font, narrow margins, and minimal use of white space to squeeze in more information. Aim for both quality of information and quality of presentation and communication. If you do go over two sides of A4, then re-read the letter of application to see whether you can reduce it without suffering loss of quality. If you can reduce it and not lose quality then do so, otherwise retain the original length in the hope that the quality of the letter will retain the interest of the readers sufficiently for them to read it in full.

Covering letter

The covering letter is just a short note, containing your name and address (include your contact telephone number(s) and email address), confirming the name of the post for which you are applying (include any reference number and the name of the school), identifying the enclosures you are including with the letter (e.g. a completed application form and letter of application) and confirming that you wish to apply for the post.

Practical task

Writing a letter of application

Identify a job for which you are going to apply.

Create a chart like the one below. In the first column write down the criteria/attributes contained in the person specification which could be evidenced through the letter of application. For each entry made in the first column write examples about yourself and your experience/practice which demonstrates that you meet the criteria/attributes. Try to include a range of examples which cover, as far as you are able, all the roles and responsibilities contained in the job description. In the third column, for each entry in columns one and two write down the key skills and qualities you used, the learning gained, specific strategies or resources used, and how your thinking about learning and teaching have developed and been extended.

Criteria/attribute in the person specification	Examples of your experience and practice which evidences the criteria/attribute	Key skills, qualities, capabilities, strategies, approaches, resources used. Learning and development gained.

Now use this chart to help you to write your letter of application. Check to see if there is any other information about the job in the further details that you need to address/cover in the letter of application. Ask a friend to read your letter of application and give you feedback about how to improve it.

Case study

What information are you inadvertently sharing with the selection panel?

A person on a PGCE course was doing particularly well. She was achieving high grades for her teaching in school and was regarded as having huge potential. Her second placement school would have loved to have kept her but had no vacancies, so she has been applying for jobs. Everyone assumed she would obtain one quickly. Her references were excellent and she was confident, hard-working and talented.

A teaching post was advertised near to where she lived, so she applied and was immediately invited for interview. Obviously the application form and supporting letter had hit the mark. All that remained was to prepare thoroughly for the interview and do herself justice. As the day loomed she read widely, rehearsed possible questions and asked for advice from her mentor and other colleagues. The headteacher of her school even did a short practice interview with her.

All was going well until the night before the interview. She received a call from the headteacher of the school she had applied to. Her invitation to interview was cancelled. When asked, the headteacher said that pictures of her on a drunken night out had been seen on a social networking site. The selection panel had decided that this did not constitute professional conduct and so they no longer wished to consider her for the post.

- What are your views about this case study? Do you think the headteacher was being unfair?
- Do you think that what you do 'in your own time' should not influence a selection panel or impact on judgements about your professional conduct?
- Do you use social networking sites? What impressions of you as a person and as a teacher do they give?
- What lessons might this case study teach you about social networking and applying for posts in teaching?

Selection

Ideally a school would wish to advertise any vacant posts as widely as possible to ensure that they attract the strongest possible candidates, appoint the most capable person that they would be able to attract and ensure that they have been fair and equitable in their selection and recruitment process and practices. Generally, from the full number of applicants, the selection panel will choose whoever they feel to be the strongest candidates and short-list these for interview.

Short-listing meeting

In this short-listing meeting the selection panel will consider all applicants and match the information contained in their applications with their selection criteria, which should be informed by the capabilities and characteristics identified in the person specification. Some of these capabilities and characteristics might be essential, others desirable, and some may have greater weighting than others. Generally, however, the closer the match the application suggests that the applicant is to the person specification, the greater the chance that person will be invited to interview. To increase equity and fairness at the short-listing stage, the short-listing increasingly takes place 'blind', i.e. applications are numbered and the selection panel are not told the names or ages of the applicants. This is an important point for you. If you know that your application will be matched to the person specification, then in order to increase your chances of an interview, when you write your application you must ensure that you are really focusing on demonstrating that it matches the person specification

The selection panel will need to decide a selection process which is realistic and manageable. They need to decide whether the process will consist of just an interview of the short-listed applicants, or whether to include additional activities, such as asking applicants to make a presentation, meeting staff and/or meeting or working with groups of learners. Depending on the number and strength of the applications, a selection panel will short-list about four applicants (it would be unusual to short-list less than two or more than six).

The interview

At the interview stage questions should be carefully chosen by the selection panel to compare the applicants with the characteristics in the person specification, where it has not been possible to do so through the written application, e.g. social skills, verbal skills, group, team, practical skills. A selection panel should only short-list candidates who they feel have the potential to be offered the job – it would be a waste of time to do otherwise. Thus, if you get an interview, the assumption is that the selection panel think that you are 'appointable' – so it is up to you to demonstrate to the selection panel at interview that you are 'more appointable' than the other candidates and so end up being offered the post.

Generally at interview you will be asked some questions which relate directly to your application – to enable the selection panel to check out areas that they wish to clarify or explore further. These questions might not be asked of the other candidates. It is likely that some questions will be asked of all candidates, because these are deemed to be the best questions to ask in order to enable the candidate to present themselves in such a way

However many people are on the interview panel, they should make every effort to put you at your ease. They will be keen for you to do your best so they gain an accurate picture of what you have to offer their school

Source: MBI/Alamy

that the selection panel can make judgements about whether the candidate has certain capabilities, characteristics or qualities that the panel are looking for. Additionally, the panel may believe that, if they ask all the candidates more or less the same questions, they are following a procedure which is fair and equitable to all the candidates. You are likely to have an opportunity to ask the panel any questions which you care to ask.

Don't be surprised if members of the selection panel are writing notes as you speak during your interview. This may be off-putting for you because you may feel that you have lost eye contact with the panel members and that they are not listening to you. However, it is more likely that they are not ignoring you, but actually writing down evidence and reactions to what you are telling then and comparing it with the selection criteria. It may be that the more they record, the more you are sharing things which relate to the selection criteria.

The aim of an interview should be for the panel to be fair and enable you to present yourself as effectively as possible. The aim is not to give you the 'third degree' or anything similar in order to have a negative impact on your 'performance'. However supportive and skilful the selection panel is, attending for interview is still likely to be a stressful situation for most of us, and so it is worth considering what strategies you might use to help you to manage any stress you experience, as constructively as possible.

If you are offered the job it might be conditional – on condition that a number of things are carried out and are acceptable, e.g. receipt of references which have not yet arrived, checking qualifications if this has not already taken place, confirming eligibility to work in the UK, CBR checks, etc. It is usual now for you to be asked to bring with you certain information, e.g. proof of identity, etc. – to meet child protection and related policies. It is possible that, in interview, you will be asked questions relating to child protection and how you model effective child protection strategies in your teaching and in your wider role as a teacher.[4]

Every interview will be different but there are likely to be some common stages.

Generally, during your interview, avoid being negative or critical about schools, school placements, learners or colleagues that you have previously worked with. It may be that, if you are over-critical, any judgement made by the selection panel might be made about, and against *you*, rather than against the people whom you have criticised. However negative a previous experience might be, there are learning opportunities to be gained from it – and sometimes we will learn more from a negative experience than from a positive one. So, if you are asked a question which might invite you to be negative or critical, then simply focus on what you learned and gained from the experience.

Introduction and welcome

Be aware of your body language during the interview. Attempt to use behaviour which conveys that you are relaxed, positive and assertive, open and communicative. Remember to smile, shake hands with the interview panel if you get the opportunity, and convey your feelings that it is nice to meet them and that you are pleased that you have the opportunity to attend for interview for the post.

Making you feel comfortable and settled

You will usually be asked some easy, more personal questions at the beginning of the interview to help you feel comfortable and to settle your nerves. These questions might vary from whether you had a good journey to the school, whether you know the area, to saying something about yourself and asking why you are interested in applying for the post and working at the school. However irrelevant you think the initial questions might be, do not forget that it is part of the interview process and the interview panel may be observing how you answer and respond to them.

Questions about learning and teaching (and subject knowledge)

These questions will be geared to exploring your teaching experience and expertise, your understanding of current developments and initiatives in learning, teaching, assessment, subject knowledge and educational issues, and will include questions specific to the actual post and specialist teaching subject area.

---

[4]If you cannot attend on the date offered to you for interview then inform the school and ask whether you can be offered an alternative time and date. Although the selection panel are not obliged to offer you an alternative date and time, if they really want to try to appoint the best candidate then they might consider whether they are able to do so. If you cannot attend because of a disability, or for a religious reason, then you should inform the school of this, since, if they do not give regard to this then they might be discriminating against you and we must make the assumption that panels would not wish to do this. If you have a disability, it is in your interests to let the school know of any particular provision you might need at interview in order for you to perform on an equal footing with the other candidates. The more notice you can give the school, the more time they have to cater for your needs. Obviously if you cannot attend because you are on holiday or have tickets for a concert that day or another social commitment, then the panel might be less likely to rearrange the interview for you.

Questions about you

These questions will be geared to exploring your capabilities in areas such as organising, leadership and managing skills, communication and interpersonal skills, your attitudes and values.

Opportunity for you to ask questions

This is an opportunity for you to ask questions about the post and the school.

Concluding the interview

This enables the selection panel to check how you feel the interview went, whether you feel that you have presented yourself as well as you had wanted, whether you are still a firm candidate for the post and whether you would be in a position to accept the post if you were offered it. You may be asked if there is anything you wish to add. If you have not covered all the key points which you want to get across then now is your opportunity.

The panel will want to check how they can contact you after the interview process to inform you about the decision of the panel and also about any arrangements there might be of giving you feedback about your interview performance, if you wish to receive it.

Exiting the interview

Remember to thank the interview panel, to keep positive and, if appropriate, to shake hands with the members of the panel.

Examples of questions that you might be asked at interview

Introductory questions

- Did you find the school OK?/have a good journey?
- Tell me about a little bit about yourself? (This is probably the most frequently asked question in interviews so you may wish to plan for this question, or something very similar, and have your answer ready. Try to keep your response to one or two minutes maximum)
- What do you know about our school? What do you think of the school now you have been shown around it?
- Why do you want to teach at our school?
- Why do you think that you are suitable for the post?

Learning and teaching specific questions

- Describe your teaching style.
- What were the (three/four/five) most significant accomplishments in your last school experience/placement?
- If your learners are experiencing a difficulty learning a skill or understanding a new concept, what would you do?

- How would your learners describe you, as a teacher?

- How do you differentiate/ensure personalised learning/meet individual needs?

- What do you understand as inclusive learning? How do you ensure you are meeting all the learners' needs?

- How do you keep your learners motivated/engaged/interested?

- How do learners best learn (your subject)? How you would organise your classroom and plan your learning and teaching activities to reflect this?

- What strategies would you expect a school to have in place to ensure that needs of all children are being met including, higher attainers and those with special educational needs? How will you apply this to your teaching?

- What are the key factors associated with establishing and maintaining good behaviour in the classroom and in school? How would you deal with a learner who persistently failed to behave in an appropriate manner?

- How would you make use of formative assessment activities in teaching to effectively monitor progress and understanding?

- Describe the best session you ever taught/you were proud of? What was so good about it/were you proud of it?

- How would you use technology/ICT to support learning, teaching and assessment activities?

- How do you evaluate your teaching?

- Raising standards is a focus for all schools. How would you ensure standards are improved?

- What do you dislike about teaching?

- Describe something which you have initiated yourself?

- How should learners be treated?

- What qualities make an excellent teacher? Which of these do you have?

- We are keen to develop links with parents and the wider community. How do you feel this can be best undertaken in school?

Questions about yourself

- What can you do for us that someone else can't?

- What are you looking for in this job?

- What would be your short-term objectives/aims, should you be offered the post?

- If you were offered the post, how long would it take for you to make a meaningful contribution?

- How does this post fit with your overall career plans?

- What do you believe is the most difficult part of being a teacher?

- How would your colleagues describe you?

- How would a previous boss describe you?

- How would you describe yourself?

- How will you compensate for your lack of experience?

- Can you work well under deadlines or pressure?
- How do you keep up with current developments in teaching/education/your subject?
- How did you prepare for this interview?
- What are your strong points?
- What are your weak points?
- What do you expect to be doing in five years' time?
- What have you undertaken recently to develop yourself?
- Why would you be an asset to this school?
- What makes you think that you will be successful/effective in this post?
- What did you find was your biggest problem/mistake during your last teaching placement? What did you learn from this?
- What questions didn't I ask you that you expected me to have asked?
- What skills and qualifications are essential for success in this job?
- What motivates you?
- What kind of teacher do you most admire?

Questions you might ask

- What equipment/resources are available for teaching my subject(s)?
- How much support is there for new staff and/or for NQTs, e.g. mentorship?
- Are then any planned developments in the school/department/subject?
- What are the school's/department's biggest challenges – how is the school addressing these?
- What would you like to be done differently by the next person who fills this post?

Practical task

Preparing for interview

Expect to be asked 'Say something about yourself', 'Why have you applied for this post?' and 'What makes you a strong candidate for the post?' at interview. Prepare your answers to these and practise your responses. Aim to get your replies across to the interview panel as prepared, natural and thoughtful. Don't let them sound parrot-fashion and memorised.

Read your letter of application. What questions might an interview panel ask about what you have written? What might they ask you to tell them more about, explain further or give illustrative examples. Expect the interview panel to ask you these questions and think how you would respond.

Look at the person specification for a post you are going to apply for and identify ten questions that you expect to be asked at your interview which would check whether you match with the specification requirements. Think how you would respond to these at interview.

Identify ten things which you would want to get across at an interview. Consider how you will proactively do this (by design rather than leaving it to chance!)

Whether you are offered the job or not, if you have the opportunity, seek feedback on your interview performance and learn from the experience. Consider how you might apply this learning to future interview (or similar) situations.

Giving a presentation

If you are asked to give a presentation as part of the job selection process, you will find ample resources, including many on the internet, which will help you think about doing this. The references below are not meant to be exhaustive, but they offer a representative sample of the resources which could give you ideas to draw on and inform your thinking about your approach to planning, preparing and delivering an effective presentation. Think about the pressures of the day and make sure you have planned something that you can deliver in a relaxed and calm manner – without rushing through lots of PowerPoint slides.

There have been some examples of people arriving to give a presentation only to be told that the projector is broken or the computer has 'gone down'. Take alternatives if using ICT – handouts, for example. Remaining calm and being able to present amidst the confusion of technical problems shows you to be highly professional and well prepared.

Teaching a sample lesson

If the delivery of a short lesson is part of the selection process, this will require some careful thought. You are likely to be presented with a topic to teach and an idea about the size and age group of the students in the class. This is a chance for you to shine and to demonstrate your skills. Though only you will know how innovative and daring you wish to be, it is essential to cover the basics.

- Plan a sensible amount of time for the activity. Don't try to cram a full lesson that worked well for you last week with your Y8 group into 20 minutes.
- Cover the topic you have been asked to cover, not what you would prefer to cover.
- Attempt to gauge the learners' prior understanding at the start.
- Have very clear objectives and share them with the learners.
- Introduce yourself confidently and calmly and try to get to know the learners by name – have a seating plan or badges.
- Involve the learners as much as possible – small group work or an individual or paired activity, for example.
- Ask targeted questions and give lots of praise for correct answers and attempts. Don't dismiss incorrect answers but ask why the student said what they did.
- Be firm (the observers may be watching for how you cope with small-scale disruption) but smile.
- Keep the learners busy and give clear tasks and instructions so they always know what to do and what is expected.
- Make sure your own subject knowledge of the topic is very good.
- Finish with a clear summary and a way of trying to measure how much learning has taken place.

In other words, try to cram as much good practice into your teaching session as you can, but not as much content. Always discuss your plans with your mentor or other colleagues and try out any activities. Finally, make sure that everything you take will be there, will work and that you have an alternative if it doesn't.

What if you are applying for jobs but not getting any interviews?

First, review the quality of your application (i.e. the application form and letter of application). For example, are you spending enough time honing your letters of application, seeking both to improve the quality of the content and presentation and to tailor it to the actual job for which you are applying? Do you make claims in your letter of application about your capabilities which you are failing to justify through the examples you give of how to use these capabilities in your teaching? Are you underselling yourself, perhaps writing in an overly modest way, either through your use of language or use of examples? Alternatively, are you using a style which gives the impression of your overconfidence to the reader? You want your letter of application to make you appear capable, but not that you believe that you can do everything, that you are 'perfect', since this might suggest that you have an unrealistic view of your capabilities as an NQT and a beginner. If need be, tear up your existing letter of application and re-write it, maybe in three or four different ways and styles. Use these to apply for jobs and see if any one format is more successful than the others in gaining you an interview.

Second, review the jobs for which you have applied to check whether they are appropriate for you. Are you limiting yourself unduly in the range of jobs for which you are applying (perhaps by only applying for posts which receive a large number of applications, which will reduce your chances of gaining interviews), or applying for jobs which are a poor match between the nature and requirements of the job and your own levels of experience and expertise?

If you have reviewed the above and are still not getting an interview then consider one or more of the activities below:

1 Extend and improve your experience and expertise. Perhaps you could gain some supply teaching for a while or even seek a voluntary placement in a school. Not only will this give you an opportunity to develop your experience and expertise, but it should also provide you with more examples to include in your letter of application as evidence of your increasing experience and professional development (as well as taking the initiative, being proactive, etc). It will also enable you to find out more about the schools where you might apply. Should they have a future vacancy, it will give you opportunities to network and to get yourself known in schools.

2 Consider how you might get professional feedback on the quality of your applications, e.g. from a headteacher or senior leader of a school or from the careers service of the university you attended. Use this feedback to improve your applications.

What if you are being invited for interviews but not getting a job?

Review your interview technique. Evaluate every aspect of the interviews you have attended, from the clothes you wore, to your interpersonal behaviour, to the nature of your answers to the questions you were asked. Really try to get feedback from the interview panels and examine it to see whether there are any common threads to the feedback which you need to change and improve. Do you feel that you are presenting yourself and coming across at interview in a way that you would like? If not, what do you need to do differently so as to present yourself as you want to?

Use friends and, in particular, any friends who are fellow teachers or who have experience of interviewing to undertake some mock interviews and, if possible, record these. Evaluate the mock interviews with your friends to identify how you might both build on your interviewing strengths and identify how you might respond differently to address weaker areas of your interviewing approach.

The job

Congratulations! You have a job! During your NQT year you can expect a range of support strategies to be put in place to help you. For example, you will be allocated an induction tutor and a mentor. You will be given 10 per cent remission from your timetable as an NQT and a further 10 per cent, as with all teaching staff, as PPA time (preparation, planning and assessment time). So, this will be equivalent to one day per week. However, how schools allocate this will vary, so do not assume that it will be allocated to you as one full day per week. It might be spread over the week as a number of smaller sessions or perhaps given to you in blocks at different times during the school year.

During some of your NQT time you may be invited to attend courses and workshops for NQTs, often organised by the LA.

During your NQT period (a minimum of one academic year), although the gudelines suggest that you should not be expected to take on responsibility for a subject or curriculum area, in practice there may be opportunities for you to become involved and you should take advantage of these. This will increase your experience and understanding of aspects of school development and will confirm you as being proactive and eager to learn more about school.

During your NQT induction period you will be expected to meet the Professional Standards for Teachers (QTS) standards (you were assessed against these during your Initial Teacher Education programme when you qualified as a teacher). During your NQT induction period you will be assessed against the Professional Standards for Teachers (core) standards at the end of each term. The idea is that you use your career entry and development profile (CEDP) to help you reflect on and record your progress and achievements and to help you identify your continuing professional development needs, goals and targets, and action plan.

When you have completed your NQT induction period your school will inform the General Teaching Council for England (GTC), whether or not you have met the core standards. The GTC will inform you whether or not you have passed – if you have, they will issue you with a certificate. The core standards and the career entry and development profile (CEDP) can be downloaded from the Training and Development Agency web-site (*http://www.tda.gov.uk*).

You can expect lesson observations (by the induction tutor and probably a senior leader of the school), but you can also expect to have opportunities to observe other staff in the school as well as visit other schools.

Your NQT period is at the beginning of your teaching career, at a time when you are at your least experienced, but also at an exciting time when you have much to learn and consolidate. It is a time when you can draw on all your enthusiasm and energy and throw yourself into what, hopefully, will became a positive, happy and rewarding career for you. You will, no doubt, have your ups and downs in what will be a busy, tiring and sometimes stressful time. Consider how you will make the most of this exciting period of your career; be open to feedback and do not be afraid to ask questions; and draw upon the experience and support of your new colleagues (particularly your mentor and your induction tutor).

Schools will differ in the way they provide support, but the following offers a frame-work within which most schools will operate.

Your induction tutor

The role of the induction tutor is, principally, to:

- Coordinate effective guidance and support for the NQT's professional development
- Liaise and collaborate with all partners in the NQT's induction process
- Monitor the NQT's progress towards satisfactory completion of induction, gathering evidence for fair and rigorous assessments
- Inform the headteacher about the NQT's progress
- Contribute to the school's monitoring and evaluation of the school induction provision.

Teacher Training Agency (TTA) (2003) *The Role of the Induction Tutor*, Teacher Training Agency (accessible at http://www.tda.gov.uk/upload/resources/pdf/r/roit.pdf).

Mentorship

Generally the mentorship scheme for NQTs will include in its aims:

- To improve the rate at which an NQT adapts to their new teaching role within the school
- To support NQTs in their learning and development
- To contribute to the improvement of staff performance and capability within school.

    As a consequence this means that you, as an NQT, should receive:

- Induction support
- Support for your professional teaching role
- Support for the transfer and development of the understanding and skills acquired from your initial teacher education course into your new role as a teacher
- Support in your specialist teaching subject(s) and learning, teaching and assessment activities
- Support from a critical 'friend' outside the direct line of management.

And as a consequence you will:

- Settle into your job and role more quickly and easily
- Build up a professional network more quickly and effectively
- Avoid feeling isolated and peripheral
- Receive positive encouragement and constructive feedback
- Have access to a critical friend
- Have help with problem solving
- Gain an additional perspective and insight into your own performance and development
- Identify personal and professional development needs and opportunities
- Learn from your mentor as a role model
- Optimise your learning from your professional practice.

What you need to do to get optimum benefit from the support available:

- You should aim to be open and honest with both your induction tutor and mentor.
- You should accept gradual and increasing responsibility for managing these relationships, so gradually developing your professional autonomy.
- You should share responsibility for the relationships, through the stages of building the relationship at the beginning, maintaining the relationship during the induction, and winding down and dissolving the relationship at the end of the induction period. Of course, after this time, you and your colleagues might still have a professional relationship, but it will be different, for a different professional purpose, and it will not be a relationship that is part of the NQT induction scheme.

You can help achieve this by:

- Ensuring that your colleagues are kept up to date on your progress and any problems that you might be encountering
- Asking for support when you need it
- Actively preparing for the meetings with your induction tutor and mentor, and thinking about what you want to gain as outcomes of the process
- Being responsible for your own development
- Following through actions and decisions that you have agreed
- Meeting with your colleagues regularly – more frequently in the earlier stages.

What else can you do to help yourself?

- Ask for copies of important documentation which tells you about school policies, processes and procedures. If you are lucky, this might all be contained within one document – a School Handbook. Otherwise, the information might be quite dispersed with some information provided at whole-school level, some at department level, some in hard copy, and some in electronic form – for example, on the school website. In fact, looking at the school website every now and again might be a very useful way of helping you to keep up to date about school.
- Make yourself familiar with the Professional Standards for Teachers (Core) standards and the information about the induction period for NQTs. Use these to inform your

thinking about your improving practice. Consider and discuss with your induction tutor the evidence which you will need to generate to show you are meeting these standards.

- Find out if there are any other NQTs starting at the same time as you. Contact them and explore how you might support each other and build up a support network.
- Ask for help and support when you need it – and be prepared to support others when they need your support.
- Ensure that you give enough time and thought to the planning of your teaching, setting of homework and your marking.
- Join a teachers' trade union – maybe consider joining the one which has the largest number of members in your school.
- Build relationships – with other staff, teaching and non-teaching. Participate in any social events that might be arranged.
- Consider how you might contribute to the wider life of the school, e.g. extra curricular/out-of-school activities.
- Make your classroom visually attractive, through use of display and technology.
- Be positive – smile and enjoy!!!

With luck, at the end of your first academic year you will pass your NQT period. Do not forget that it is during your second year that you will find that you might lose some support mechanisms. For example, you will no longer have allocated to you the 10 per cent NQT time and the development opportunities (and sometimes breathing space) that this provided you with. You will no longer have an induction tutor and may no longer be allocated a mentor. This may be a bit of a shock to you, and you need to take stock of your new situation. Reflect on your new and emerging professional development needs and plan how at least some of these might be supported through the performance-management process of the school. Consider how you might continue to have support mechanisms, whether these might be more formal by exploring any opportunities for continued mentorship, or informally, by building on and strengthening the support network that you developed during your first year in post. As you gain experience, you will, no doubt, have the opportunity to offer support to others, perhaps new NQTs who are appointed. Remember how important and useful the support and help you received was when you began your career and consider how you might support others in the same way, when the opportunity arises. Giving support to others, whether it be formally or informally, is a significant learning and development opportunity for the supporter, as well as for the supported.

Summary

In this chapter we have discussed the processes of applying for and getting a job in teaching. You have been asked to consider your strengths and match these to the appropriate post. In order to do this effectively you have been encouraged to obtain as much information about the job as possible. Investigate the nature of the school and the key points about the position. Obtaining a job, or filling a position if you are on the other side of the recruitment process, is a matching exercise. You are trying to get the best job possible, and they are trying to find the most suitable candidate. Knowing exactly what you are applying for is a sensible first step, so do your homework.

The chapter has also given you much practical advice about how to complete the application process, and especially the letter. Notice that you have been strongly encouraged to keep matching what you say about yourself and your experiences to the job specification, role description and person specification. Being the right person for the wrong job, or the wrong person for the right job is not a scenario you would wish to be involved with.

Then there is the selection event. You have received a great deal of advice about how to conduct yourself at the interview and during other tasks you may be asked to carry out. It is easy to suggest that you relax and be yourself, but the better you prepare, the more confident you will be. Remember that the panel will expect you to be nervous – it shows you care and want the job – but they will also expect you to control your nerves. The chapter contains some very useful advice about interview questions and how to prepare.

Finally, remember this is a matching exercise and not a popularity contest. If you do not get the post don't take it personally and do use it as a learning experience. Ask for feedback and use it to improve your application and interview performance. The correct teaching post is out there waiting for you, so don't lose confidence.

References

Cowley, Sue (2003) *How to Survive your First Year in Teaching*, London: Continuum International Publishing Group.

Training and Development Agency website at *http://www.tda.gov.uk*.

Further reading

Bromberg, Peter (2008) *Talking Good; Giving Effective Presentations*, Library Garden accessible at *http://librarygarden.blogspot.com/2008/02/talk-good-giving-effective.html* (Accessed 7 August 2008).

DesJardin, Marie (2006) *Giving Effective Presentations*, University of Maryland, Baltimore, Maryland, USA accessible at *http://www.cs.umbc.edu/courses/graduate/CMSC691B/spring06/slides/presentations_feb20.ppt* (Accessed 7 August 2008).

Health Education Resource Exchange (1998) *Tips for Giving Effective Presentations*, Washington State Department of Health accessible at *http://www3.doh.wa.gov/here/Howto/images/present.html* (Accessed 7 August 2008).

Kerr, Gillian (2006) *Giving Effective Presentations*, Ourmedia: Channels of Creativity, accessible as *http://ourmedia.org/node/150464* (Accessed 7 August 2008).

Teacher Training Agency (TTA) (2003) *The Role of the Induction Tutor*, Teacher Training Agency (accessible at *http://www.tda.gov.uk/upload/resources/pdf/r/roit.pdf*).

The Writing and Communication Center, (2001) *Building Your Oral Communication Skill*, East Tennessee State University, Tennessee, USA accessible at *http://www.etsu.edu/wcc/oral_communication_skills/sld001.htm* (Accessed 7 August 2008).

Wertheim, Edward (undated), *Making Effective Oral Presentations*, Northeastern University, Boston, MA, USA, accessible at *http://web.cba.neu.edu/~ewertheim/skills/oral.htm* (Accessed 7 August 2008).

Index